NEVER
CAUGHT

Also by Erica Armstrong Dunbar

*A Fragile Freedom: African American Women and
Emancipation in the Antebellum City*

NEVER CAUGHT

THE WASHINGTONS' RELENTLESS PURSUIT *of* THEIR RUNAWAY SLAVE, ONA JUDGE

ERICA ARMSTRONG DUNBAR

37INK

—

ATRIA

New York   London   Toronto   Sydney   New Delhi

ATRIA BOOKS 37INK

An Imprint of Simon & Schuster, Inc.
1230 Avenue of the Americas
New York, NY 10020

First 37 Ink/Atria Books hardcover edition February 2017

37INK **/ ATRIA** BOOKS and colophons are trademarks of Simon & Schuster, Inc.

For information about special discounts for bulk purchases, please contact Simon & Schuster Special Sales at 1-866-506-1949 or business@simonandschuster.com.

The Simon & Schuster Speakers Bureau can bring authors to your live event. For more information, or to book an event, contact the Simon & Schuster Speakers Bureau at 1-866-248-3049 or visit our website at www.simonspeakers.com.

Interior design by Amy Trombat

Manufactured in the United States of America

10 9 8 7 6 5 4 3 2 1

Library of Congress Cataloging-in-Publication Data is available.

ISBN 978-1-5011-2639-0
ISBN 978-1-5011-2643-7 (ebook)

For my mother
Frances Chudnick Armstrong
&
My husband
Jeffrey Kim Dunbar

Contents

Author's Note

I MET ONA JUDGE STAINES IN THE ARCHIVES ABOUT TWENTY YEARS ago. I was busy conducting research on a different project about nineteenth-century black women in Philadelphia, and I came across an advertisement about a runaway slave in the *Philadelphia Gazette*. The fugitive in question was called "Oney Judge," and she had escaped from the President's House. I was amazed. I wondered how could it be that I had never heard of this woman? What happened to her? Was George Washington able to reclaim her? I vowed to return to her story.

Those of us who research and write about early black women's history understand how very difficult it is to find our subjects in the archives. Enslavement,[1] racism, and sexism often discarded these women from the historical record, and as historians we are frequently left unsatisfied with scant evidence. Much of the earlier historical record was written by other people, typically white men, who were literate and in positions of power. Fortunately, Ona

---

[1] I prefer to use the term "enslaved" when referring to men, women, and children who were held in bondage because it shifts the attention to an action that was involuntarily placed upon millions of black people. However, throughout the text, I chose to use the word "slave" for the purpose of narrative flow.

Judge Staines left the world just a bit of *her* voice, and, hopefully, time will reveal new information about this incredible woman. Although she remained in hiding for more than half a century, I don't believe that she ever wanted to be forgotten.

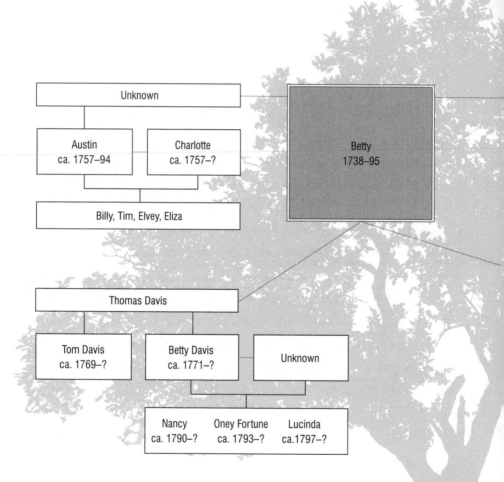

Ona's Family Tree

This family tree shows the relationships, as far as they are known, between Ona Judge's mother, Betty, and her children and their descendants.

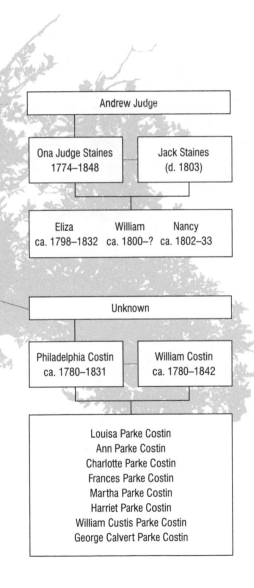

Andrew Judge

Ona Judge Staines
1774–1848

Jack Staines
(d. 1803)

Eliza   William   Nancy
ca. 1798–1832   ca. 1800–?   ca. 1802–33

Unknown

Philadelphia Costin
ca. 1780–1831

William Costin
ca. 1780–1842

Louisa Parke Costin
Ann Parke Costin
Charlotte Parke Costin
Frances Parke Costin
Martha Parke Costin
Harriet Parke Costin
William Custis Parke Costin
George Calvert Parke Costin

Foreword

SPRING RAIN DRENCHED THE STREETS OF PHILADELPHIA IN 1796. Weather in the "City of Brotherly Love" was often fickle this time of year, vacillating between extreme cold and oppressive heat. But rain was almost always appreciated in the nation's capital. It erased the putrid smells of rotting food, animal waste, and filth that permeated the cobblestone roads of the new nation. It reminded Philadelphians that the long and punishing winter was behind them. It cleansed the streets and souls of Philadelphia, ushering in optimism, hope, and a feeling of rebirth.

In the midst of the promises of spring, Ona Judge, a young black slave woman, received devastating news: She was to leave Philadelphia, a city that had become her home. Judge was to travel back to her birthplace of Virginia and prepare to be bequeathed to her owner's granddaughter.

Judge had watched six spring seasons come and go in Philadelphia. Each spring she watched the rain fall on a city that was slowly cleansing itself of the stain of slavery. She watched a burgeoning free black population grow such that by the end of the century, it would count nearly six thousand people. Although a slave, Judge lived among free people, watching black entrepreneurs sell, along with other provisions, their fruits, oysters, and pepper pot soup in the streets. On Sunday mornings she witnessed the newly erected "Bethel" church welcome its small but growing black membership. And what she didn't witness firsthand, she would have heard about. Stories about organizations such as the Pennsylvania Abolition Society, who helped enslaved men and women find or protect their freedom, and beyond. Philadelphia represented the epicenter of emancipation, allowing black men and women the opportunity to sample a few of the benefits that accompanied a free status.

As a slave in Philadelphia, Ona Judge was actually in the minority. In 1796 fewer than one hundred slaves lived within the city limits. Not only did her status as an enslaved person separate her from the majority of free black Philadelphians, but she was further distinguished by the family she served. Judge was owned by the first president of the United States and his wife, George and Martha Washington.

Judge's sojourn from Mount Vernon in rural Virginia to the North began in 1789 when she accompanied the presidential family to New York, the site of the nation's first capital. In November of 1790, the capital moved to Philadelphia, where Judge encountered a new world, one in which, on occasion, she strolled through the streets, visited the market, and attended the theater without her owners. The rigid laws of Southern slaveholding were difficult to integrate into a free Philadelphia, and when told she'd be given away to the famously mercurial granddaughter of the "first lady," she made a very dangerous and bold decision: she would run away from her owners. On Saturday, May 21, 1796, at the age of twenty-two, Ona Judge slipped out of the president's mansion in Philadelphia, never to return.

Very few eighteenth-century slaves have shared their stories about the institution and experience of slavery. The violence required to feed the system of human bondage often made enslaved men and women want to forget their pasts, not recollect them. For fugitives, like Ona Judge, secrecy was a necessity. Enslaved men and women on the run often kept their pasts hidden, even from the people they loved the most: their spouses and children. Sometimes, the nightmare of human bondage, the murder, rape, dismemberment, and constant degradation, was simply too terrible to speak of. But it was the threat of capture and re-enslavement that kept closed the mouths of those who managed to beat the odds and successfully escape. Afraid of being returned to her owners, Judge lived a shadowy life that was isolated and clandestine. For almost fifty years, the fugitive slave woman kept to herself, building a family and a new life upon the quicksand of her legal enslavement. She lived most of her time as a fugitive in Greenland, New Hampshire, a tiny community just outside the city of Portsmouth.

At the end of her life, Ona Judge made another bold decision: she would tell her story. She granted interviews to two reporters for abolitionist newspapers, the first of which, with Thomas H. Archibald, appeared in the *Granite Freeman* in May of 1845, almost forty-nine years to the day of her escape. Judge's second, and final, interview appeared in 1847 on New Year's Day in the *Liberator,* the nation's most powerful abolitionist newspaper. Judge's interviews are quite possibly the only existing recorded narratives of an eighteenth-century Virginia fugitive. Her oral testimony allows us to learn about the institution of slavery not only through the lens of white abolitionists and slave owners, but through the voice of a fugitive.

It is my pleasure, indeed an honor, to reintroduce Ona Judge Staines, the Washingtons' runaway slave.

NEVER
CAUGHT

One

Betty's Daughter

*List of slaves at Mount Vernon, 1799. Courtesy of Mount Vernon
Ladies' Association.*

In June of 1773, the unimaginable happened: it snowed in Virginia.

During the first week of June, the typical stifling heat that almost
always blanketed Virginia had not yet laid its claim on the colony.
Daytime temperatures fluctuated from sultry warmth to a rainy
chill during the first few days of the month. Even more peculiar yet,
on June 11, it snowed. As he did most days, Colonel George Washington sat down and recorded the unusual weather, writing, "Cloudy
& exceeding Cold Wind fresh from the No. West, & Snowing." His

diary went on to note, "Memorandum—Be it remembered that on the eleventh day of June in the year one thousand seven hundred and seventy three It rain'd Hail'd snow'd and was very Cold."

⁓⟨♋⟩⁓

The men and women who lived on George and Martha Washington's estate must have marveled at the peculiar snow, but whatever excitement the unusual weather brought was most certainly replaced by concern. Shabby clothing and uninsulated slave cabins turned winter into long periods of dread for the enslaved men and women at Mount Vernon and across the colony of Virginia. Although the intense heat of summer brought its own difficulties, winter brought sickness, long periods of isolation, and heightened opportunities for the auction block. To exacerbate matters, the selling of slaves frequently occurred at the beginning of the year, connecting the winter month of January to a fear of deep and permanent loss. The snow in June, then, could only be a sign of very bad things to come. For the nearly 150 slaves who labored on the Mount Vernon estate in 1773, a mixture of superstition, African religious practices, and English beliefs in witchery must have intensified a sense of fear. Things that were inconsistent with nature were interpreted as bad omens, commonly bringing drought, pestilence, and death. As for what this snow portended, only time would tell.

Sure enough, eight days after the snow fell, Martha Parke Custis, daughter of Martha Washington, fell terribly ill. The stepdaughter of George Washington, just seventeen, had long struggled with a medical condition that rendered her incapable of controlling her body. Plagued by seizures that began during her teenage years, "Patsy" Custis most likely suffered from epilepsy. The early discipline of medicine was far from mature, offering few options for cures outside of bleeding and purges. Her parents had spent the last five years consulting with doctors and experimenting with unhelpful medicinal potions, diet, exercise modifications, and of course, deep prayer.

Their faith was tested on June 19 when Patsy Custis and a host of invited family members were finishing up with dinner a little after four o'clock. Although sickly, Washington's stepdaughter had been "in better health and spirits than she appeared to have been in for some time." After dinner and quiet conversation with family, Patsy excused herself and went to retrieve a letter from her bedroom. Eleanor Calvert, Patsy's soon-to-be sister-in-law, went to check on the young woman and found her seizing violently on the floor. Patsy was moved to the bed, but there was very little anyone could do. Within two minutes, she was gone.

The June snow and Patsy's death combined to create an eerie feeling of uncertainty. House slaves understood that Martha Washington would need to be handled with more care than usual, especially since this was not the first child that she had lost. Two of her toddlers had succumbed to the high childhood mortality rates of colonial Virginia, and Patsy's death left the devastated mother with only one living child. George Washington wrote to his nephew, breaking the news of his stepdaughter's death and his wife's emotional distress, stating, "I scarce need add [that Patsy's death] has almost reduced my poor Wife to the lowest ebb of Misery." George Washington wasn't the only one attuned to Martha's emotional state. Slave women who worked in the Mansion House tended to the devastated Martha Washington, taking great care to respect their grieving mistress, while helping the household prepare for Patsy's funeral.

Yet while the mistress Martha Washington wept over the loss of her daughter, a slave woman named Betty (also known as Mulatto

Betty) prepared for an arrival of her own. Born sometime around 1738, Betty was a dower slave; that is, she was "property" owned by Martha Washington's first husband, Daniel Parke Custis. As a seamstress and expert spinner who was among Mrs. Washington's favored slaves, the bondwoman had a long history with her mistress, one that predated the relationship between Colonel Washington and his wife and one that had seen Martha endure great heartbreak. In 1757 Betty watched her mistress survive the sudden loss of her first husband, followed by the death of her four-year-old daughter, Frances. She also watched Martha reemerge from sorrow's clutch. Betty continued to spin and sew as her mistress took control of the family business, which included six plantations and close to three hundred slaves that fed Virginia's tobacco economy. With the death of her husband, Martha Parke Custis stood in control of over 17,500 acres of land, making her one of the wealthiest widows in the colony of Virginia, if not throughout the entire Chesapeake.

Before her move to Mount Vernon, Betty worked in the Custis home known as the White House on the Pamunkey River in New Kent County, Virginia. Two years after the death of her owner, Betty learned that her mistress was to remarry. She most likely received the news of her mistress's impending second marriage with great wariness as word spread that Martha Custis's intended was Colonel George Washington. The colonel was a fairly prominent landowner with a respectable career as a military officer and an elected member of the Virginia House of Burgesses. His marriage to the widowed Martha Custis would offer him instant wealth and the stability of a wife and family that had eluded him. For her part, the young widow had managed to secure a surrogate father to help raise her two living children. She had also found a partner with whom she could spend the rest of her days. Nevertheless, a huge yet necessary transition awaited Martha Custis as she prepared to marry and move to the Mount Vernon estate, nearly one hundred miles away.

For Betty, as well as the hundreds of other slaves that belonged to the Custis estate, the death of their previous owner and Martha's marriage to George Washington was a reminder of their vulnerability. It was often after the death of an owner that slaves were sold to remedy the debts held by an estate. Betty and all those enslaved at New Kent had no idea what kind of financial transactions would transpire, which families would be split apart, never to be united again. For enslaved women, the moral character of the new owner was also a serious concern. When George and Martha Washington married in January of 1759, Betty was approximately twenty-one years old and considered to be in the prime of her reproductive years. She was unfamiliar with her new master's preferences, or more importantly, if he would choose to exercise his complete control over her body. All of the enslaved women who would leave for Mount Vernon most likely worried about their new master's protocol regarding sexual relations with his slaves. But of greater consequence for Betty was the future for her young son, Austin. Born sometime around 1757, Austin was a baby or young toddler when his mistress took George Washington's hand in marriage. To lose him before she even got to know him, to have joined the thousands who stood by powerlessly while their children were "bartered for gold," as the poet Frances Ellen Watkins Harper wrote, would have been devastating.

As she prepared to move to Mount Vernon, Martha Washington selected a number of slaves to accompany her on the journey to Fairfax County. Betty *and* Austin were, to Betty's relief, among them. The highest-valued mother-and-child pair in a group that counted 155 slaves, they arrived in April of 1759.

Betty managed to do what many slave mothers couldn't: keep her son. Austin's very young age would have prohibited the Custis estate from fetching a high price if he were sold independently from his mother. Perhaps this fact, in addition to Betty's prized position in the Custis household, ensured that she would stay connected to her child as she moved away from the place she had called home.

As Martha Washington settled into her new life with her second husband at Mount Vernon, a sprawling estate consisting of five separate farms, Betty also adapted, continuing her spinning, weaving, tending to her son, and making new family and friends at the plantation. The intricacies of Betty's romantic life at Mount Vernon remain unclear, but what we do know is that more than a decade after giving birth to Austin, Betty welcomed more children into the world. Her son, Tom Davis, was born around 1769, and his sister Betty Davis arrived in 1771. Unlike Austin, these two children claimed a last name, one that most likely linked them to a hired white weaver named Thomas Davis.

George and Martha Washington placed their most "valued" and favored slaves inside the household. Martha Washington allowed only those slaves she felt to be the most polished and intelligent to toil within the walls of the main house, and that included Betty, whose skills as a clothier ranged from knowledge of expert weaving to the dyeing of expensive and scarce fabric. Betty and a corps of talented enslaved seamstresses not only outfitted their masters but also stitched together clothing for the hundreds of slaves at Mount Vernon.

Now, in 1773, fourteen years after she watched her mistress experience the death of her first child, Betty witnessed her mistress come undone once again. The loss of her daughter Patsy left Martha Washington almost inconsolable and stood in contrast with Betty's relative good fortune. Martha Washington had lost young Frances in 1759, just as Betty was blessed with the arrival of her son Austin. Now, the circumstances were nearly identical, for as Martha Washington grieved over the loss of her daughter, Betty began preparing for the arrival of another child. June snow served as a marker of death for the Washingtons but issued a very different signal to Betty. It marked the beginning of a life that would be as unusual as summertime winter weather. Sometime around or after the June snow of 1773, Betty gave birth to a daughter named Ona Maria Judge. This girl child would come to represent the complexity of slavery, the limits of black freedom, and the revolutionary sentiments held by many Americans. She would be called Oney.

Betty, like other bondwomen, increased her owner's wealth each time she bore a child. Although she called George Washington her master, he owned neither Betty nor her children. As a dower slave, Betty was technically owned by Martha Washington and the Custis estate. The birth of Ona Judge would not add value to George Washington's coffers, but her body would be counted among the human property that would produce great profit for Martha Washington and the Custis children and grandchildren.

Similar to Betty's other children, Ona had a surname. It belonged to her father, Andrew Judge, an English-born white man. On July 8, 1772, Andrew Judge found his way to America via an indenture agreement, contracting himself to Alexander Coldelough, a merchant from Leeds, England. In exchange for his passage to "Baltimore or any port in America" as well as a promise of food, clothing, appropriate shelter, and an allowance, Judge handed over four years of his life. Although indentured servitude served as the engine for population growth in the early seventeenth century, Andrew Judge entered into service at a time when fewer and fewer English men agreed to hand over their lives for an opportunity in the colonies. Why did he come? Indenture agreements never made clear the circumstances from which a person was exiting, so it is quite possible that Judge was running from debt or a life of destitution. Whatever the problem, the solution for Judge was life as a servant in the colonies, uncertainty and all.

He landed in Alexandria, Virginia, where George Washington purchased his indenture for thirty pounds. Mount Vernon relied primarily upon slave labor; however, Washington included a number of white indentured servants in his workforce. White servitude had its advantages, but by the late eighteenth century, planters like Washington often complained about their unreliability, their tendency for attempted escape, and their laziness. Yet Andrew Judge did not appear as the target of Washington's ire in any of his correspondence. In fact he became a trusted tailor relied upon by the colonel for outfitting him at the most important of moments. By 1774 he appeared in the Mount Vernon manager's account book as responsible for creating the blue uniform worn by Washington when he was named commander in chief of the American forces. Judge was responsible for making clothing for the entire Washington family, which would have required him to make frequent visits to the main house, where he would come into contact with Betty. In her mid- to late thirties, Betty became acquainted with the indentured tailor.

Interracial relationships were far from uncommon in Virginia at the time, and many mixed-race children were counted among the enslaved. Perhaps Betty and Andrew Judge flirted with one another, eventually engaging in a mutual affair. Maybe the two bound laborers fell in love. If either of these scenarios were true,

Betty probably chose her lover, a most powerful example of agency in the life of an enslaved woman. Understanding the inherited status of slavery, Betty would have known that any child born to her would carry the burden of slavery, that any child she bore would be enslaved. Nonetheless, a union with Andrew Judge could facilitate a road to emancipation for their child and perhaps for Betty herself. Eventually Judge would work through his servitude agreement and become a free man. If he saved enough money, he could offer to purchase his progeny, as well as Betty and her additional children. Although a legal union in Virginia between a white man and a black woman would not be recognized for almost two centuries, Judge's eventual rise in status out of the ranks of servant to that of a free, landholding, white man offered potential power. Andrew Judge may not have been able to marry Betty, but if he loved her, he could try to protect her and her family from the vulnerability of slavery.

Love or romance, however, may not have brought the two bound laborers together. Although he was a servant, Andrew Judge was a white man with the power to command or force a sexual relationship with the enslaved Betty. What is lost to us is just how consensual their relationship may have been. Perhaps Judge stalked Betty, eventually forcing himself upon her. As a black woman, she would have virtually no ability to protect herself from unwanted advances or sexual attack. The business of slavery received every new enslaved baby with open arms, no matter the circumstances of conception. What we do know is that their union, whether brief or extended, consensual or unwanted, resulted in the birth of a daughter. We also know that however Judge defined his relationship to his daughter, it wasn't enough to keep him at Mount Vernon.

Eventually Andrew Judge left and built upon the opportunity that indentured servitude promised. By the 1780s Andrew Judge lived in his own home in Fairfax County. Listed among the occupants of his home were six additional residents, one of whom was black. It's uncertain if Andrew Judge owned a slave or if he simply hired a free black person who lived on and worked his land. What is clear from the evidence left behind is that Judge left Mount Vernon and his enslaved daughter behind. Perhaps he attempted to purchase Betty and his child but was refused the opportunity by the Washingtons. Or maybe Judge simply didn't want a complicated relationship with an enslaved woman and a mixed-race daughter. Whatever hope, if any, Betty had placed upon the relationship with Andrew Judge collapsed quickly, leaving her at Mount Vernon to raise Ona and her siblings, including Philadelphia, a daughter she gave birth to after Ona but before Judge left, sometime around 1780.

Leaving his child behind at Mount Vernon, Andrew Judge's parting gift to his daughter was a surname and a unique first name. The name is both African and Gaelic, and no other slave at Mount Vernon or the White House on the Pamunkey River was named Ona. Perhaps even more exceptional was that she was given a middle name, Maria. Her distinctive name set her apart from her siblings and from the majority of the other bondmen and bondwomen who toiled with her in Virginia.

⁂

The slaves who were directly connected to the work at the Mansion House lived across the road from the blacksmith's forge in the communal space known as the Quarters, or House for Families. Betty and other women who worked in the Mansion House were typically required to be present from sunrise to sundown, preparing meals, mending clothes, cleaning, spinning, and performing other domestic tasks, leaving most enslaved children separated from their parent or parents most of the day. Many of the children at Mount Vernon began structured labor between the ages of nine and fourteen, but most performed odd jobs just as soon as they were physically able. As very young enslaved children were unhelpful and sometimes considered a nuisance, they were often left in the Quarters without much supervision beyond the older slave women, who were deemed incapable of working in the fields and no longer up to the task of domestic work.

Bushy haired, with light skin and freckles, a young Ona probably spent some of her days playing with her siblings and other enslaved children in the Quarters. More often than not, though, she had to learn how to fend for herself. Judge and the other children at Mount Vernon cried out in loneliness for their parents, witnessed the brutality of whippings and corporal punishment, and fell victim to early death due to accidental fires and drowning. Childhood for enslaved girls and boys was fleeting and fraught with calamity. Many perished before reaching young adulthood. Judge's childhood wasn't shortened by a plantation fatality. Instead, hers ended at age ten, when she was called to serve Martha Washington up at the Mansion House.

A good number of children at Mount Vernon did not live with both of their parents, a circumstance created by the separation of enslaved spouses. Washington may not have broken up slave marriages by selling away husbands and wives, but he was not averse to separating slave couples by placing them on different farms. While he may not have purposefully disrupted slave unions, the business of slavery and the needs of Mount Vernon always came first. For slave couples and enslaved families, this meant that they would see each other only when permission was given.

Just like other enslaved children, Ona Judge did not spend the majority of her youth with two parents. Andrew Judge had the privilege of white skin and the power anchored in a male body that allowed him to slip away from a life of unpaid labor. Betty had neither gender nor race on her side, and spent the entirety of her life in human bondage in Virginia, a colony that would eventually become the slave-breeding capital of a new nation. Ona Judge learned valuable lessons from both of her parents. From her mother she would learn the power of perseverance. From her father, Judge would learn that the decision to free oneself trumped everything, no matter who was left behind.

Two

New York–Bound

George Washington taking the presidential oath of office, Federal Hall, 1789.

On Christmas Eve 1783, George Washington returned to his family and beloved Mount Vernon a very changed man. For eight and a half years, Washington had led his countrymen as commander of the Continental Army, a poorly outfitted and undertrained band of men who took on the Herculean fight that many believed would end in failure. It had been a terrible war that lasted far longer than anyone had ever predicted. There were never enough shoes, blankets, or shirts for the men who enlisted. Even gunpowder was hard to come by. General Washington held the lives of more than one hundred thousand men in his hands, men who had agreed to bear arms in the new Continental Army, men who risked their limbs and lives in order to create a new country. More than thirty thousand American soldiers perished in the war, many from direct combat, and others from slow-moving disease and infection that ravaged makeshift infirmaries and camp hospitals. Unknown numbers of men died in the most dreadful ways—accidentally shot by comrades, crushed by old and unstable heavy wagons, falls from horses, and accidental drowning. Simply unable to live with the violence of war, some men took their own lives, leaving wives and children to face poverty and starvation.

The general was a lucky man. He would return home without the visible markers of war that thousands of his countrymen carried to their graves. Even though he had escaped the ailments that plagued his soldiers, the amputation of legs, blindness, and grotesque facial disfigurement from musket fire, his health was far from stable. Now in his fifties, he had aged considerably.

In the eighteen months before his return home to Mount Vernon, Washington witnessed the collapse of the mighty British Army. After the surprising victory at Yorktown, earnest negotiations began in Paris, resulting in a signed peace treaty and the evacuation of British troops. Washington left his post in New York and headed to Annapolis, Maryland, where he would resign as commander of the Continental Army. He had been home to visit only one time during the Revolution, and he wanted desperately to return to the life he once enjoyed. He missed his wife and longed for the privacy that his estate offered. Having completed his duties, the general looked forward to a restful Christmas holiday with his family and friends and returned to Virginia with a sense of great accomplishment for doing what most had imagined impossible: he had won the Revolution. But very few Americans had much faith in the new nation, including Washington. The United States of America was fragile; its infrastructure was anything but secure as the former colonies took their time forming a more cohesive country. Making matters worse, the new nation was on the brink of financial collapse. Dependent upon foreign loans, America was broke.

His return to civilian life at Mount Vernon was brief; Washington could not remove himself from the politics and the concerns of the new nation, even when he tried. When invited to serve on Virginia's delegation to the Constitutional Convention, Washington declined. It would take months for friends and political acquaintances to convince the retired general that he must attend the convention in Philadelphia. A reluctant yet duty-bound Washington was unanimously elected as the convention's president where the new nation's Constitution was created—but no one knew if it would work.

Washington left Philadelphia and returned to Mount Vernon feeling trapped. He avoided conversation about the possibility of becoming the first president of the United States, dodging questions about his intentions and denying a desire to lead the new nation. But once the Congress set the timetable for the presidential election, Washington had to make his feelings known. Presidential electors were to be chosen in January of 1789, and an election would quickly follow. Washington sent his trusted secretary, Tobias Lear, to New York to establish and secure good housing in the city that would become the nation's first capital. With considerable pressure and reassurance from friends and politicians, Washington had made up his mind; if elected the first president of the United States, he would accept the position.

On April 14, 1789, Charles Thomson, secretary of the Congress, arrived on horseback at Mount Vernon. It was Thomson's responsibility to inform the general that he had been unanimously elected to serve as president, capturing all sixty-nine electoral votes. Thomson read aloud a letter, penned by Senator John Langdon of New Hampshire, president pro tempore of the Senate.

Sir, I have the honor to transmit to Your Excellency the information of your unanimous election to the Office of the President of the United States of America. Suffer me sir, to indulge the hope, that so auspicious a mark of public confidence will meet your approbation, and be considered a sure pledge of the affection and support you are to expect from a free and enlightened people.

For Washington, the letter confirmed that his life would never again be the same, and it set into motion a chain of events that irrevocably altered the lives of George and Martha Washington. The president-elect prepared to leave for New York quickly, but not before borrowing £600 from Captain Richard Conway. Just like the new nation, Washington was cash-strapped. Poor crop harvests and delinquent taxes had placed the soon-to-be leader of the new nation in dire straits. He would need to borrow money (at 6 percent interest) to keep Mount Vernon afloat and to finance his trip to New York. All of this weighed heavy on the president-elect's mind as he wrote, "I am inclined to do what I never expected to be reduced to the necessity of doing—that is, to borrow money upon interest."

Concerned about his failing plantation, unhappy about a northern relocation, and uncertain about the fragile new nation, Washington left for New York, the seat of the nation's capital, with

a great deal on his mind. But he was not the only one with concerns about leaving Mount Vernon; there were others who would
travel with the president and his family, people who had no choice
in the matter. Seven slaves would accompany the Washingtons to
New York, including a sixteen-year-old Ona Judge. The fear of the
unknown, the separation from loved ones, and the forced relocation must have felt apocalyptic for the bondmen and bondwomen
who would travel to New York. Not that the cares and concerns of
Mount Vernon's slaves entered into the mind of the new president.

Eager to keep the new nation running, Washington left for New
York on April 16, leaving a tremendous amount of the relocation
work in the capable hands of Martha Washington, who would join
him later. Prior to his departure, the president selected an acting
master and mistress for the Mount Vernon estate. George Augustine Washington, the eldest son of the president's brother Charles,
was already living at Mount Vernon, serving as a manager, and was
deemed the appropriate choice to fill his uncle's shoes. His wife,
Fanny Bassett (the daughter of Martha Washington's sister) would
look after all things connected to the running of the house and
would remain in close contact with George and Martha Washington via the post.

Fear, regret, and concern spilled onto the pages of the president's diary. He wrote of his departure from Mount Vernon not in
the fashion of a famed general ready for new challenges, but as a
man who was extremely tentative: "About ten o'clock, I bade adieu
to Mount Vernon, to private life, and to domestic felicity; and with
a mind oppressed with more anxious and painful sensations than I
have words to express." He doubted himself and the enterprise he
had already accepted. Washington explained that he had the "best
dispositions to render service to my country in obedience to its call,
but with less hope of answering its expectations."

Washington's journey north took him through Philadelphia, where nearly twenty thousand men and women lined the streets to greet their new president. The crowds couldn't compensate for the grueling nature of the trip; the muddy roads and constant festivities slowed the pace of travel. By the time Washington arrived in New York, he wanted nothing more than to enter the city as inconspicuously as possible and to begin his work leading the new nation. Washington wrote to New York governor George Clinton, stating, "I can assure you with the utmost sincerity, that no reception can be so congenial to my feelings as a quiet entry devoid of ceremony." Although the governor offered the president lodging in his private home until a residence was secured for the new first family (a more modern term not used in the eighteenth century), Washington declined the offer, stating that it was simply too much of an imposition. The president planned to take "hired lodgings, or Rooms in a Tavern" until the details of the Washingtons' new home were settled. Just one week before his arrival, the Congress leased a home for the president at 3 Cherry Street, located in what was then the northeastern section of the city, very near the present-day Brooklyn Bridge.

Washington began the work of leading the new nation in a city that was very different from his Mount Vernon home. By the late 1780s, New York was the second-largest city in America, with a population of about thirty thousand people, and it was characteristically American. The city displayed signs of opulence and wealth all while maintaining a parochial nature that allowed for great diversity within its public spaces. People from all walks of life found themselves conducting business on the cobblestoned streets. Men, women, white, black, enslaved and free, all resided within the city limits, adding richness to a bustling commercial port city. The streets of New York could be adventurous and filled with opportunity, but they could also be rough terrain to navigate.

On April 30, 1789, George Washington took the oath of office and issued an inaugural address from the balcony of New York's federal hall. Notably absent from the ceremony was his wife. While the first lady had traveled to see her husband during the American Revolution as he led the colonists in battle against the British, she wanted nothing more than to stay put and resented her husband's call to public service that was taking them away from their Virginia home.

For his part, though he had spent a great deal of time separated from his wife over the course of the previous decade, it wasn't his preference. The new president missed having his wife by his side and began to wonder just how long it would take for Mrs. Washington to arrive in New York. She was, certainly, taking her time. Rather than immediately traveling to New York, she remained at Mount Vernon, attempting to come to grips with the path of her new life, one that would keep her away from her Virginia home for many years. Unsettled and displeased about the move to the nation's capital, she expressed her discontent to her closest confidants and stalled for time. Even the president's trusted secretary got involved. On May 3, Tobias Lear wrote to George Augustine, describing the new home on Cherry Street and offering bits of information that might entice Mrs. Washington to hurry along in her journey north. Lear wrote that they had hired "Black Sam as Steward & superintendent of the kitchen, and a very excellent fellow he is in the latter department." Lear knew that the first lady enjoyed seafood, and so he reported on the culinary wonders performed by the head chef, hoping that it would "hasten her advancing towards New York." The president's secretary made it clear that everyone was awaiting the arrival of the first lady; he wrote, "For we are extremely desirous of seeing her here." In convincing Martha Washington that there was much to look forward to, he had his work cut out for him.

The slaves at Mount Vernon knew all too well about the displeasure of their mistress and had to add that to their list of concerns. Ona Judge, in particular, one of the favored house slaves, responsible for tending to her mistress's needs, both emotional and physical, had to balance the first lady's deep sadness, resentment, and frustration with her own fears about the move.

The young Ona Judge was far from an experienced traveler. The teenager knew only Mount Vernon and its surroundings and had never traveled far from her family and loved ones. For Judge the move must have been similar to the dreaded auction block. Although she was not to be sold to a different owner, she was forced to leave her family for an unfamiliar destination hundreds of miles away. Judge would have had no choice but to stifle the terror she felt and go on about the work of preparing to move. Folding linens, packing Martha Washington's dresses and personal accessories, and helping with the grandchildren were the tasks at hand, and it wasn't her place to complain or question. Judge had to remain strong and steady, if not for herself, then for her mistress who appeared to be falling apart at the seams. Like Judge, Martha Washington had no choice about the move to New York. Her life was at the direction of her husband, who was now the most powerful man in the country. Mrs. Washington and Ona Judge may have shared similar concerns, but of course only Martha Washington was allowed to express discontent and sorrow: Martha Washington was unhappy, and everyone knew it, including her frightened slave.

The president's nephew Robert Lewis would also soon be made aware of it. When he arrived at the estate on May 14, things were in disarray. Lewis, who served as Washington's secretary between 1789 and 1791, was chosen to escort his aunt and her grandchildren to New York but was surprised and a bit concerned when he arrived to find a frenzied and hectic scene. Lewis wrote, "Everything appeared to be in confusion," the manifestation of Mrs. Washington's conflicting feelings.

Robert Lewis described the departure, which finally took place on May 16, 1789, as an emotional moment for the slaves and the first lady:

"After an early dinner and making all necessary arrangements in which we were greatly retarded it brought us to 3 o'clock in the afternoon when we left Mt. V. The servants of the House, and a number of the field negros made there [sic] appearance—to take leave of their mistress—numbers of these poor wretches seemed greatly *agitated, much affected*—My Aunt equally so."

Betty, Ona Judge's mother, must have been one of those agitated slaves. Not only was she losing her sixteen-year-old daughter, but she was also losing her son Austin, who would serve as one of the Washingtons' waiters. Austin's wife, Charlotte, and their children would have joined in the mourning. Betty watched her children leave Mount Vernon, a reminder of what little control slave mothers had over the lives of their children. If she found any comfort that day, it would have been that brother and sister were traveling together. Austin was older and male and could look out for his younger sister. Still, Betty knew that her relationship with her children would never be the same.

The grieving mother was not the only slave to wrestle with a feeling of dread at the sight of her mistress's departure. Every slave on the Mount Vernon estate knew that the order of things was in transition. With George and Martha Washington hundreds of miles away, their lives were now in the hands of George Augustine and the overseers. Would the slaves at Mount Vernon be treated decently? Would the nature of their work change, and if so, how? The uncertainty of life and the involuntary separation of family members reminded every black person at Mount Vernon that the system of slavery rendered them powerless.

Not everyone was disturbed with the plans for Northern living, however. Traveling north may have also stirred some feelings of hope or excitement in the minds of the slaves who were chosen to accompany the Washingtons. Freedom and opportunity were at play in many Northern states that boasted growing free black populations. News about Northern emancipation reached the information-hungry slave communities of the South, often prompting slaves to risk everything and attempt escape. The commonwealths of Pennsylvania and Massachusetts had already loosened the shackles of slavery through gradual abolition laws, while New York struggled with such decisions. Just a year prior, in 1788, Connecticut and Massachusetts forbade its residents from participating in the slave trade, but New York enacted a new comprehensive slave law, one that kept all slaves currently held in bondage as slaves for the entirety of their lives.

It is impossible to know how familiar the slaves at Mount Vernon were with the specifics of the changing laws of the North, of one state's mandate versus another's, but what is certain is that Judge had witnessed the act of running away. The slaves at Mount Vernon who successfully escaped reminded the bond people who remained that there were alternatives to the dehumanizing experience of slavery. Freedom, of course, was risky, and was never considered without great caution and planning, but perhaps a trip to New York would yield opportunities never imagined by the slaves who lived at Mount Vernon? Maybe life would be better in New York and perhaps they could find their way to freedom? As the slaves pondered what the move to New York might mean for them, they did so subtly. A slave could not appear to be too calculating or strategic, and no one wanted to spook the Washingtons, especially the very fragile Martha Washington.

The president and his wife were well aware that the practice of slavery was under attack in most of the Northern states. They also knew that though New York's residents still clung to bound labor, public sentiment regarding African slavery was changing. Unwilling to even think about abandoning the use of black slaves, the president and the first lady were careful in their selection of men and women who traveled with them from Mount Vernon. Their selections involved only those slaves who were seen as "loyal" and therefore less likely to attempt escape. Skills in the art of house service were also a necessity.

William Lee, the president's body servant, elbowed his way to the front of the line of the bondmen who would travel north. He was Washington's number one slave, the valet who knew the president better than any other enslaved person at Mount Vernon. Born circa 1750, William Lee was a teenager when he was purchased by George Washington. Sold alongside three other slaves, Lee earned the position as butler in part because of his complexion. Believing that interracial slaves were more attractive and intelligent, Washington preferred to buy "yellow-skinned" men and women. Lee was offered fine clothing and learned the art of caring for his master from older, more seasoned house slaves. He would perfect his duty of dressing his master's hair and preparing his clothing.

Washington's manservant also became known for his expertise in riding, an activity much enjoyed by his master. The trusted bondman was noted as a "fearless horseman" who was "sturdy, and of great bone and muscle." Washington and Lee would ride together several times a week, forming the closest kind of relationship appropriate for a master and slave. Once Washington announced that he would accept the position of president and move to New York, William Lee was determined to go with him. Lee had traveled north once before—albeit to Philadelphia for the Continental

Congress, fifteen years earlier, not New York—and good memories must have prompted him to want to return. For it was during his first northern sojourn that Lee found both his voice and love.

While we know virtually nothing about Lee's first experience in the North—other than the fact that Washington attired him in new shoes and garments—we can surmise that the trip changed him. Prior to leaving Mount Vernon, members of George and Martha Washington's family often referred to Lee as "Billy." Washington frequently listed him as "my boy Billy" in his account books, but Lee returned from the Northern city with a proper name, one that he chose on his own. His master wrote that his enslaved valet began "calling himself William Lee." Presumably, revolutionary rhetoric and the beginnings of black freedom in the North affected Lee, giving him the impetus to move away from the nickname of "Billy" and to adopt the surname that directly tied him to the plantation on which he was born. Not only did William Lee name himself after that trip to Philadelphia, but in doing so, he openly connected himself to his former owner, whom he must have considered to be his biological father.

However, it was his meeting and courtship with Margaret Thomas, a free black woman in Philadelphia, that changed Lee's life. The couple requested that they be kept together, and Margaret Thomas made the odd and dangerous decision to move south with her beloved. Although the marriages of enslaved people were not recognized by the law in Virginia, Washington supposedly granted their request that Thomas be allowed to travel to and live with Lee at Mount Vernon. What happened next is lost. There is no written evidence that Lee and Thomas lived together at Mount Vernon, though as a freewoman she would not have appeared in Washington's account book. It is possible that she either died or left the marriage. What's more probable is that Thomas changed her mind about exchanging what little stability she had in Philadelphia for dangerous uncertainty in Virginia. By leaving Philadelphia, Thomas would've walked into the mouth of the slave-hungry South, placing her free status in serious jeopardy. In this instance, perhaps, love was not a strong enough pull to compete with freedom. Lee's chance for love with a freewoman, and a future complete with free heirs, never came to fruition. Still, he was marked by this experience, and he was keen, indeed determined, to travel to New York with his master.

Lee's desperate wish to travel to New York was in danger, however, because of his failing health. In April of 1785, Lee was injured during a surveying expedition and "broke the pan of his knee." Reduced to hobbling around on crutches or a cane, Lee dealt with his constant pain through the consumption of alcohol, and lots of it. Three years later on a cold and snowy day in March, Lee was sent to fetch the mail from Alexandria. During his errand the already disabled slave fell again, this time shattering the other knee. His body was broken, and his usefulness was lost. Lee became somewhat of an invalid, unable to perform any tasks that required him to walk or move. In his late thirties, Lee's duties shifted to that of a shoemaker, a demotion. Fortunately, Washington felt a sense of closeness with his faithful slave and agreed to bring Lee to New York as a member of his team of slaves, even though he was unable to perform the duties of a respected valet. William Lee, therefore, began the journey to the nation's capital with the president-elect and his aides Tobias Lear and David Humphreys. Hours away from fulfilling his dream of living in another Northern city, he experienced yet another setback. He fell behind the president's entourage. Unable to keep up with the hectic pace of traveling, he was left in Philadelphia to see a doctor and to recuperate. He was fitted for braces and appeared in New York on June 22, 1789, more than two months after Washington.

Also joining the first family would be two other slaves known only as Giles and Paris. Similar to William Lee, Giles and Paris had traveled outside of the Virginia colony when they accompanied the president to the Constitutional Convention in 1787. Proving themselves reliable outside the rural limits of Virginia, they were to serve the Washingtons as postilions—drivers for the president's horse-drawn carriages—a duty that would require a quick study of the streets of New York. As illiterate slaves, these men would have to form fast friendships with New York coachmen, relying upon word of mouth and a circle of New York postilions to learn the geographical layout of the city. That wouldn't prove too difficult. For one, they were serving the decorated commander of the Revolutionary War. And they were fortunate to find other blacks performing the same duty. Black postilions and footmen were seen as symbols of wealth for the rural gentry in New York. The Washingtons could thus maintain their Virginia customs far from Mount Vernon and do it in style.

The president was conscious of the appearance of his slaves, especially bondmen like Giles and Paris, who stood as symbols of urban wealth. He surveyed their grooming habits and attire, asking his secretary to purchase new clothing for them when their outfits became frayed or tattered. Deciding that the caps worn by Giles and Paris were unacceptable, Washington even wrote to Tobias Lear, "I therefore request that you will have two handsome ones [caps] made, with fuller and richer tassels at top than the old ones have." Giles and Paris needed to look good. Washington's image depended upon it.

Austin, Ona Judge's half brother, and Christopher Sheels, the nephew of William Lee, were also to serve the Washingtons in New York as waiters/butlers. These men were undoubtedly accustomed to eighteenth-century Southern protocol, and not only were they seen as reliable slaves, but they were presentable to a new Northern social circle. They were most likely trained by the ailing William Lee, who knew the likes and dislikes of his master more than any other bondman. Lee would serve as Mount Vernon's transplanted institutional memory, the reminder of a slow and steady Virginia past in a hectic New York present.

Christopher Sheels was a dower slave born during the revolutionary era, probably around 1774. Similar to Austin, he belonged to the Parke Custis heirs and was not counted as one of Washington's personal slaves. Like Ona Judge, he was young and had a familial connection that placed him among the most trusted of house slaves. Mount Vernon historian Mary Thompson suggests that Sheels was one of the few slaves who were literate on the Mount Vernon estate. This skill would most certainly be useful in the new capital city. Older than both Sheels and Judge, Austin offered reliability as well as maturity.

The only bondwomen who were set to travel to New York were Ona Judge and Moll, a fifty-year-old seamstress. Judge and Moll would serve the first lady as housemaids and personal attendants. Judge would draw her mistress's bath, prepare her bed clothing, brush her hair, tend to her when she was ill, and travel with her throughout the city on social calls. Moll would be responsible for the grandchildren who lived with the Washingtons. Moll would wipe noses, calm anxious souls awakened by nightmares, and make certain that the Washingtons' grandchildren were well fed and dressed. Ona would help Moll in whatever way she could above and beyond fulfilling Martha Washington's needs. The two women worked all day and every day under the careful watch of their mistress. The life of an enslaved domestic carried grueling and constant demands. Private time, time away from their mistress and master, was all but fleeting.

Mrs. Washington traveled a similar route to that of her husband, arriving first in Philadelphia, where she was to make a few social calls and take a short respite, before traveling onward to New York, to much fanfare. Judge watched as a cavalry and honor guard greeted them at the outskirts of the city, welcoming Mrs. Washington and her entourage to Philadelphia. While the first lady reacquainted herself with her old friend Mary Morris, wife of well-known financier Robert Morris, Judge tended to her mistress and started to acclimate herself to a new Northern pace. They were still several days' travel away from New York, but the time in Philadelphia marked an important transition. Philadelphia was Judge's first encounter with the North, this exhilarating place where enslaved and free blacks comingled. Inevitably, Judge was confused and excited by the examples of black freedom she witnessed, for it was unlike anything she had ever seen.

With close to forty-four thousand residents living and working in the growing city, Philadelphia was teeming with people. Nearly three hundred slaves still tethered to the institution of slavery called the City of Brotherly Love their home, yet they were in the minority. When Judge arrived in the city in May of 1789, there were nearly five times as many or close to 1,800 free blacks living within the city limits. Early antislavery literature distributed by Philadelphia publishers forced the city's inhabitants to look at the institution of slavery through new eyes. When Judge arrived in Philadelphia, the most well-known abolitionist broadside, *Description of a Slave Ship*, had already made an appearance. The eighteenth-century poster laid bare the brutality and inhumanity of African slavery, creating a visual supplement for all who were interested in the subject of the transatlantic slave trade.

In the same month that Ona Judge traveled to Philadelphia, printer Matthew Carey produced the broadside for the newly reorganized Pennsylvania Society for Promoting the Abolition of Slavery and for the Relief of Free Negroes Unlawfully Held in Bondage—later known as the Pennsylvania Abolition Society. *Description of a Slave Ship* documented how Africans were mercilessly packed into slave ships with no regard to space or hygiene, let alone humanity. The broadside buttressed the constant Quaker conversations about the evils of slavery. It also reminded Pennsylvanians about their decision to prepare for the end of slavery in the commonwealth. Some of the most revered Philadelphia statesmen joined the crusade to release men, women, and children from the grasp of perpetual bondage, even former slaveholders such as Benjamin Franklin.

Franklin was not unlike many other white Philadelphians in that it took him some time to accept and support the ending of African slavery. Yet toward the end of the Revolution, Franklin ceased his connection to human trafficking. He had held a handful of slaves, most of whom ran away or died while in his service, and in 1787 became the president of Pennsylvania's abolition society. That same year, the year that Ona Judge came to Philadelphia, Franklin penned several essays that supported national abolition. Martha Washington would make certain to avoid the likes of Franklin during her brief stay in Philadelphia. She had no interest in releasing the slaves at Mount Vernon, who numbered in the hundreds. Instead, she would move quickly to join her husband in New York, shielding her slaves from the contagion of liberty.

As Judge started to familiarize herself with Northern life, expert astronomer and African American scientist Benjamin Banneker's predictions of a solar eclipse came true. Although the hybrid solar eclipse was not visible in the skies of North America,

Banneker foretold of the event, much to the surprise of his white peers. In ancient times, it was feared that the shadow of the sun signified either death or the end of an era, and in many ways, this was true for the bondmen and bondwomen who found themselves laying over in Philadelphia. On Sunday, May 24, 1789, the moon sailed in front of the sun. The next day the party from Mount Vernon left Philadelphia and headed for New York, marking the beginning of a new life for the young slave girl.

Three

New York in Black and White

For Sale,

A LIKELY, HEALTHY, YOUNG
NEGRO WENCH,

BETWEEN fifteen and fixteen Years old:
She has been ufed to the Farming Bufi-
nefs. Sold for want of Employ.——Enquire at
No. 81, William-ftreet,
New-York, March 30, 1789.

"Sale in New York."

Fugitive slaves lived in the shadows of eighteenth-century cities, searching for anonymity among the masses. In New York, a fugitive named Molly looked for domestic work and stayed close to her new friends. She lived her life looking over her shoulder for kidnappers or officials of the law, all of whom were anxious to lay claim to her vulnerable black body. We do not know where Molly was from or what family, if any, she left behind in bondage. But we know that she selected New York as her hiding place, a city that still clung to slavery but had cracked open the door to black opportunity. Molly's carefulness, however, was simply not enough to keep her from the reach of a local constable who had every intention of following the new nation's constitution. It was his responsibility to arrest men and women who stole themselves from bondage and to make certain that human property was restored to its rightful owner. Molly had to be returned to slavery.

Perhaps she fought the constable, however unsuccessfully, succumbing to his strength as he dragged her to the river to board a boat that would return the fugitive to her owner. A mixture of fear and anger would have coursed through the runaway's body as she confronted the failure of her escape and the realization that her re-enslavement was imminent. The constable approached the watercraft and prepared to load his newly found human property, when a group of men, white men, appeared. Lawrence Embree, a New York attorney and member of the New York Manumission Society, was among the men who were determined to save the fugitive. They hurled their bodies in front of the constable, "took hold of him," and refused to let him carry out his slave-catching task. While Embree and his friends detained the constable, Molly was spirited away. The fugitive was safe, for the time being. Embree would face charges of interfering with the law, charges that the prosecutor eventually dropped.

The men who had come to Molly's rescue were among a small group of New Yorkers who were ready to end the institution of slavery. These influential men had gathered together, just a few years before, to form the New York Manumission Society and began the difficult task of persuading New Yorkers to gradually release their slaves. Becoming important allies to black New Yorkers, the New York Manumission Society was committed to thwarting shadowy slave catchers and to preventing the public sale of slaves. These men offered legal aid to fugitives and opened the first of several African Free Schools for black children. Some of the most well-known nineteenth-century black leaders were educated at the African Free

School, including Alexander Crummell, Henry Highland Garnet, and James McCune Smith among others.

As this early band of New York reformers challenged black slavery, free blacks worked to improve life for themselves. Committed black men came together in the tradition of West African societies to form the African Society. Cloaked in secrecy, its founding date is uncertain; however, it is clear that the organization was up and running by 1784 when the poet Jupiter Hammon was invited to speak to the organization. This active and influential black society paved the way for nineteenth-century political and social organizations that focused on the issues of free and enslaved people of African descent. Eventually, among its other goals, this organization would take the charge in fighting for the burial rights of black men and women. In 1788, the year before George Washington's arrival in New York, black residents uncovered the dubious practice of white medical students: in need of cadavers for dissection and research, white students raided black graves, removing bodies for study and then leaving their remains in bags by the docks. Infuriated blacks came together and petitioned the Common Council to put an end to this practice, but the fight to protect the rights of the deceased and the respect of black bodies crossed over into the 1790s.

White reformers who came to Molly's aid and those who fought for the burial rights of black people faced almost insurmountable obstacles. Molly's rescue was a victory, but slavery would live on in New York for decades. Perhaps it was New York's legal safeguarding of black bondage that allowed the new president to feel comfortable bringing his slaveholding customs to his new Northern residence.

George Washington met his family and the estate's slaves on May 27 in Elizabethtown, New Jersey, where they were greeted in almost the same manner as was the president. In Martha's entourage was Judge, who likely alternated between helping Martha and attending to Eleanor Parke "Nelly" Custis and George Washington Parke "Wash" Custis—the Washington grandchildren—as they crossed the river and arrived in Manhattan. In a little less than two weeks, Ona Judge transformed from a rural Virginia slave to one of the most high-profile bondwomen in the new nation. The Washingtons quickly became familiar with the city's social and political movers and shakers, moving around and entertaining at home, with their slaves ever present. It was a very new kind of life, but the Washington family adjusted in good time. Martha Washington made friends, immersing herself into the new role of the first lady, which included running the President's House as well as managing Mount Vernon from afar.

Although private correspondence reveals Martha Washington's personal struggles with the new demands placed upon her, Ona Judge, an illiterate teenager, left behind no such trace. We can only imagine what Judge's transition to Northern life must have felt like; it had to have been terrifying or at the very least, unsteadying.

Yet the young bondwoman handled the abrupt change like a seasoned slave. Judge adapted to her new life and work in New York, a routine that offered little in the way of sentimental comfort or familiarity. Her new role as Martha Washington's top servant thrust her into a tornado of constant preparation. The young slave was Martha's "go-to girl" for just about everything, and it was Judge's duty to know the desires of her mistress before Martha Washington knew them herself. A slave always had to be prepared, for anything.

Her responsibilities were varied. Coming from a family of talented seamstresses, Judge was responsible for Martha Washington's appearance. She selected her gowns, made small repairs on aging skirts, removing stains whether they be from food or the dirt from the unpaved streets, and then dressed her. What appeared to be the mundane task of wardrobe selection for the first lady was actually quite important. A wardrobe lay at the root of one's appearance, and the mistress and her slave girl fashioned an image for the new American aristocracy. Although the first lady was far from unrefined, her Virginia ways were revamped during her residency in New York. The Washingtons were precedent setters—and citizens and foreigners alike examined their manners and public displays of quotidian life. The President's House on Cherry Street became much more cosmopolitan as the first family found themselves adapting to a bustling city with a demanding social calendar.

When Mrs. Washington arrived at Cherry Street, she found the accommodations to be more than acceptable, writing, "The House he is in is a very good one and is handsomely furnished all new for the General." Just a few blocks away from the countryside, a reassuring reminder of Mount Vernon for the new first lady, it faced the East River and was three stories high and five windows wide. Leased from attorney Samuel Osgood for a sum of $845 per year, a substantial amount of money was required to refurbish the home before the arrival of the president and his family. Similar to other elite New York homes of the eighteenth century, the house counted seven fireplaces as well as the relatively modern convenience of a pump and cistern in the yard. Rooms were enlarged and remodeled for the president's comfort and business affairs with an extended drawing room for entertaining and a larger and more appropriate stable and washhouse. An office, large dining room appropriate for formal receptions and dinners, and a smaller, more intimate dining room were located on the first floor. Just above, a drawing room and bedrooms for the family occupied all the space on the second floor. The secretaries had two bedrooms on the third floor, leaving the rest of the third floor and attic to be shared by the servants and slaves.

Even with the extensions and adaptations, however, the Cherry Street house was quite full. In addition to the president and Mrs. Washington, two grandchildren, seven slaves (William Lee arrived later in June), and additional members of the staff resided with the president. Tobias Lear, personal assistant to George Washington, and four additional secretaries: David Humphreys, William Jackson, Thomas Nelson Jr., and Washington's nephew Robert Lewis all made their home on Cherry Street.

There was absolutely no way that Ona Judge and her six enslaved companions could complete all of the necessary work of running the president's household on their own, and Tobias Lear had already begun to assemble additional staff. Fourteen white servants were hired as both live-in and day servants, including coachmen, porters, cooks, waiters, and housemaids. The servants lived in shared tight quarters with Judge and the other Virginia slaves. For Judge, this was most likely the first time that she lived in such close contact with free white servants. Although there were white artisans and overseers employed at Mount Vernon, Judge would have had infrequent interaction with free whites, who worked physically demanding jobs in order to squeeze out a meager living. At home in Virginia, Judge would have spent the majority of her day serving her masters, but she would have lived in the slave quarters, which were separate and distinct from the main house at Mount Vernon. Things were very different in New York, for not only would Judge learn of a free black population, she would sleep, eat, and share other intimate spaces with white servants.

We know almost nothing about the lives of the servants who were employed by Tobias Lear, and we know even less about their relationships with the seven enslaved men and women with whom they cohabited. What we can imagine is that just as Judge witnessed the "freedom" possessed by Washington's servants, she also noticed its limitations. White servants grappled with a frightening closeness to poverty, the vulnerability of a job market that still clung to enslaved and indentured labor, and a lack of opportunity that often prevented them from climbing out of destitution. Still, while her white roommates may indeed have been subject to the hostility of poverty, they were free, and Judge was not.

Everyone who resided at the Cherry Street mansion, from the new commander in chief down to the scullery maid, was learning new responsibilities. The learning curve was steep for Judge. In addition to her priority of service to the first lady, the leisure time activities of Nelly and Wash Custis likely became Judge's responsibility as well. The Washingtons' granddaughter was ten years old, and her brother was eight, and after her own children died, the Washington grandchildren moved into the center of Martha Washington's life. Although busy with many new duties, the first lady focused on finding the appropriate tutors and educating the children. According to most accounts, Nelly enjoyed formal learning, while her brother was less enthralled with his academic lessons. During the first few months of his stay in New York, little Wash worked with a private tutor, while Nelly began working with her music teacher, Alexander Reinagle, an Austrian composer and performer. Nelly Washington also learned the art of painting, an eighteenth-century symbol of nobility and refinement. By the fall of 1789, the Washington grandchildren were enrolled in new schools, Wash at a small private school that counted seven additional boys, and Nelly became a day student at a newly opened boarding school, Mrs. Graham's School, on Maiden Lane.

The whirlwind of New York life intensified the demands of

Mrs. Washington, and Judge's responsibilities became increasingly formal and public. To complicate matters, the young bondwoman had to interact with her mistress in a much more delicate manner. Martha Washington was homesick and complained about her new life almost constantly, later referring to her time in the North as "the lost years."

Mrs. Washington wasn't the only one struggling to adjust. New York was both the metaphorical and the literal gateway to an urban early republic. The streets were filled with new adventures in entrepreneurship, culture, and a growing urban citizenry. As the Washingtons adapted to their new life, they did so with trepidation and a longing for the simpler life of Mount Vernon. Washington's life was filled with so many ceremonial duties that he complained about the loss of his own personal time. Washington wrote, "I had no leizure to read or answer the dispatches which were pouring in from all quarters." After his return from war, Washington grew accustomed to and appreciated the five and a half years of a slower-paced life at Mount Vernon. His preferred lifestyle all but vanished in his new post, and the new president struggled to create boundaries between the personal and the public, a chore that was almost impossible. Anxious not to appear antidemocratic, Washington wanted to maintain an open relationship with "the people," but he needed to reel in the constant social and semipolitical demands placed upon him and his family. Weekly levees, small receptions where visitors could speak directly to him, seemed a perfect compromise. These audiences with the president began at three o'clock every Tuesday afternoon and lasted no longer than an hour. The president was a punctual man but also somewhat socially distant. He did not like socializing with strangers; it made him uncomfortable. Four o'clock on Tuesdays couldn't come soon enough for Washington.

The president's levees were open to male visitors only, so every Friday, Martha Washington would open the home on Cherry Street to her female friends and acquaintances. Beginning at seven o'clock in the evening, Mrs. Washington greeted her guests with tea and coffee, as well as lemonade and ice cream. Unlike her husband, Mrs. Washington did not cut her social gatherings short, allowing guests to stay until ten o'clock. In addition, on Thursday evenings Mrs. Washington and her husband hosted a formal dinner party for which great care was taken with the guest list. It was important for the president to appear impartial, and therefore the dinners hosted on Cherry Street had to include people from all walks of political life. Foreign ministers, senators and congressmen, as well as cabinet members were invited to dine with the Washingtons, an event where Mrs. Washington often carried most of the socializing. (Aside from her husband's natural reticence, Washington also suffered from awful dental problems that often caused pain and embarrassment.) Mrs. Washington complained about the lack of personal time and solitude she experienced in New York, but few would know her true feelings. She served well as the president's social partner, transmitting an image of grace and respectability.

For her part, Ona Judge would have looked forward to these occasions. While the preparation for Mrs. Washington was intense prior to each event, Judge found herself with a bit of free time, a few stolen moments for herself, once the dinners and socials began. More downtime came on Saturdays when the president and his family went out for a ride in the coach, sometimes riding around town or traveling out to the countryside. On occasion, the Washingtons followed the "fourteen mile round," a popular path that took travelers through lower Manhattan. Leaving at eleven in the morning, the president and his family spent a few hours away from the house, offering Judge what must have seemed like a luxurious amount of time apart from her masters.

In a home that was filled to the rafters with guests, family, secretaries, servants, and slaves, Judge would have relished this time. In her stolen moments of leisure, it is very likely that she spent time talking to Austin, her brother, or the other slaves about current events or reminiscing about loved ones back at home in Virginia. Perhaps, in these moments, Judged talked with some of the hired servants about New York and its environs. These fleeting respites from her owners allowed for moments of autonomy that helped the young bondwoman come to know her new city and refine her understanding of freedom and slavery in New York.

For decades, New Yorkers grappled with the issue of black emancipation. The Revolutionary War found men in the coffee shops of Philadelphia, Boston, and New York discussing the topics of freedom and citizenship, prompting some New Yorkers to rethink their commitment to slavery. But the drive to maintain human bondage was a slow-burning fire that stayed lit well into the nineteenth century. So, Washington's decision to bring seven slaves from Mount Vernon to his new home on Cherry Street in 1789 was not considered unseemly or unusual. As was the case for many other elite whites, Washington's use of slave labor was acceptable. Governor George Clinton owned eight slaves, and New York resident Aaron Burr owned five of his own. Yet these men were also involved in the New York Manumission Society, as were John Jay and Alexander Hamilton. Although the society engaged in conversation about gradually ending slavery, most of New York's leaders remained uncommitted to this goal. Slave ownership was still a sign of upper-class status, so slavery in New York lived on.

Politicians and learned men were not the only ones who raised concerns about the system of human bondage. By the 1770s, religious groups were pushing for, or at the very least discussing, the ending of slavery. The Quakers in Philadelphia jumped to the front of the movement to abolish slavery by disowning all members of the Society of Friends who engaged in the traffic of human souls. Their early ban on slavery not only affected the Quakers in Philadelphia but also slowly spread across the North. Other religious groups such as the Methodists also began to rethink their affiliation with the institution of slavery, and Anglicans, who had appeared more committed to un-free labor, started to educate and baptize black New Yorkers. Yet New York was not quite as progressive as Philadelphia. When Judge and her enslaved companions stopped briefly in the City of Brotherly Love on their sojourn to New York, they inevitably recognized that slavery was on the wane. This realization would have stirred hope and optimism in the heart and mind of a Southern slave. But a strange reversal followed Judge once she left Philadelphia and traveled north. As she entered New York, she found herself surrounded by slaves again, albeit mixed with a significant number of free blacks.

As the city continued to grow in size, so too did its population of enslaved men and women. But New York would never claim as large a black population as Washington's home state of Virginia. As a black woman, Judge was now in the minority, a stark difference from her world back home at Mount Vernon. Ten percent of New York's population consisted of black people, and of them about two-thirds were enslaved. Judge would interact with these men and women, noticing that the wealthiest white men and women owned a large percentage of the city's slaves, though poorer whites were not absent from the slave trade game, as was the case with a small grocer named Hastings Stockhouse. The grocer lived on

Cherry Street but owned no real property and struggled to make a living. Although relegated to the lower end of the socioeconomic ladder, Stockhouse owned a slave.

It would have only taken a short time for Judge to figure out that the majority of whites who owned slaves didn't own a great number of them. Unlike an estate such as Mount Vernon, which counted its bondmen and bondwomen in the hundreds, most slaveholders in New York City held one or two slaves. The majority of those who claimed human property were artisans, such as Stockhouse, living above their small stores and rented shops, placing their human property in the attics and cellars of their already cramped homes. New York slave owners simply couldn't own more than a couple of slaves, for there was nowhere to lodge them, unlike the slave quarters and cabins at Mount Vernon, which allowed slaves to sleep, eat, laugh, and love each other outside the walls of a master's house.

What may have been even more surprising to Judge as she settled into residency in New York was that the majority of the blacks with whom she became acquainted were women. Although artisans and other slaveholders who invested in slave labor preferred male slaves, black women (both slave and free) were a significant presence in the city. Northern slavery was different from what the young Virginian knew. In cities of the North and Mid-Atlantic, slavery was an institution that depended upon black women not for their ability to reproduce but for their agility with the most arduous kinds of domestic work. Meal preparation, cleaning, and sewing were extremely taxing in the eighteenth century, and without the luxuries of running water or electricity, much of the work required lifting heavy buckets of water and cooking in unbearably hot kitchens or freezing sheds. For most black women who toiled as domestic slaves or servants, their bodies were broken, and their time was never their own.

Because of her owner's revered status, however, Judge was most likely spared from the most physically taxing labor in the home, as she had to be on call to assist Mrs. Washington and to accompany her on her many social visits. While she wouldn't be asked to assist with cooking or heavy cleaning, in many ways, her work would be much more demanding and extremely unpredictable.

It was Judge's job to serve the first lady without being seen. When Mrs. Washington entertained her close friends, Judge was always within earshot. Sunny days prompted Mrs. Washington to call for her carriage, where she could chat with friends and enjoy the fresh air. Passersby always recognized the first lady and took note of her entourage.

> *Preceded by a Servant about ½ mile ahead, and two young Gentlemen on Horseback, Just before them, a Mulatto girl behind the carriage and a Negro man Servant on Horseback behind.*

Judge, the "Mulatto girl," was always careful not to intrude on her mistress and her guests. She perfected the responsibilities of a domestic slave; she was always available but never present.

But only one month after Judge's arrival in New York, the frantic pace of life on Cherry Street came to a hard stop. The president was in danger—he was gravely ill.

⁘

Over the course of his eight-year war experience, Washington's health had deteriorated. Difficult and sometimes unsanitary conditions at war, as well as his advancing age, had taken their toll on the president's body. Having survived the war, no one expected the president to battle for his life after he contracted a fever in June of 1789. His febrile body worsened, and a large tumor developed on his left leg. As the tumor grew, Washington became debilitated by pain, was unable to sit, and the situation grew worse by the hour. Well-respected physician Samuel Bard diagnosed the president's condition as a cutaneous form of anthrax and feared the worst. Washington knew that he might not survive, which must have been nothing short of devastating to Mrs. Washington. Having already buried one husband and all of her children, Martha Washington was most likely consumed with fear.

Though they wanted to keep his condition private, the physician's extended stay at the President's House must have proven curious to the Washingtons' close friends and family. When servants and/or slaves were asked to cordon off Cherry Street, even the public began to wonder what was happening. Straw was placed on the street outside the president's home to dampen the noise of foot traffic, and all who resided within the walls of the president's home understood the seriousness of the situation. By June 17 Dr. Bard had no choice but to operate on the president's leg. All surgery in the late eighteenth century was horribly painful, as analgesics and anesthesia were yet to be invented. The surgery was quite serious, and Dr. Bard was forced to remove the tumor, which Tobias Lear later described as "very large and the incision on opening it deep." Washington survived the ordeal but was left debilitated and unable to sit or walk for weeks, forcing the president to attend to his duties from his bed or sofa.

Martha Washington continued to worry about her husband's health even after he regained his strength by early September. Judge's task was not only to care for Lady Washington, as she had been doing, but also now to help calm her nerves and soothe her soul. Still distraught about leaving Mount Vernon, Martha Washington was forced to deal with the mortality of her husband and to imagine what life would be like without her partner. For three months, Martha Washington's mood remained apprehensive. Even after the president appeared to be on the road to full recovery, the first lady remained leery about her husband's health, worried that his responsibilities would take him to an early grave.

Finally, with the president relatively healthy—his dental condition never left him pain-free—in February of 1790 the first family relocated to a much larger home on Broadway. The new home was a spacious four-storied building that allowed for the president and his wife to entertain with much more grandeur. Views of the Hudson River, fine carpets, and beautiful furniture appeared more appropriate for the Washingtons and allotted all who resided in the president's house a bit more space.

Once his leg was completely healed, the president's obligations increased, forcing him to travel from state to state, often with little rest. And yet again, the president was betrayed by his own body. The first lady's apprehension about her husband's fragile health seemed a premonition. A few months after the Washingtons settled into their new home on Broadway, the president developed another fever, which refused to disappear.

This time the president couldn't hide his infirmity, and friends and colleagues began to talk openly about their concerns. Pennsylvania congressman George Clymer wrote, "But it is observed here with a great deal of anxiety that his general health seems to be declining." Influenza spread through the city, striking without regard to status or position, and the president was no exception. By late April of 1790, Washington came down with the virus that served as a gateway for pneumonia. The contagion that ripped through the city and president's body would claim many lives and robbed Washington of much of his hearing. When Dr. Bard along with other well-known physicians were summoned to his bedside,

Judge once again witnessed the mood of the president's house turn from great optimism to despair. The president coughed up blood, and his fever worsened, leading the president's doctors, aides, and his wife to fear the worst. But their deep concerns would soon dissipate because, once again, Washington beat the odds. In a little more than a month, the president appeared to be out of harm's way.

When the summer arrived, the Washingtons and their slaves packed up once again. This time Judge prepared to return home to Mount Vernon for an extended visit, one in which everyone could take a step back from the frantic pace of Northern life. Judge returned to Virginia a changed woman. She had been thrust into the spotlight of serving the most powerful family in the nation during a year that had been particularly strange and perilous. As she watched her owners take their place at the top of the political ladder, she subtly monitored the beginnings of Northern black freedom. Though only sixteen years old, Ona Judge was no longer a child; she was an experienced housemaid whose eyes had seen plenty.

Four

The Move to Philadelphia

"Residence of Washington in High Street, Philadelphia."

In the summer of 1790, after a year and a half in New York, the Washingtons traveled back to Mount Vernon for a nearly three-month visit. The contents in the house at 39-41 Broadway had to be packed and prepared for transport to two locations. While some of the family's personal items would follow along back to Mount Vernon, the rest of Washington's property would be sent on to Philadelphia, the new site for the nation's capital. Very little information exists to document this sojourn back to Mount Vernon, but Ona Judge must have looked forward to the familiarity of home and to meeting a new family member. Judge's sister, Betty

Davis, had given birth to little Nancy sometime in 1790. Meeting her niece and visiting her family and friends at Mount Vernon would be bittersweet, as it rekindled her most intimate relationships while reminding Judge of a childhood lost and an entrenched system of plantation slavery. Now in her late teenage years, she had become one of the Washingtons' most-valued house slaves and had witnessed things her family members could only dream of. Neither her siblings nor her mother had traveled to the North; only Judge's brother Austin could claim the same kind of worldliness that she knew.

When the carriage returned Judge to the curved driveway at the Mount Vernon estate, the bondwoman would alter her frame of reference. Her eyes would miss the spotting of free black men and women in the marketplace, and her ears longed for discreet conversations about black freedom. On her return trip to Virginia, Judge would confront the fixed reality of her life as a slave. While her lifestyle and duties may have appeared desirable, even glamorous, to the enslaved at Mount Vernon, Judge knew that black Northerners could enjoy much more than she could. Laying eyes upon little Nancy would remind Judge of the deepest dilemmas of slavery; slave births were moments of celebration and mourning. She would welcome this new baby girl into the family, knowing all too well the kinds of danger, degradation, and violence that lay in wait for her. But Judge was Nancy's aunt, not her mother, and whatever dreams she had of raising her own family were packed away. There was no place in the Executive Mansion for an infant slave. Motherhood would have to wait for Ona Judge.

Martha Washington, who had been so reluctant to join her husband in New York, now found herself saddened that as a result of a political compromise, brokered by Alexander Hamilton and Thomas Jefferson, the capital was moving to Philadelphia. She had grown accustomed to her new status and her expanding circle of friends, and now she had to start over again in a different city. While a holiday back at Mount Vernon most likely tempered her anxieties about the impending move to Philadelphia, the first lady was burdened with another relocation to plan. Plagued with thoughts of a long and grueling road trip to Virginia, the Washington household made its way through the streets of New York in a farewell procession. *The Federal Gazette* reported that "Mrs. Washington, also, seemed hurt at the idea of bidding adieu,"—which they did on August 30.

New Yorkers bid farewell to their president and to their claim on the nation's capital. Following the American Revolution, the location of the seat of government was a point of great debate, with thirty or more cities competing for the right to house the new center of power. New Yorkers and Philadelphians argued that the site of the nation's capital should be along the Eastern Seaboard, with its quick and easy access for business transactions. Philadelphians were shocked when the Congress abandoned the Pennsylvania State House (later called Independence Hall) and took up residence in New York. In 1788 New York became the official meeting place for the first Congress under the Constitution.

Yet behind closed doors, some members of Congress were holding quiet conversations and private dinners, where they developed plans to create a "Federal City" that was separate and apart from any other city or state government. Southerners like James Madison led the charge in what would become a decadelong drama around the location of the new seat of power. Virginians, in particular George Washington, were insistent that the permanent location of the nation's capital reside within a Southern orbit.

The Federal City would be splendid, and the hands of slaves would build it. The new federal government rented hundreds of slaves to clear the land, making way for paved streets and thoroughfares. These same slaves would bake the bricks and saw the lumber needed to erect buildings on what had been a desolate swamp. Black men and women's unpaid labor would lay the foundation for what would become the seat of America's power.

It was Alexander Hamilton and Thomas Jefferson who brokered the famed compromise between Southern and Northern coalitions in which the federal government assumed all state debt related to the American Revolution in exchange for landing a permanent nation's capital along the Potomac River. The construction of the capital would take close to a decade, and Philadelphia's consolation prize was the temporary relocation of the capital for a period of ten years starting in 1790. Philadelphians hoped that the decadelong window of opportunity would allow Pennsylvanians to persuade members of the Congress to rethink their decision. Some congressmen were still uncertain about the construction of a capital on the swampy, mosquito-infested shores of the Potomac, and Philadelphians believed that the modernity and cosmopolitan nature of their city could change minds. A grandiose President's House was constructed for the Washington family in Philadelphia, but the president avoided any connection to the opulent structure. As a Virginian, the president was committed to the Potomac location and chose to maintain a residency in the Morris House on High Street.

George and Martha Washington spent the summer months readying themselves for the transition to Philadelphia. The couple had learned quite a bit about Northern urban living from their New York experience and took great care to plan for an appropriate staff for the Philadelphia residence. Questions about the propriety of slavery notwithstanding, the president and Mrs. Washington had no plans of leaving behind their slaves, and in fact, chose to bring additional slaves with them this time. Concerned about a shortage of white laborers in Philadelphia and displeased with some of the Northern practices of white servants, the Washingtons thought long and hard about who should accompany them in November. The president, ever concerned about appearances, would no longer tolerate white servants who appeared unkempt. He revealed to his secretary Tobias Lear that he would not rehire his previous chefs, noting, "The dirty figures of Mrs. Lewis and her daughter will not be a pleasant sight in view (as the Kitchen always will be) of principal entertaining rooms in our new habitation." Instead, he chose to bring his slave Hercules, known for his fine cooking skills. Clearly, the Washingtons were more concerned with the image of cleanliness and refinement than they were about the growing debate over slavery in Philadelphia.

The culinary master ran his kitchen with authority. When Hercules's commands were made known, "his underlings flew in all directions," trying desperately to please the extremely demanding chef. Hercules must have been respected not only by the slaves at Mount Vernon, but also by his masters. He knew what kinds of foods his master liked and could eat with or without his dental prosthetics. Moreover, George and Martha Washington were confident that he would prepare impressive and splendid meals for heads of state and foreign dignitaries.

Hercules knew that he carried some social capital with his owners and that his work as a chef was desirable, for he managed to parlay his new assignment in Philadelphia into an opportunity for his son. Richmond, a young and inexperienced slave at Mount Vernon, traveled north with his father to serve as an assistant in the kitchen. The president was less than enthusiastic about his arrangement with Hercules:

Austin & Herculas go in this days Stage, & will, unquestion-
ably arrive several days before us. Richmond and Christo-
pher embarked yesterday by Water—the former not from his
appearance or merits I fear, but because he was the Son of
Herculas & his desire to have him as an assistant, comes as a
Scullion for the Kitchen.

Unimpressed with Richmond, the president nonetheless acqui-
esced, giving the young Richmond an opportunity to travel out of
Virginia, to learn his father's trade, and to remain connected and
attached to Hercules.

Six of the seven slaves who had traveled to New York also
accompanied the Washingtons to Philadelphia. Ona Judge, Moll,
Austin, and the horsemen Giles, Paris, and Christopher Sheels
were all selected to serve the president and his family in their
new home on High Street. Hercules and Richmond would bring
the total to eight, with a ninth slave joining them during the
president's second term. William Lee's worsening physical disabilities prohibited him from serving as the president's valet. He
was removed from service and left behind at Mount Vernon.

Four moves in less than eighteen months was a tiring grind for
the entire family, but for the eight slaves who moved north with
their masters, it was more taxing. A new set of rules would have to
be learned, new communities would need to be formed, and separation from family and friends would once again be experienced.
How would Philadelphia differ from New York? How would their
new home be outfitted, and would their duties change? Many
questions must have filled the minds of Washington's slaves who
traveled north, but they could show no trepidation. Little did Ona
Judge know that this move would begin a sojourn toward freedom.
The journey would be treacherously slow and would take six years

to complete, but for Judge, Philadelphia would serve as the birth-place of her own freedom.

The "President's House" stood at 190 High Street (also known as Market Street) between Fifth and Sixth Streets, less than six hundred feet from Independence Hall. The house was known by many names, including the Masters-Penn House, the Robert Morris House, 190 Street, and the Washington Mansion, but the name most often used by Washington in his correspondence was the President's House. The building was one of the largest homes in the city and had housed several well-known people. Colonial governor Richard Penn (grandson of William Penn), British general William Howe, American general Benedict Arnold, and financier Robert Morris had all spent time in the house on High Street, but beginning in November of 1790, it became home to the Washing-tons, albeit with some modification. Adjustments would need to be made for his family and large staff to live with relative com-fort in the home. A wall was demolished, and bow windows were installed—a fashionable statement for the times. Additional rooms were created for servants near the servants' hall and in the attic. Forty-five feet wide and fifty-two feet deep, the home was the size of two adjacent rowhomes. With three floors and an attic, the Pres-ident's House would be bursting at its seams once the Washingtons and their entourage arrived.

George and Martha Washington, along with their grandchil-dren Nelly and George (Washy), would find themselves sharing living quarters with the president's four secretaries and chief of staff, Tobias Lear. Lear's wife, Mary, and their toddler, Benjamin, also lived at High Street with eight slaves and approximately fif-teen white servants. Judge would spend the next six years of her life living in a household that counted between twenty-five and thirty residents. Privacy was an impossibility for the slaves and servants who lived at the President's House; it was hard to come by even for the Washingtons themselves.

The wide stoop of three white marbled steps greeted the family. When entering the house, the first family met a long hallway, approximately fifty feet in length, that was carpeted in green and extended up the stairs. Wainscoting was painted along the passageway walls, and mahogany doors accented the two dining rooms, one used for the family and another for more formal state dinners that could seat up to thirty people. In the center of the first floor was the kitchen, a large room that was now in the hands of Hercules and John Vicar from Baltimore, who was later replaced by Samuel Fraunces, also known as "Black Sam." Attached to the kitchen were a washroom, a servant's dining hall, the steward's room, two bedrooms for white servants and their wives, and a closely located bathing room. The rear of the property included a stable, a cow house, a coach house, and a smokehouse that was converted to accommodate sleeping space for slaves. Hanging glass lamps, mahogany-railed stairs, and the "house clock" perched on the second-floor landing provided a stately decor for the new home of the president.

The second floor was the exact same size and scope as the first floor, but functioned in a different capacity. The second floor served as a salon to entertain guests, but it also housed the bedrooms of the Washington family. Toward the front of the house, a large room called the Yellow Drawing Room became Martha Washington's social domain. The long yellow drapes and furniture brightened the room where she served afternoon tea to her friends and acquaintances. Once a week the space was filled with several dozen guests who came to socialize during the Friday evening "drawingrooms." Adjacent to Martha Washington's social room was the State Drawing Room, a larger space in which the family hosted social receptions for dignitaries and friends from across the country and the Atlantic.

The president knew that space was at a premium, but he made certain that he would have his own small private office. Washington had the original bathtub removed and created a private study for himself on the second floor. A separate servant quarters for the lodging of laundresses and kitchen maids also claimed space toward the rear of the second floor. Off the hallway were two smaller rooms that had been customized for the grandchildren. Each had his or her own room; however, each child slept with one of the slaves. Ona Judge and Moll were assigned to sleep with the Washington grandchildren and while Moll was specifically responsible for the care and well-being of the children, it would have been next to impossible for Judge to escape this responsibility as well. One of the grandchildren's bedrooms shared a door to the president and Mrs. Washington's bedroom, most likely the room in which Judge slept. She would be available to soothe the Washingtons' grandchildren when they were sick and when they had nightmares, but would be unavailable for any child of her own. Moreover, she would be on call to tend to the grandchildren at night but also expected to respond to the needs of her mistress both night and day. Her service was endless.

Most bondwomen dreaded the sleeping accommodations for house slaves, as living in the same quarters as their owners put them at risk for sexual attack. They preferred the slave cabins offered to field slaves on larger plantations. While the dirt-floored slave cabins were rough, with very little to no insulation during the cold Virginia winters or the terribly hot summers, they provided what house slaves longed for: privacy. Slaves who lived in cabins

with friends and family slept in a place of refuge from the constant demands of white owners. Enslaved men and women could
talk, laugh, and pray together in the crude wooden structures that
served as their homes. But for house slaves like Judge, there was
no refuge.

The Executive Mansion on 190 High Street was teeming with
secretaries, servants, and slaves, most of whom were male. Ona
had to be vigilant. How would Judge avoid the advances of male
staff, servants, or slaves who might try to force themselves upon
her? She was in constant jeopardy of rape, and very little could
prevent a knife-wielding assailant from forcing himself upon her.
Many slave women feared their male owners (and their owners'
sons) more than any other man, and a room adjacent to an owner
could mean many sleepless nights for the female slave. Judge never
accused Washington of such licentious behavior, although whis-
pers about an encounter between the president and his brother's
slave named Venus lived on at Mount Vernon. For now, as long as
Washy, with whom she probably shared a room, was a small boy,
Judge didn't have to worry about attack.

The third floor, similar to the second, contained more spaces for
living and for presidential business. Tobias Lear and his wife, Mary,
claimed a sleeping compartment that they shared with young Benjamin, and the two other bedrooms were shared by Washington's
secretaries: Maj. William Jackson, Howell Lewis, Bartholomew
Dandridge, and eventually Robert Lewis (all but William Jackson
were the nephews of George and Martha Washington). The secretaries' living spaces on the third floor were conveniently located
near the President's Business Office, where Washington and all
who arrived on official business conducted meetings. The third
floor was also home to the "Summer Room," a spacious addition
that provided the necessary living quarters for family and friends

to visit with the Washingtons. In the garret or the attic, rooms were cordoned off for the remaining slaves and servants who needed a place to rest their head. Next to the kitchen, the attic was the warmest place in the house and almost unbearable during the summer months. Hercules, Richmond, and Christopher most likely slept there with Paris and Giles sleeping in either the stables or the smokehouse.

So, men and women, free and enslaved, lived in very close proximity to one another at 190 High Street. The president failed to realize how such tight quarters would jeopardize his fortune. The Washingtons' slaves in Philadelphia would learn a great deal from the free white servants who toiled alongside them. They watched their comrades receive pay for their labor, move about the city with relative ease, and make decisions about their lives, including, even, the right to leave their employer. These were important lessons for all the slaves who lived on High Street, lessons that Ona Judge would study and commit to memory.

Five

The Blacks in the Family

Logo of the Pennsylvania Abolition Society, founded in 1775.

With the family settled in Philadelphia, Washington began a grueling Southern tour, a tiresome three-month trip that took him from Maryland down to Savannah, Georgia. Whenever possible, the president would return to Mount Vernon, checking in on his estate, which stubbornly avoided financial success. He also used his home visits as moments to rest and reenergize from the constant and almost maddening pace of presidential business. Mount Vernon was Washington's safe harbor, but the tranquility he so desperately needed was shaken when the president read through his mail. A troubling letter, written by Tobias Lear on April 5, 1791, aroused deep concerns for the president. His finances were once again in jeopardy, not because of a poor tobacco harvest, but because of his investment in human bondage.

Attorney General Edmond Randolph appeared at the Executive Mansion, wanting to speak with the president regarding a pressing concern. The former governor of Virginia would have preferred talking to the president about such delicate matters, but Washington was in Virginia, and just as she had done so many times in the past, Martha Washington stood in as her husband's social substitute. Perhaps the two sat in the Yellow Drawing Room, exchanging brief pleasantries while they waited for the Washingtons' slaves to serve tea or lemonade. She would quickly discern that her visitor was upset, and that Randolph's visit would require delicacy. Mrs. Washington typically had Ona Judge by her side, but she would have dismissed her slave before such a sensitive conversation took place.

Angry and frustrated, the attorney general confided in the first lady, telling her about a problem that plagued slaveholders who resided in Philadelphia. Three of his slaves had run off, and the attorney general knew that he would not be able to get them back. As the top-ranking lawyer in the nation, Randolph never believed that his slaves would quote the law of Pennsylvania back to him, but they did just that, and to make matters worse, they were correct. Randolph told the first lady that his slaves had boldly "given him notice that they should tomorrow take advantage of a law of this State, and claim their freedom." Pennsylvania was a place, he warned, where visiting slaveholders, like the Washingtons, could lose their property, thereby suffering great financial loss. Slaveholders in Philadelphia were vulnerable.

Randolph reminded the first lady that Pennsylvania law required the emancipation of all adult slaves who were brought into the commonwealth for more than a period of six months. The attorney general either took for granted that his slaves would never learn of the law or believed that they were unfathomably faithful and would decide to remain enslaved to their master, even when the law did not require it. Randolph offered his own experience as a cautionary tale, suggesting that the president's family be careful about their own slaves, fearing that "those who were of age in this family might follow the example, after a residence of six months should put it in their power." This warning gave Martha Washington reason to pause.

The first lady understood the seriousness of the house call as well as the need for discreet and swift action. She listened to Randolph intently, thanked him for his visit, and quickly began discussions with Lear about the best plan of action. Her husband had to be notified immediately, and the slaves who lived on High Street needed to be kept from such inflammatory news. But the President's House was not spacious, and voices carried through the hallways. Very little remained private in a space that was typically filled by twenty or more people. Just as Randolph's slaves came to understand and utilize the gradual abolition law, so, too, might the Washingtons' slaves. It would be painfully embarrassing and financially damaging if the president's own slaves turned the laws of the state against him.

Tobias Lear knew that the Washingtons were sitting on a powder keg, and it was his responsibility to make certain that it didn't blow. As the sixth-month mark since the first family had taken residence in Philadelphia was fast approaching, Lear's letter to the president asked for advice and guidance and for Washington to "give directions in the matter respecting the blacks in this family."

The president was aware that Philadelphia's popular sentiment surrounding the issue of slavery was unlike what he had encountered in New York. There was little public chatter about the Washingtons and their caravan of enslaved Africans arriving in New York in the spring of 1789, but things were different in Pennsylvania. While he was familiar with the gradual abolition law, the president was caught off guard about the precarious status of his own slaves, and within a week's time, Washington responded to Tobias Lear's request for advice. The president had given the issue quite a bit of thought, rationalizing his circumstances as different from those of the attorney general. Writing from Richmond, Virginia, Washington told his trusted secretary that Randolph was in some ways responsible for his own misfortune. So that he could practice law in the commonwealth, the attorney general made the decision to become a citizen of Pennsylvania. Randolph chose to "take the Oaths of Citizenship," therefore agreeing to observe all the laws of the state, one of which was to emancipate his slaves within six months of his arrival. Washington rationalized his situation was different. He lived in the commonwealth of Pennsylvania as a necessity of his employment, stating that "my residence is incidental as an Officer of Government."

But even with a justification in place, the president was cautious. Washington wrote to his secretary that there were some citizens, abolitionists—who were in the "practice of *enticing* slaves *even* when there is *no* colour of law for it." The president worried that his own slaves were in danger of exposure to the epidemic of black freedom, and although Washington believed that his slaves were better served and cared for in his possession, he understood the power and the allure of freedom. Washington wrote, "For although I do not think they would be benefitted by the change, yet the idea of freedom might be too great a temptation for them to resist."

He asked Lear to continue with an investigation of the laws of Pennsylvania, and in the meantime, the president, Mrs. Washington, and Lear crafted a plan of circumvention; the Washingtons would not break the law—they would simply work around it.

Ona Judge learned quickly that life in Philadelphia was quite different from what she had come to know in New York. Her slave status was somewhat of a rarity in her new city, and unlike New York, there was a much more strident abolition movement. In terms of thinking and legislating freedom for all people, Pennsylvania was advanced compared to New York or New Jersey, becoming the first state to gradually dismantle slavery. Philadelphia took the lead in the state's movement to unhinge lifelong bondage, and by the time Ona Judge moved to High Street, slavery was on its deathbed.

Pennsylvanians wrestled with the moral dilemma of African slavery as early as the seventeenth century. The colony was only seven years old when the first group of Quakers began to question human bondage. Founded by William Penn in 1681, Pennsylvania became a colony known for its significant number of Quakers who did, indeed, own slaves. Many Quaker slaveholders agreed with founder George Fox, who advocated for the humane treatment of those held in bondage. Good treatment was relative, and compared to the life-shortening tobacco farms in Virginia or the rice plantations in the Carolinas, Pennsylvania slavery did enjoy a kinder reputation than did its southern neighbors. Nonetheless, slavery continued, and within the Society of Friends a great debate over human bondage brewed for nearly a century. Beginning in 1688, a number of Germantown Quakers declared slavery oppositional to their religious beliefs, but their cries fell upon deaf ears as Friends began to shun their own members, labeling them troublemakers, going as far as to cause financial calamity to the small business owners who dared to question the morality of slavery. Although they were a consensus-driven religious organization that believed in equality and the "light of God" within all men, the financial gains connected to slavery and the racial stereotypes that bred fear of a free black community halted a meaningful seventeenth-century abolitionist movement.

It was the Quakers living outside the city who took the first bold move to push the Society of Friends to ban African slavery. In 1711, Friends from Chester County asked the Yearly Meeting to prohibit Quakers from purchasing new slaves. While no formal mandate was issued, it was recommended that Friends withdraw themselves from the slave trade. What the Quakers began on the outskirts of Philadelphia would culminate in the first antislavery law in the new nation.

This monumental piece of legislation, passed March 1, 1780, tackled the explosive issue of slavery and set the standard for gradual emancipation in the North. It still allowed white owners to squeeze every bit of uncompensated labor out of enslaved black bodies until they were twenty-eight years old—middle-aged for the eighteenth century—leaving broken bodies and weary souls to find new ways for living after emancipation.

The process was slow, but Judge found herself living in a city that had promised to end slavery and was in the midst of doing so.

***

Surrounded by antislavery sentiment and laws that undermined their financial investments, the Washingtons knew they had to work quickly and quietly if they were to protect their wealth and their reputation. The president needed a solution to the problem of slaveholding in Philadelphia—one that would work for many years. So the Washingtons devised a plan: the couple would shuffle their slaves to and from Mount Vernon every six months, avoiding the stopwatch of Pennsylvania black freedom. If an excursion to Virginia proved a hardship for the family, a quick trip to a neighboring state such as New Jersey would serve the same purpose. The hourglass of slavery would be turned over every six months, and the president knew there was no time to waste.

Still in Virginia, the president sent clear and direct orders back to Philadelphia; the slaves at the Executive Mansion needed to leave the state, and soon. Washington decided that his wife should plan an expedited trip home to Virginia, bringing all of their slaves back to the safety of Southern laws. The president was primarily concerned with his adult slaves, who he (erroneously, as it turned out) believed were the only ones capable of freeing themselves under Pennsylvania law.

But while the president was adamant about protecting his human property, he was only two years into his first term, and in no hurry to agitate the powerful antislavery forces in Philadelphia. Washington preferred to handle his private affairs with discretion and "to deceive" the public if necessary. The president directed his secretary to reveal his intentions to no one except his wife, stating, "I request that these Sentiments and this advise may be known to none but *yourself & Mrs. Washington.*"

Just as she had prepared for the move to New York, Martha Washington executed important plans in the absence of her husband, but this time it had to be done in secrecy. Although they faced significant time constraints, the president wanted his wife to quickly gather up their human property without setting off any alarms. The slaves had to be kept in the dark, for if they knew why they were to accompany Mrs. Washington on her trip to Virginia, they might run off, just like Randolph's slaves. As directed, Martha Washington began to think strategically about a trip back to Virginia. She always looked forward to her Mount Vernon visits, but now, her trips would not only be for rest and relaxation. The first lady was tasked with protecting an investment in human property, property that would eventually be passed down to her heirs.

On April 19, just seven days after the president corresponded with Tobias Lear, Mrs. Washington wrote to her niece Frances "Fanny" Bassett Washington, who was back home at Mount Vernon. She inquired about family and friends and prodded for news, hoping that she would hear word about an impending pregnancy. But most importantly, embedded in the first lady's letter was an excuse for why Ona Judge's brother, Austin, would be returning to Mount Vernon (ahead of the others) on such short notice. Mrs. Washington explained to her niece that while she was really in no position to spare Austin's services in Philadelphia, she needed "to fulfill my promises to his wife" and to allow Austin to reunite with his family. Austin's stay in Virginia would be short, a gift from a benevolent slave owner, or so it would seem.

The first lady never let on to her niece the real reason for sending her slave back to Mount Vernon: Austin's six-month residency limit was about to expire, and Mrs. Washington needed an excuse to shuffle him out of state. The Washingtons must have trusted Austin, for not only did they allow him to travel back to Mount Vernon alone, but they gave him resources with which to do it. Austin was given a total of $11.66 for the trip, an amount that would take care of the cost of the stage to Baltimore, transportation from Baltimore to Alexandria, and food and lodging throughout his journey.

The Washingtons began to breathe a little easier, knowing that the plan to move Austin out of Philadelphia was securely under way. Martha Washington could now focus on preparing for the family's trip back to Mount Vernon, an excursion that would bring the rest of the slaves on High Street back to Virginia. But Tobias Lear interrupted the Washingtons' fleeting relief with more bad news. The first family needed to worry about the residency clock for all of their slaves, not just the adults.

Washington had been confident that Christopher, Richmond, and Ona Judge were exempt from Pennsylvania's gradual abolition law because of their status as minors, but Lear reported that the president's beliefs were incorrect. After another discreet conversation with the attorney general, Lear told the president that his three juvenile slaves could also claim freedom after six months' time. The secretary wrote to the president that "those Slaves who were under the age of 18, might, after a residence of six months, apply to the Overseers of the Poor, who had authority to bind them to a master until they should attain the age of 18, when they would become free." This report was a misstatement, as most black children in Philadelphia were indentured until the age of twenty-eight, but according to the law, if Christopher, Richmond, or Ona Judge stayed in Philadelphia longer than six months, they would have a chance at freedom. They might have to wait, but in Philadelphia, the opportunity existed.

Imprudently believing that he could prevent his slaves from hearing about the laws, Washington insisted that the utmost discretion be used regarding their plan of slave rotation in and out of Philadelphia. More than a loss of labor was at stake. If Ona Judge and her enslaved companions uncovered the truth about their slave status in Philadelphia, they would possess knowledge that could set them free. Power would shift from the president to his human property, making them less likely to serve their master faithfully, and eventually, they might run away. Washington wrote that if his slaves knew that they had a right to freedom, it would "make them insolent in the State of Slavery." Lear had less faith in the idea that the slaves would remain in the dark than Washington. There were people in Philadelphia who would help if not encourage Ona Judge and her enslaved companions to take their freedom. Tobias Lear noted his concern to Washington, stating, "There were not wanting persons who would not only give them (the Slaves) advise; but would use all means to entice them from their masters." If Washington's slaves didn't escape, they would likely be impudent and therefore worthless, ruined by Northern freedom.

The loss of slaves would signal more than a loss of face. Still teetering on the brink of financial insolvency, Washington continued to live beyond his means, and losing property would only add to his financial woes. Ona Judge, Moll, Austin, Giles, Christopher Sheels, and Richmond belonged to the Parke Custis estate, and it was the president's responsibility to manage its human property. If anything happened to his wife's slaves, George Washington would be held responsible. In his letter to Tobias Lear, the president wrote, "It behooves me to prevent the emancipation of them, otherwise I *shall* not only loose the use of them, but may have them to pay for."

It was clear. All the president's slaves would need to be carefully monitored. By April 24, Austin was back at Mount Vernon and Richmond was scheduled to sail to Alexandria on the following day. Mrs. Washington took no chances and quickly organized a trip to Trenton, New Jersey, taking both Ona Judge and Christopher with her, restarting their six-month residency clock. With Giles and Paris accompanying the president in Virginia, Moll and Hercules were the only slaves left on High Street who needed rotating. Moll would not immediately travel back to Mount Vernon, a suggestion that the president and Mrs. Washington must have trusted her not to attempt escape. But the Washingtons had deep concerns about the remaining enslaved member of the household—Hercules, the cook, would need close watching, for many reasons.

As the president's famed chef, Hercules cultivated a relationship with the Washingtons that earned him an elevated status and a modicum of respect. Viewed as a crucial member of the staff on High Street, he prepared the president's breakfast hoecakes, white corn-mush patties, and Saturday evening meals of salt fish hash. The Washingtons relied upon Hercules and allowed him the opportunity to make an income by selling unwanted kitchen "slops." Used tea leaves, animal skins, and leftover stock could fetch a decent price at market, permitting the enslaved chef to earn between one and two hundred dollars a year. With his personal income, Hercules purchased fine clothing that he displayed on his evening walks. Dressed in a velvet-collared coat with bright metal buttons, shiny shoes, and a pocket watch, Hercules left his master's house to socialize with his new Philadelphia friends. His gold-headed cane and cocked hat reminded everyone of his elevated financial status, even though he was a slave.

The Washingtons were quick to believe that if any of their slaves would use the law to find freedom, it would be Hercules. After all, he had the financial resources to support himself. They would not risk it. They decided to send Hercules to Mount Vernon ahead of the family's annual summer travel to Virginia, an odd mandate that would have raised questions given what a prominent role he played, but a move that was necessary to pause the stopwatch of freedom.

Though the Washingtons got away with the subterfuge surrounding Austin's return, the lies and reasons given for Hercules's premature departure were exposed, even with heightened discretion. There was an information breech in the President's House, though the perpetrator remained unknown. Someone did, indeed, tell Hercules that under the laws of the state he could free himself and that it was now obvious his owners were making excuses to send him home. He knew that the Washingtons did not trust him.

Hercules had decisions to make, and he had to make them quickly. If the chef took advantage of the law, he would have to choose between his freedom and his family, a dilemma faced by every enslaved person who considered escape. His daughters Evey and Delia were motherless small children back at Mount Vernon, and his son Richmond (who was no favored possession of the president) worked at his side in Philadelphia. If Hercules refused to return to Mount Vernon, he would in essence walk away from his family. The reprisals that his children would surely confront drove the chef to think seriously about his options.

Hercules chose his family over freedom. Perhaps it was an easy decision, or maybe he arrived at his choice after much deliberation. In any case, once his decision was made, the chef knew that he needed to prove himself trustworthy to the Washingtons. In order to remain in his position in Philadelphia, he must erase their concerns about his loyalty. Hercules needed an opportunity to make his case to the president's secretary, and he would not have to wait long.

By the end of May, Lear informed Hercules that he would travel back to Virginia and watched the chef for an unusual or stubborn response. Lear wrote to the president, "If Hercules should decline the offer which will be made him of going home, it will be a pretty strong proof of his intention to take the advantage of the law at the expiration of six months."

The secretary told Hercules that the first family was aware of the information breech, and what happened next told the Washingtons exactly what they needed to know.

Hercules appeared agitated and desperate when he explained to the secretary that he had no intentions of leaving his owners and that his faithfulness had never swayed. Whatever theatrics Hercules employed were convincing, and the secretary accepted all that the enslaved chef told him. Lear wrote to the president that "[Hercules] was mortified to the last degree to think that a suspicion could be entertained of his fidelity or attachment to you." The chef managed to convince Mrs. Washington and Tobias Lear that he could be trusted to stay with the family in Philadelphia beyond the month of May and the expiration of his six-month residency. On June 3, Lear purchased two new shirts for Hercules and gave him at least $7.20 to cover the cost of his transportation, food, and lodging for his trip back to Virginia. Lear's confidence in Hercules was stronger than ever as he wrote to the president that the enslaved chef "has accordingly continued here 'till this time, and tomorrow takes his departure for Virginia." His performance worked, and Hercules was once again in the good graces of his owners. He would have to wait another six years before he had the opportunity to take his freedom. On February 22, 1797, Hercules ran away and was never seen again. It was George Washington's birthday.

The Washingtons' plan to circumvent the law was successful, and for five years, from 1791 to 1796, the president and Mrs. Washington carefully transported their slaves to and from Pennsylvania. Tobias Lear assisted his employers in their slave shuffle, but he also made certain to voice his opinions about human bondage to the president.

You will permit me now, Sir, (and I am sure you will pardon me for doing it) to declare, that no consideration should induce me to take these steps to prolong the slavery of a human being, had I not the fullest confidence that they will at some future period be liberated, and the strongest conviction that their situation with you is far preferable to what they would probably obtain in a state of freedom.

Both Lear and Washington held fast to paternalistic assumptions about African slavery, believing that enslaved men and women were better off with a generous owner than emancipated and living independent lives. Decades later, Southerners would justify the institution of slavery with descriptions of the supposed benefits that came with enslavement. According to many Southerners, slaves were better cared for, better fed, sheltered, and treated almost as though they were members of the family. Northern emancipation left thousands of ex-slaves without assistance, and Southerners charged that free blacks were living and dying in the cold alleyways of the urban North. Many believed Northern freedom to be a far less humane existence, one that left black men and women to die in the streets from exposure and starvation.

But Washington must have suggested to Lear in earlier conversations that he would eventually release his slaves from bondage, prompting Lear to continue assisting the president. He would safeguard the Washingtons' secrets and continue shuffling Ona Judge and the other slaves at the Executive Mansion from the North to the South every six months at least. On each lengthy trip back to Virginia, Ona Judge would have thought about what she lost and gained by going home, understanding the growing divide between the orbits of the slaveholding South and the fragile freedom of the North.

Six

Life in Philadelphia

Bethel A.M.E. Church, the first Colored Methodist church in Philadelphia, established in 1787.

On a Tuesday evening in early June, Philadelphia's Southwark Theatre prepared to welcome the president and his family for a production of *The Beaux' Stratagem*, a comedy written by George Farquhar. The Washingtons arrived at the theater and were promptly taken to the east stage box from which hung the United States coat of arms. The box was decorated with red drapery and cushioned seats, and soldiers secured the entrances at each stage door. Filled with racy scenes and irreverent innuendo, the produc-

tion thoroughly entertained the Washingtons, and they left the
theater wanting to share their experience with friends and family,
even with their slaves. The following day, Ona Judge was given
permission to attend the same theater with her brother Austin and
the always well-dressed Hercules.

An eighteenth-century stage performance was typically a four-
or five-hour affair that included music and dance performances.
Judge took her seat, perhaps in the pit or in the rear of the balcony,
and watched a story unfold about two young men who had lost
their fortunes and were determined to find wealthy wives. The
lead characters are confronted with many obstacles on their quest
to find fortune, but in the end, meet with love and wealth. (While
the performance entertained theatergoers, it would have reminded
Judge about her station in life. She was gifted a ticket to the play,
but she would never be able to look for love and fortune, not while
she remained a slave.)

The slaves at the President's House enjoyed the cosmopolitan pleasures of their new city. In addition to the theater, Judge
attended the circus and went to see the tumblers perform whenever her owners would allow it. Sometimes the president or Mrs.
Washington would give small financial gifts to their slaves and
allow them to shop. On February 22, 1791, the president's birthday, Judge, Austin, Hercules, and Moll received one dollar from the
Washingtons with a suggestion that they purchase gifts for their
family members and send them home to Mount Vernon. Christopher only received fifty cents, an implication that his owners were
less than pleased with his service. Christopher had big shoes to fill,
since the disabled William Lee had returned to Mount Vernon.
Washington had a notable bond with the longtime service of Lee,
and it's likely that no one else could build such a relationship with
the president.

Judge experienced life as an urban slave, growing familiar with Philadelphia, its cultural venues, and the social elite. Accompanying Mrs. Washington on her social calls, the slave girl matured into a young bondwoman who met many of the city's leaders and influencers. Although she was not an invited guest, her presence among the wives of policy makers, bankers, and politicians exposed her to extremely sophisticated people. Judge would never have socialized with Mrs. Washington's friends, but she certainly became familiar with the slaves and servants of the nation's top movers and shakers. She became a recognizable face among both white and black Philadelphians.

But there were places and venues that Judge would not have visited. The watchful eyes of her masters were omnipresent, and the Washingtons would never allow their slaves to interact closely with the free blacks of Philadelphia. Three years before Judge's arrival, a group of free blacks, including Richard Allen and Absalom Jones, came together to form the Free African Society. It was the first black mutual aid society in Philadelphia, and its goals were to help widows, the poor, and fugitive slaves, who were unable to provide for themselves. Donations of firewood, clothing, and food were offered to black Philadelphians who found themselves mired in paralyzing poverty, and financial contributions were distributed for decent burials. The Washingtons would have stopped at nothing to keep their slaves away from the city's black leaders and trailblazers. But this was an almost impossible mission. Inevitably, Ona Judge became acquainted with free black Philadelphians, some of whom, when she made the decision to flee, would become the most supportive friends imaginable.

Judge spent the next five and a half years (albeit rotating every six months back to Mount Vernon or out of state) in Philadelphia, serving her masters while she watched the rest of Philadelphia's

enslaved population break free from the bonds of slavery. Her interactions with paid servants, contracted hired help, and with her own
enslaved housemates informed her thoughts about her life and the
possibilities of freedom. After the information breech regarding the
Washingtons' slave rotation, it would have been virtually impossible to keep Judge in the dark about the laws of the state. If Hercules
knew the law and the Washingtons' intentions, then Judge most
certainly did, too.

Judge may have believed that as a minor, she could not claim
freedom as easily as Hercules or one of the other adult slaves who
lived in the President's House. If she escaped her masters before
their calculated trips out of state, and hid among the free blacks
of Philadelphia, she could contest her slave status, but the risk was
high. Because Judge was under the age of eighteen years old, her
enslavement would convert to a contract of servitude, one that
could place her fate into the hands of an unknown person until
she reached the age of twenty-eight. She could be hired out to
serve a particularly cruel employer, someone who might demand
a more physically taxing or dangerous type of labor. Worse yet,
her new owner could exploit her sexually, a fear that every female
slave and servant harbored when presented with new labor assignments. While Judge may have preferred freedom, she must have
felt relatively safe in the President's House and made the decision
to stay put for the time being.

Ona Judge was not the only person in Philadelphia who wondered about the future. While emancipation touched the lives of
many black men and women who lived in the commonwealth of
Pennsylvania, it was a process that was slow and cumbersome. Pennsylvania may have been revolutionary in its move to gradually end
African slavery, but for black Philadelphians, especially those who
were enslaved, change didn't come fast enough. Some refused to

wait for freedom, choosing to live the vulnerable life of a fugitive. During the 1780s, more than 160 slaves took their chances and headed north from the city, looking for freedom and anonymity. Most runaways were young black men, but the few women who attempted escape in Philadelphia often did so to join free husbands scattered about New England, often with their children in tow.

Although the number of free people continued to grow, black men and women always remained in the minority in Philadelphia. It must have been strange to live in a land that was predominantly white. Aside from living on a plantation that counted more than two hundred enslaved people, Fairfax County, Virginia, where she had spent the majority of her life, was home to a large proportion of black residents. There were close to 4,500 blacks living around Mount Vernon, though only 135 of them were free. Judge was accustomed to living around enslaved black people, and Philadelphia was, in reality, a white city. In 1790 the first federal census takers counted more than forty-four thousand residents who made their home in Philadelphia and its surrounding counties. Black men and women comprised only 5 percent of the city's population.

Judge watched as slave owners emancipated their male slaves at a much faster rate than their women, creating a larger pool of female slaves who would spend much more time in bondage. As domestic help was a necessity and a labor shortage evaporated the pool of good servants, artisans and merchants held tight to their female slaves. Judge must have known some of the enslaved women living in Philadelphia, a reminder that she was not alone. But she would have also calculated that her peers would eventually find freedom through the laws of the state, and that this was not a possibility for her.

Most of the black women who lived in Philadelphia labored long hours as domestics. Employment opportunities outside of cleaning homes and washing clothes were nearly impossible for women of any race, but especially for women of African descent. Free black women took in laundry, sold pepper pot soup and fruits and vegetables on the streets, or took to rag picking, the latter only by those who were destitute. Searching through trash heaps, they gathered discarded clothing or bits of cloth and cleaned them for resale. It was dirty work and offered the smallest of financial rewards, but it was work, and it often allowed black women and their children to evade hunger and malnutrition. Judge witnessed black poverty and understood that freedom was by no means an easy endeavor.

Judge also watched black men and women make their way out of slavery through indentured servitude. Just like George Washington, many slave owners who moved to Pennsylvania (and there was a flood of them as a result of the revolt during the 1790s in Saint-Domingue, which would become Haiti) looked for ways around the law that stripped them of their human property after six months. Many whites in Pennsylvania acknowledged that abolition was a fait accompli, so to slow it down, slave owners emancipated their slaves and indentured them for lengthy periods of time.

But there were amazing things about the city that Judge would have to witness from afar. Free black communities were organizing, creating churches, schools, and social societies, all within a stone's throw of Judge's residence. While Judge probably rode or walked by the buildings owned by free blacks, she would not have stopped to interact with its members. If Judge were caught speaking to or socializing with free blacks, she would put her presence on High Street in jeopardy. She had seen how the Washingtons handled the transgressions of her enslaved housemates. The Washingtons would simply not tolerate the contagion of freedom seeping into the lives of their slaves. If there was the slightest suspicion of fraternizing with free blacks, Judge's life could be turned upside down.

Judge knew that no one's place, including her own, was secure on High Street. The spring of 1791 brought the first round of change at the President's House, beginning with the enslaved postilion, Giles. While on a Southern tour with the president, Giles was severely injured, perhaps thrown from a horse, a common and life-altering accident. His injuries were so grave that Washington had no choice but to remove Giles from service and to leave him behind in Virginia, never to return to Philadelphia. This must have been devastating to Giles for several reasons. Aside from being forced to return to Virginia for good, he would no longer serve the Washingtons in a position of distinction. Giles was to be trained in some other form of service, but this would most likely be something such as broom making or clay digging, jobs that were the least desirable for slaves at Mount Vernon.

Like Giles, the young slave Paris would also not return from Mount Vernon to work in the President's House in Philadelphia, but for very different reasons. Paris also accompanied the president on his tour of the Southern states, but his service was unacceptable to Washington. The president wrote to his secretary,

> *Paris has become so lazy, self willed & impudent, that John (the Coachman) had no sort of government of him; on the contrary, Jno. say's it was a maxim with Paris to do nothing he was ordered, and everything he was forbid. This conduct, added to the incapacity of Giles for a Pistilion, who I believe will never be able to mount a horse again for that purpose, has induced me to find Paris some other employment than in the Stable—of course I shall leave him at home.*

Perhaps Paris had been contaminated by the contagion of freedom in Philadelphia, or maybe a difficult Southern trip brought out the impudence in the young slave. Whatever the reason, Paris remained at Mount Vernon for the next two years before illness claimed his life. The removal of Paris was still fresh in the minds of the slaves at the President's Mansion when Christopher Sheels, the only literate slave on High Street, was sent back to Virginia. It is possible that his literacy left the first family uneasy, deciding that his residency in Philadelphia was too great a risk. Having lived with Sheels for two years, Judge would have likely been saddened by his departure.

The transition at the Executive Mansion was no excuse for Judge to slow down or to reflect about loss. In fact, it required all the slaves on High Street to work faster, complete extra work assignments, and to simply carry on. Judge understood that as a slave, most of what happened in her life was beyond her control, but she would not stand alone in her vulnerability. All the residents of Philadelphia, including the Washingtons, would soon confront the fragility and unpredictability of life's circumstances.

During the late summer of 1793, one of the worst public health crises hit the nation's capital with unabated destruction. Men and women suffered from headaches, chills, sharp pains, stomach upset, and jaundice, followed by the spewing of black vomit and internal bleeding. Yellow fever sickened and killed many, and thousands of citizens fled from the city, including George and Martha Washington, who along with Judge, retreated to Mount Vernon to escape the death and devastation connected to the dreadful outbreak. Eighteenth-century medicine was still far from a stable science and few understood the actual cause or transmission of the disease. Although yellow fever is acquired via the bite of a mosquito, many believed the illness was associated with foul air, throwing physicians far off the track of preventive care or a possible cure. The yellow fever outbreak did not dissipate until the first frost in November, and the death toll was staggering. Between four and five thousand Philadelphians perished, including the wife of Washington's secretary Tobias Lear. One of the first victims of the dreaded fever, Polly Lear died on July 28 at the age of twenty-three.

Yet out of what could only be considered a grim situation, black community leaders Richard Allen and Absalom Jones saw an opportunity for black residents to gain footing in the struggle for black rights in Pennsylvania. Unfortunately, their hopes were based upon the faulty beliefs of the well-known physician Benjamin Rush. As one of the top doctors in Philadelphia, many turned to him for guidance during the outbreak. Rush believed incorrectly that people of African descent were immune to the disease. Proclaiming that no black men or women had come down with the fever by September, he reached out to the famed black leaders of Philadelphia asking for their help in recruiting black men and women to lend a hand as nurses and grave diggers.

Allen and Jones saw this request as an opportunity to uplift the profile of blacks in the city. As emancipation moved forward, the pursuit of racial equality became a priority in emerging black churches and among the growing free population. In the minds of Jones and Allen, assisting whites would prove that black men and women were capable of being good citizens and were worthy of the abolitionist assistance offered to them by leading Philadelphia Quakers. Black leaders saw this moment as an opportunity for African American residents to reverse the detrimental stereotypes of blacks as lazy, impudent, and unreasonable emancipated men and women. If black assistance during this horrible epidemic could help alleviate the growing racial tension in a city that fitfully accepted emancipation, then Jones and Allen were ready to recruit significant numbers of black men and women to help nurse the sick, to hold the hands of the dying, and to dig the graves of those who perished. And they did so with great optimism.

The problem with their plan was that Benjamin Rush was wrong. His assumptions about black immunity to the disease were incorrect, and blacks died at the same rates as did white Philadelphians. As the city trembled under the heat of the summer, the plague not only took the lives of white Philadelphians, but it also struck the city's black population. Indeed, African Americans represented 10 percent of all deaths related to the fever. Yet insult was added to injury when whites began to hurl accusations of black impropriety during the outbreak of fever. Blacks were accused of exploiting white vulnerability by robbing dying men and women and by ransacking abandoned homes. An opportunity to ease racial animosity between white and black Philadelphians was lost, reminding free blacks, servants, and the enslaved that gradual emancipation would not end centuries of racial violence, stereotypes, or tension overnight.

The epidemic did do something positive for Judge, however. Fear of contagion prompted the Washington household to pack up for a visit back to Mount Vernon. Once back at her birthplace, she got to know her new niece. Betty Davis had given birth to another daughter, a baby who would share a name with her aunt. Little Oney would remind Judge of the importance of family and of the gift of motherhood, two things that she would never have while serving the Washingtons in Philadelphia. Once again, the trip back home to Mount Vernon was bittersweet.

As autumn ushered in cold weather, killing disease-carrying mosquitos in the nation's capital, the yellow fever epidemic of 1793 finally came to a close. The Washingtons and their slaves, including Judge, returned to Philadelphia in December, laying eyes upon the ravaged city. As Philadelphians mourned the loss of five thousand residents, Judge would have noticed more than just grief in the air; the city was rife with racial tension of a sharper kind. Blacks had just buried their own family members only to suffer accusations of hideous behavior. Judge most certainly heard the stories of black anger and resentment from those who had lost loved ones in a grand attempt to prove themselves worthy of freedom and equality.

No matter the status, free or enslaved, black people were still considered the inferior race. Even when people of African descent offered up their lives to help whites, they were still rejected and scorned. This was a valuable lesson for free black leaders like Richard Allen and Absalom Jones, but it was also a cautionary reminder to people like Ona Judge. Life as an enslaved person robbed her of her dignity and her personhood, but life as a free person, although preferable, would not serve as a conduit to easy living. She thought deeply about her circumstances and about her future, but her reflections came to a sudden stop when she received devastating news about her brother Austin.

Like Judge, Austin served the Washingtons in New York and Philadelphia and traveled back and forth to Mount Vernon every six months. Austin was scheduled to return to Virginia in December of 1794, and was eager to see his wife, Charlotte, and their five children. As one of the more trusted slaves, Austin was sent home unescorted to Mount Vernon with twenty dollars to cover the cost of his travel and lodgings. Three days after his departure, a letter arrived for the president from Maryland telling of a terrible accident. Austin had experienced tremendous difficulty navigating a river in Harford near Havre de Grace, Maryland, and was "with Great Difficulty . . . Dragged out of the water." He was "likely to Lose his Life." Indeed, shortly after being dragged from the river, only in his midthirties, Austin died, leaving behind his family at Mount Vernon and his sister in Philadelphia.

The news of Austin's death no doubt shocked Judge. Austin had been her only familial link during her stay in New York and

Philadelphia, and now she would be forced to endure the rest of her time in the North without any kinfolk.

The news was too much for Austin's mother to bear. An elderly Betty, now in her late fifties, was sickly and worn thin from a life of enslavement. To make matters worse, winter, always a difficult time for the aged, especially those who suffered from chronic illness, and for the enslaved who lived in uninsulated cabins, was just around the corner. She did indeed grow ill, and in January of 1795, George Washington was notified about her death. The president saw her death as merciful, relieving the slave from her debilitating illness. He wrote, "It is happy for old Betty, and her children and friends, that she is taken of[f] the stage; her life must have been miserable to herself, and troublesome to all those around her." As a slave owner, Washington thought not only about the misery that Betty endured, but he thought practically about her required care. Elderly or sickly slaves were considered a nuisance and a financial drain, as the cost of feeding and clothing them was never recouped. For Washington, Betty's death was a financial relief, but to Betty's family, it was an insurmountable blow.

In 1795 the only four of the original slaves to arrive on High Street—Moll, Hercules, Richmond, and Ona Judge—welcomed a new slave by the name of Joe to the Washington household. There were psychological changes afoot as well. No longer a young girl, Judge, now in her early twenties, had matured and had maintained her respected status as Martha Washington's first attendant. Judge stayed on in the President's House as Washington served his second term, becoming accustomed to her episodic trips back to Mount Vernon. Following the death of her mother and brother, the world that she once knew so intimately at Mount Vernon had vanished, perhaps reminding Judge that Mount Vernon was less a home to her than was the North.

Seven

The Wedding

Elizabeth "Betsey" Parke Custis.

The enslaved who lived at the Executive Mansion measured their triumphs in the smallest of ways. Victories were days marked by the first lady's good mood and defeat was palpable when the president was angered. For Ona Judge and the other slaves who served the Washingtons, the future was never predictable, and the smallest of matters, such as an accidental overcooking of a meal or

antagonistic political news, could change the mood of their owners
with the snap of a finger. By his peers, the president was not considered a violent slave owner, but all of the slaves who worked for
him in Philadelphia and at Mount Vernon knew that on occasion,
he did lose his temper. And in February 1796, a letter arrived that
prompted everyone, slave and servant, black and white, to tread
lightly around George and Martha Washington.

The president and the first lady enjoyed the correspondence
they received from Virginia, especially the letters written by close
family and friends. The stories and reports that arrived via the mail
were reminiscent of a simpler life at Mount Vernon, and sometimes they remedied Martha Washington's homesickness. However, the post could also bring the most dreadful news, such as
death announcements or descriptions of poor tobacco harvests.
When the president opened a letter from his step-granddaughter,
he wished for good news, but he was disappointed.

Nineteen-year-old Elizabeth Parke Custis (called Betsey by her
family and Eliza by her adult friends) lived in Virginia. She had
news to share, urgent news, that needed swift attention from her
grandparents. Without their knowledge, Eliza had taken a suitor
and, much to the surprise of everyone, the relationship quickly
turned serious. The unknown boyfriend was named Thomas Law,
a British businessman who had immigrated to America in 1794,
and in a short period of time he had become heavily involved in
land development in and around the Federal City. There was a lot
of money to be made around the future site of the nation's capital, and Law was determined to get in on the ground floor of land
speculation and construction.

He had lived in India for quite some time, serving as a policy
maker on behalf of the British government, and now, Thomas Law
found himself in the most peculiar of positions in his new coun-

try. He had fallen in love with the president's granddaughter, a woman who was twenty years his junior. Thomas Law and Eliza Custis promised themselves to one another, but they both knew that their union would need to be approved by the most powerful man in the new nation.

Though she initially concealed the relationship from her grandparents, Eliza now turned to them for support, asking the president to give the news of her engagement careful consideration before rushing to judgment. She also asked the president to wait until he had heard from her intended before he made a decision. Eliza knew that her grandparents, especially her grandmother, would be uneasy with this news.

Ona Judge witnessed deep concern envelop the first lady, an unsurprising response for a woman who had outlived all of her children. For Martha Washington, her grandchildren were the only remaining connections to her deceased heirs. Two of her babies (Daniel and Frances) from her marriage with Daniel Parke Custis had been snatched by death's indiscriminate hand before they reached their fifth birthdays. Young Patsy's seizure had extinguished her life at the age of seventeen, and her brother John would succumb to illness at the age of twenty-seven. Martha Washington was middle-aged with no living children, so she turned all of her attention and care toward her grandchildren Nelly, Washy, Eliza, and Martha (called Patsy by her friends).

George and Martha Washington's marriage never yielded children. Although Martha Washington was only twenty-seven years old when she married the president (she was eight months older than George), she never bore him a child. This must have been a disappointment to the couple, especially for the president, but they would eventually receive an opportunity to share the experience of child-rearing. After the death of Martha's only surviving son,

John (affectionately called Jacky), Martha and George Washington welcomed two of his small children into their home. The president and the first lady became the caregivers for Nelly and little Washy Parke Custis while older siblings Eliza and Patsy remained with their mother in Virginia. Martha Washington was committed to the lives of all four of her Parke Custis heirs.

Now, one of her grandchildren had made a monumental, life-changing decision, pending Washington's approval, and there was much to be concerned about. Thomas Law arrived in America with two of his three children, both of whom were the offspring from a relationship with an Indian woman. His biracial children and his age most certainly raised concerns for the Washingtons; however, it was his British citizenship that gave Martha and George Washington reason to pause. Would their dear Betsey be taken away to a foreign country with her new spouse, or would Law agree to remain in America?

Tension filled the rooms of the Executive Mansion. Although this was family business, everyone who lived within the walls of the President's House knew exactly what was happening, including Ona Judge, who was, in some measure, responsible for her mistress's happiness. Judge would have worked with care and caution as she tended to the needs of Martha Washington.

The first lady had been busy with preparations for the upcoming "birth night" ball in honor of the president's sixty-fourth birthday and was completely unprepared to deal with her granddaughter's explosive announcement. Judge was accustomed to watching tense situations unfold in the President's House, so she did what she was trained to do: be attentive, say little, but hear everything.

Three days later, George Washington received a letter from Thomas Law announcing his intentions of marrying Eliza and undoubtedly asking for approval and a blessing. The president and

Mrs. Washington discussed the situation, and as the snow began to fall, the president sat down to write both his granddaughter and Thomas Law. In his letter to Eliza dated February 10, 1796, Washington acknowledged that he had obeyed his granddaughter's request; he had not responded to her letter until he heard from her intended. He asked Eliza if she was certain that Law was the man of her choice. The president wrote,

> If Mr Law is the man of your choice, of wch there can be no doubt, as he has merits to engage your affections, and you have declared that he has not only done so, but that you find, after a careful examination of your heart, you cannot be happy without him—that your alliance with him meets my approbation. Yes, Betsey, and this approbation is accompanied with my fervent wishes that you may be as happy in this important event as your most sanguine imagination has ever presented to your view.

Responding to Thomas Law's letter with a cool hint of annoyance, Washington made it clear that the intended union between Law and his granddaughter was a complete surprise. But the president did nonetheless offer the approval of both grandparents, adding that he offered "best wishes that both of you may be supremely happy in the alliance."

He closed by emphasizing his family's desire that Eliza stay stateside, saying, "We shall hope that your fortunes (if not before) will, by this event, be fixed in America; for it would be a heart rending circumstance, if you should seperate [sic] Eliza from her friends in this country." The president's not-too-subtle suggestion that Law remain in America with his granddaughter was followed by an invitation for a visit at the Executive Mansion.

The years that Martha Washington spent as first lady taught her the art of public appearance. She refused to make her concerns public knowledge, and instead acted as though she could not have been more pleased about her granddaughter's impending marriage. The first lady told all who would listen about the upcoming wedding, pretending to be a proud and excited grandmother. It was clear, however, that the Washingtons' inner circle of friends and family viewed the upcoming nuptials as anything but normal. The tongues of political insiders began to wag, and even ally and vice president John Adams contributed to the presidential gossip when he wrote to his wife Abigail:

> *I have a great deal of News to tell you.- Mrs Washington told me the last time I dined at the Presidents that Betcy Custis is to be married next Month, to Mr Law the English East India Nabob. The good Lady is as gay as a Girl and tells the story in a very humerous stile. M^r. Law says he is only 35 Years of Age and altho the Climate of India has given him an older look Yet his Constitution is not impaired beyond his Years. He has asked Leave and a Blessing of the President & Mrs W.- He is to finish a House in the Federal City and live there. He has two Children born in India: but of whom is not explained.*

As politicians and acquaintances talked about the president's granddaughter, Martha Washington went from concealing her concerns to making peace with the worrisome union. Always the protective grandmother, she diminished the irregularity of Eliza's marriage through humor and cheerful conversation as she entertained friends and dignitaries at Washington's birthday celebration. Yet behind her forced smiles and merriment, Martha Washington was devising a plan for her granddaughter's future, plans that would upend Judge's life.

Eliza's engagement distracted George Washington from his own concerns: the disappointment he was sure to provoke when he announced his future plans. He had been wrestling with the question of whether or not to run for a third term in office, and early in 1796, against the strong desires of many, the president decided to retire from public life and began to prepare a farewell address to the American people. With the decision settled, Martha knew that it would be but a short matter of time before she found herself back in Virginia, connected to her friends and family, perhaps helping Eliza navigate married life.

Judge most certainly knew that her time in Philadelphia was therefore limited, too. By the time of the wedding of Eliza Custis—which took place on March 21, 1796, in Virginia at Hope Park, an estate built by Eliza's stepfather, Dr. David Stuart—the news that Washington would retire from office was no longer a secret among family members. The slaves living at the Executive Mansion would have understood that their time in Philadelphia was drawing to a close. Judge thought long and hard about her seven-year residency in the North, and the thought of returning to Mount Vernon was not an easy sell. Indeed, Judge had no real desire to return to Virginia, nor did she possess strong feelings of attachment to Mount Vernon.

Was this not the time for Ona Judge to seize the day, leave the Washingtons, and never look back? Could she find the bravery, the grit, and the power to leave everyone and everything that she knew? Several factors influenced her decision and tipped the balance sheet in one direction over the other.

Judge's biggest concern would have been the likelihood of never seeing her extended family at Mount Vernon again. Her living siblings remained at Mount Vernon with the expectation of being reunited one day with their sister. Philadelphia and Betty Davis continued in the tradition of their mother and spent their days sewing for the Washingtons, but the welfare of Betty Davis probably weighed on Judge's mind. She knew that Philadelphia was at the Mansion House, but Betty Davis moved around a bit more. Davis spent time at both the Mansion House and Dogue Run (another farm on the Mount Vernon estate). She had tested the patience of her owners on a couple of occasions so that by 1795, Washington wrote about her with animosity. He simply disliked Davis.

The president had grown tired of the excuses, the obstinacy, and the laziness that Davis openly displayed. Many slaveholders would never tolerate such behavior and used violent punishment or the threat of sale to cure disobedience. The president cautioned his farm manager William Pearce to keep a close eye on her, believing that she would use any excuse to avoid working. Washington wrote, "If pretended ailments, without apparent causes, or visible effects, will screen her from work, I shall get no service at all from her; for a more lazy, deceitful & impudent huzzy, is not to be found in the United States." The likelihood of Betty Davis fetching a high price at auction was relatively high, as she was only twenty-five years old and still considered reproductively fit. Judge no doubt knew some if not all of this, and worried about her sister.

On the other hand was the question of Ona Judge's future once she returned to Virginia after the retirement of the president. Her duties were likely to change once she returned to Mount Vernon, and might include new tasks, ones that were more physically taxing and required for rural Southern living. Judge also understood that the small amounts of private time she enjoyed in the North would be hard to come by in Virginia. While in Philadelphia, the Washingtons' social calendar was filled with dinners and social gatherings, events that allowed Judge moments of stolen privacy where she could sew, talk with house slaves and staff, take a trip to the theater, or simply rest. This life, as she knew it, would come to an end once she returned to Virginia.

None of the slaves at the President's House knew what the future held. For Ona Judge, however, the uncertainty vanished with a startling piece of news. The marriage of Eliza Law was to cut her post in Philadelphia short. Those who served the president in Philadelphia were likely to return from the traditional summer family trip to Mount Vernon, all of them except Ona. Her time in Philadelphia appeared as though it had come to a close.

Martha Washington knew that her granddaughter was completely unprepared for her new marriage with Thomas Law. She understood that Eliza knew nothing about the duties that accompanied a new marriage, let alone about setting up a new household in the Federal City. In an effort to help Eliza ease into her new matrimony, Martha Washington stepped in, and offered Eliza the support she needed: she would bequeath Judge to Eliza Law as a wedding gift.

If Judge ever believed that her close and intimate responsibilities for her owner yielded preferential treatment, she now understood better. The bondwoman now knew for certain that in the eyes of her owner, she was replaceable, just like any of the hundreds of slaves who toiled for the Washingtons. Judge may have overheard a conversation between Mrs. Washington and Eliza Law, or maybe Mrs. Washington simply mentioned the news in passing to her slave. No matter how the information was conveyed, Judge learned that she would eventually be given to the newlywed. Every slave understood that the death of a master signaled a change in ownership, so Judge knew that one day she would no longer serve the Washingtons. But it was Eliza Law's wedding that made Judge realize that her departure from Mount Vernon might come sooner than she ever imagined, a prospect that gravely concerned her.

The bondwoman knew that nothing would change the first lady's mind. Even though Judge had claimed one of the most revered positions within the Executive Mansion, she would always be a slave, and her feelings did not matter to Martha Washington or to anyone else in power. Surprise gave way to anger, which quickly turned to fear.

The pangs of anxiety she felt were based not only on having to leave Philadelphia but also on having to work for and with Eliza Custis Law, a young woman with a stormy reputation. All who were acquainted with the president's granddaughter commented upon her stubbornness and complete disregard for protocol. Eliza was unlike many elite eighteenth-century women in that she was assertive and refused to shrink from male authority. Family members joked that in "her tastes and pastimes, she is more man than woman and regrets that she can't wear pants." Eliza did what she wanted to do, often appearing irritated and labile. On occasion, she refused to go to church and other obligatory social functions, and her quick engagement to Thomas Law was a reminder to everyone that Eliza would be the architect of her own life.

George Washington often found Eliza's antics amusing. But the enslaved men and women who served Eliza would have found her temperament difficult at best. There is no question that Ona Judge would have had plentiful interaction with her as she assisted Eliza during her visits to the Executive Mansion, most certainly experiencing the wrath of the mercurial granddaughter.

Although human bondage was horrific under any owner, there

was always room for slaves to make comparisons. George and Martha Washington were not known for flying into unprovoked rages and were relatively stable and predictable owners. For Judge, a shift to the irritable and volcanic Eliza Custis Law could doom her to a life of poor treatment.

Ona Judge would have also worried about the newest member of the Washington family, a man with a shadowy reputation. Thomas Law grew his fortune in India before arriving in the District of Columbia. The land speculator purchased close to five hundred lots around the new city, expecting to line his pockets with cash once the nation's capital moved South. While his quick engagement to the president's granddaughter painted him as an opportunist, Judge would have worried more about his principles and behavior, especially given his sketchy familial past. The new member of the family had arrived in America with two of his three sons, both illegitimate and both the children of an Indian woman. While there were many biracial children at Mount Vernon (Judge herself was one of them), Law's children spoke to every slave woman's fear: Thomas Law slept with nonwhite women, and wasn't concerned about the gossip.

Judge must have worried that she might be the next target of Thomas Law's sexual interest. She was young, attractive, and would now be a slave working within his household. It would be nearly impossible to avoid his advances, a reality of female enslavement that stoked the fears of young girls and women alike. Rape and forced breeding torturously enlarged the institution of slavery, reminding every enslaved woman that she was never safe from sexual attack. The mothers, aunts, and sisters of young girls warned their female kinfolk about the sexual dangers that came with enslavement. Knowledge of what might happen to their growing prepubescent bodies prepared them for a vulnerable future.

Author and fugitive slave Harriet Jacobs knew this vulnerability too well, and described her encounters with her new owner:

> *No matter whether the slave girl be as black as ebony or as fair as her mistress. In either case, there is no shadow of law to protect her from insult, from violence, or even from death; all of these are inflicted by fiends who bear the shape of men.*

For a young woman such as Judge, the dangers of the unfamiliar—Eliza's temper and Law's sexual profile—served as an urgent incentive to run away. Living in Philadelphia exposed Judge to the benefits not only of owning one's own labor, but of also being able to select a mate, to have the relationship sanctioned by law, and to bear children who did not belong to a white master. The Washingtons' granddaughter was now married and on her way to motherhood. A legal marriage would be a near impossibility for Judge if she was given to Mrs. Law.

Martha Washington's decision to turn Judge over to Eliza was a reminder to Judge and to everyone enslaved at the Executive Mansion that they had absolutely no control over their lives, no matter how loyally they served. Slaves all over the young nation always dreamed and wished for emancipation, but Judge didn't need to imagine anything. In Philadelphia she could see freedom, feel freedom, and experience freedom in the smallest of ways. Judge's time spent in the North along with her pending return down South and a belief that she might never return, forced her to think deeply about her future.

Eight

The Fugitive

Ten Dollars Reward.

ABSCONDED from the household of the President of the United States, on Saturday afternoon, ONEY JUDGE, a light Mulatto girl, much freckled, with very black eyes, and bushy black hair—She is of middle stature, but slender and delicately made, about 20 years of age. She has many changes of very good clothes of all sorts, but they are not sufficiently recollected to describe.

As there was no suspicion of her going off, and it happened without the least provocation, it is not easy to conjecture whither she is gone—or fully, what her design is ; but as she may attempt to escape by water, all masters of vessels and others are cautioned against receiving her on board , altho' she may, and probably will endeavour to pass for a free woman, and it is said has, wherewithal to pay her passage.

Ten dollars will be paid to any person, (white or black) who will bring her home, if taken in the city, or on board any vessel in the harbour ; and a further reasonable sum if apprehended and brought home, from a greater distance, and in proportion to the distance.   FRED. KITT, Steward.
May 24   ‖3

Ona Judge's runaway advertisement in Claypoole's American Daily Advertiser, *May 25, 1796.*

During the spring months of 1796, Ona Judge's mind was filled with dreams, nightmares, plans, and challenges. Focusing on her normal tasks would have been difficult but still a requirement. As she brushed Martha Washington's hair before bedtime, she was careful not to tug too hard on the aging first lady's scalp. Women in their midsixties lamented hair loss, so Judge was gentle with each stroke of the brush. But her mind wandered. Judge's concerns about returning to Virginia and becoming the property of Eliza Law were all consuming, and at the very least, distracting. As the household slaves and servants began to prepare for the trip back to Mount Vernon, Judge continued to be deferential and obedient on the outside while on the inside she grew more anxious. Each night, as Judge removed the stains from Mrs. Washington's dresses and scraped the mud and dirt off the first lady's shoes, she contemplated the forbidden and thought seriously about reaching out for help. Yet she was frightened, and the mere mention of the words "fugitive" or "runaway" disrupted the rhythm of Judge's heartbeat.

She remembered when the Washingtons first arrived in Philadelphia, and heard talk about a growing "fugitive slave problem." Although New York and New Jersey dragged their feet in statewide abolition, slaves in the Mid-Atlantic and the Upper South knew that freedom could be found in the towns and cities of the North, as nearly all states north of Pennsylvania had already passed some kind of gradual abolition law. Numerous hurdles stood in the way of the brave enslaved men and women who dared to leave the small farms or shops of their masters. Judge undoubtedly saw these fugitives in the streets of the new capital, and although these men and women tried desperately to hide their pasts, a Southern accent, or recognition by a former owner's acquaintance, could easily betray them.

Judge had heard the stories of just how difficult it was to run away from an owner. One of the first obstacles for fugitive slaves to confront was the issue of Northern climates. The weather in cities such as Philadelphia up to the small towns of New England fluctuated constantly, and brutal Northeastern winters prompted slaves to consider spring or summer escapes. Two to three months out of every year, the Delaware River froze over, eliminating the sea as an escape route. The small rivers and creeks across the North were also impassable, often sending brave and desperate fugitives to premature, icy deaths. Roads, impassable from heavy snow and frozen mud, disabled even the strongest and most agile fugitives, trapping men and women on the run. Many lost their lives to hypothermia as they hid in the caves, barns, and alleyways of the North, with little to no food, or a proper winter coat or shoes.

Empty stomachs steered fugitives to search for food, but the winter months drove vegetables and fruits into hibernation. Fishing and hunting proved extremely difficult in heavy snow and ice, prompting men and women on the run to steal small animals from nearby farms. This always proved a desperate act and could end a fugitive's race to freedom, as farmers would notice a missing calf or chicken.

Ona Judge was contemplating escape in the spring or early summer season, which also had its challenges. Relentless heat and humidity could send a fugitive to an early grave, as heatstroke prompted vomiting and serious confusion. Dehydration transformed already tired bodies with sunken eyes into unmovable masses, as the healthiest of fugitives could only last three to five days without access to water. Spring and summer rains transformed dirt roads into muddy swamps, simultaneously claiming lives via mudslides. Of course, high illiteracy rates made it almost impossible for most fugitives to read poorly marked signs or directions. Even if given a map, Ona Judge would not have been able to read it.

Years before the safe houses of the Underground Railroad saved the lives of men and women on the run, most fugitives had few options for shelter and protection. The forests and wilderness protected escaped slaves from the eyes of local citizens, and thick brush and dense forest beds provided secrecy, as did abandoned cabins and stone hollows.

Beyond the weather and difficult conditions, Judge likely contemplated just how few women made successful attempts at escape. Unlike Judge, the majority of fugitives—90 percent—from Pennsylvania down to Virginia, were male. The same held true for South Carolina and parts of the Upper South. There were many reasons for the extremely low number of female escapees, but historians have focused on the relationships between mothers and children as the main deterrent for female slaves.

Throughout the rural South, enslaved children were much more likely to live with their mothers than with their fathers. "Abroad marriages," relationships between enslaved men and women who lived on different properties, often placed miles between husbands and wives. The inability to form legal marriages and the indiscriminate sale of human property often tore children from their fathers, sometimes separating young slaves from their fathers forever.

Most fugitives were between the ages of sixteen and thirty-five years old, the exact age span when enslaved women tended to be pregnant, nursing, or caring for a child. Enslaved mothers worried about all those who were left behind, fearing that retribution from a scorned owner would show itself on the backs of their children. This fear, of course, tethered slave mothers to the homes and estates of their owners. Successful escapes with children in tow were extremely difficult as long-distance travel with infants and toddlers reduced the chances of success. Children's cries of hunger and fatigue were easily detectable in dark forests and cold caves. Unable to walk or move quickly, small children slowed the tempo of the run to freedom. It was hard enough for a healthy adult to escape his owner, but for women with children, the task was near impossible. Childless, Judge would not have to confront the horror of leaving one's children behind for the opportunity of freedom. Of course, if she made the decision to escape, she would cut ties from her family back at Mount Vernon, a terrible choice to consider, but one that was altogether different from leaving behind a baby.

Runaway slave advertisements appeared frequently in Ben Franklin's *Pennsylvania Gazette*, and not surprisingly, most of them sought the return of male slaves. The number of runaway ads increased over the colonial period, and by the time Ona Judge arrived in Philadelphia, an average of twenty-six advertisements appeared in the *Gazette* every year. Slave women who appeared in the ads were runaways from Philadelphia proper and the surrounding counties. In September of 1790, a runaway ad appeared in the *Gazette* for a slave woman named Kate. Taking advantage of the tail end of the summer, Kate ran away from her master on the night of August 23. The twenty-one-year-old fugitive left her Chester County home and supposedly "went off with a black man, named Charles." A four-dollar reward was offered for the "Mulatto Girl" who took with her an "old black bonnet, a long gown striped red, blue and white, two short ditto striped blue, red and white, [and] a large white shawl." A month later an advertisement for a thirty-five-year-old slave woman named Nancy appeared in the *Gazette*. An eight-dollar reward was posted for the fugitive woman who was described as "of a black cast, but not the very blackest" who was "country born, and understands farmers kitchen work very well." The newspaper ads served as a reminder to both enslaved and free black Philadelphians that freedom was elusive. Although emancipation had come to many blacks in the city, it was still beyond the grasp of the enslaved in the surrounding counties. Even though Ona Judge was unable to read the newspaper ads on her own—the president's slaves were almost all kept illiterate— an oral tradition quickly moved this kind of information through black communities and to eager listeners.

Successful escapes offered hope to those who remained in

bondage, and failed attempts reminded them of the serious consequences that came with failure. Slaves were often whipped or
beaten for running away, sometimes in the presence of kinfolk and
other slaves on the small farm or large estate from which they ran.

＊＊＊

Washington remained vigilant about any and all escape attempts
from Mount Vernon, even while he was living in Philadelphia.
Although the president reportedly avoided the tearing apart of
slave families, he was not averse to punishing or selling difficult
slaves when he deemed appropriate. During the early 1790s,
Washington sold at least two difficult slaves to the Caribbean after
their maddening defiance could not be controlled. Washington
threatened a slave named Ben that he would no longer tolerate
disobedience and that:

> *if a stop is not put to his rogueries, and other villanies by fair
> means and shortly; that I will ship him off (as I did Waggoner
> Jack) for the West Indies [sic], where he will have no oppor-
> tunity of playing such pranks as he is at present engaged in.*

In 1791, the enslaved Waggoner Jack was sold for a quantity
of wine.

Aside from knowing that her master was not beyond selling a
slave for serious infractions of the rules, Judge also understood that
the slaves at Mount Vernon were subjected to physical violence. In
January of 1793, Washington condoned the whipping of Judge's
sister-in-law, Charlotte. Mount Vernon estate manager Anthony
Whiting wrote to the president about a disobedient seamstress and
recounted Charlotte's constant insubordination. Whiting wrote that

he "gave . . . a very good Whipping" and his plans for continued physical violence were made clear when he stated that he was "determined to lower her Spirit or skin her Back." Washington responded
to Whiting, stating, "And if she, or any other—of the Servants, will
not do their duty by fair means—or are impertinent, correction (as
the only alternative) must be administered."

The month following Charlotte's brutal whipping, and with
Haitian slave insurrection on the minds of many, Washington set
out to ease some of the concerns of Southern slaveholders. A little
more than two years into his residency in Philadelphia, the president signed into law the Fugitive Slave Act, creating a legal mecha-
nism for the capturing and reclaiming of fugitive slaves. According
to this act (signed in February 1793), a slave owner or his agent
could legally seize a runaway and force the apprehended slave to
appear in front of a judge or magistrate in the locality where he or
she was captured. After written or oral "proof of ownership" was
presented by the slaveholder, a judge could order the return of the
alleged fugitive. The controversial law also stated,

> That any person who shall knowingly and willingly obstruct or
> hinder such claimant, his agent, or attorney, in so seizing or ar-
> resting such fugitive from labor, or shall rescue such fugitive from
> such claimant, his agent or attorney, when so arrested pursuant
> to the authority herein given and declared; or shall harbor or
> conceal such person after notice that he or she was a fugitive
> from labor, as aforesaid, shall, for either of the said offences,
> forfeit and pay the sum of five hundred dollars. Which penal-
> ty may be recovered by and for the benefit of such claimant,
> by action of debt, in any Court proper to try the same, saving
> moreover to the person claiming such labor or service his right
> of action for or on account of the said injuries, or either of them.

To be clear, those who purposely interfered with the recapturing of a slave, or who offered aid or assistance to a fugitive, could be fined an exorbitant amount—$500—imprisoned, and be sued by the slaveholder in question. Southerners rejoiced over the new law, considering it a legal triumph to pursue their human property across state lines. However, for Northern states that no longer enforced or practiced human bondage, the law was a reminder of the growing divide over the issue of slavery. Northern states had no choice but to accept federal intervention regarding fugitive slaves, but it is important to note that Congress did not pass the Fugitive Slave Act with a unanimous voice.

Arguing that the Fugitive Slave Law of 1793 was unconstitutional, Northern states believed that the law erased the states' rights to legislate the contested issues surrounding fugitive slaves. Shortly after the act was passed, many of the Northern states passed "personal liberty" laws requiring trial by jury for blacks accused of being fugitive slaves. Several Northern states also used personal liberty laws to make certain that the "recapture" of a fugitive slave could be viewed as a kidnapping offense if not done through appropriate measures. Southern states, on the other hand, argued that the Fugitive Slave Law protected their property rights and that the law was imperative to carry out the Constitution's provisions regarding fugitives from labor.

Just as the slaves on High Street knew about gradual emancipation in Pennsylvania, they most certainly learned about the new federal law that made escape even more improbable. Without question, then, Ona Judge knew that the consequences of running away would be steep, so her escape had to be successful. If she ran away and was captured her life would change instantly, as angry owners might punish her in the worst way imaginable: by placing her on the auction block and selling her to the highest bidder. The

Washingtons might do what they had done before: they might "put her in their pocket."

She had examined the facts—the mercurial Eliza, the biases against blacks, the treatment of blacks in the aftermath of the yellow fever epidemic, the danger of the Fugitive Slave Law—and Judge realized that if she ran away, she couldn't plan her escape alone. So she took the biggest of gambles and confided in a group of crucial associates: free black allies.

We do not know how Ona Judge made contact with the group of free blacks who would offer to help with an escape. Perhaps while escorting Martha Washington to one of her many social calls, she took the opportunity to ask for assistance. As her mistress enjoyed afternoon tea, Judge could have reached out to a free black servant, one who might know how to help her, or at least, could discreetly point her in the direction of someone else who could. Every black Philadelphian knew that there was one man who could and did help runaways, the well-known preacher Richard Allen.

As one of the most influential leaders of the early republic, Reverend Richard Allen is often given credit for building the free black community of Philadelphia. By the 1790s, Allen simultaneously served as a spiritual leader to a growing black community and was also an entrepreneur, owning and operating a chimney sweep business. His trade was dangerous, but one of the few entrepreneurial opportunities open to black men. In a short time, Allen was able to hire apprentices to help grow his business and soon climbed up the economic ladder.

Perhaps the most important person on Allen's client list was the president himself, and we know that Allen collected money from the Executive Mansion for his services in March of 1796. Perhaps, after talking with a trusted friend, Judge reached out to

Allen during his visit to the President's House. Her words and interactions with the preacher would have gone undetectable by the house staff, and in a whisper, she would have asked Allen for help. Quick words would have passed between the two, perhaps with a plan to meet somewhere else to discuss her chances for finding freedom. Allen would have been a natural person to consult about the best way to flee the city and remain undetected.

Although Judge never publicly admitted to receiving help from Allen, their paths may have crossed a second time during the spring of 1796. The well-known minister included on his impressive résumé the skills of a cobbler, and was eventually listed on the Philadelphia tax rolls as operating a shoe shop in his home on Spruce Street. On May 10, the Washingtons gave Judge $1.25 to purchase new shoes, money that she could have taken directly to the shoe shop in Allen's home. There, Judge would have had more time and privacy to discuss the possibilities of escape with the famed black leader, who was himself an ex-slave.

She never revealed the identity of her friends who helped her to think about the possibilities of escape, as aiding a fugitive slave was considered a federal crime up until the Civil War.

Judge knew what the future held should she not heed the advice of her free black associates. "She supposed if she went back to Virginia, she should never have a chance to escape." Once she learned that "upon the decease of her master and mistress, she would become the property of a grand-daughter of theirs by the name of Custis," she knew that she had to flee. She imagined that her work for the Laws would begin immediately, not after the death of her owners, prompting a fierce clarity about her future and her dislike for Eliza Custis. "She was determined never to be her slave." Her decision was made. She would risk everything to avoid the clutches of the new Mrs. Law.

Judge was well-informed, and knew that her decision to flee

was far more than risky. But still, she was willing to face dog-sniffing kidnappers and bounty hunters for the rest of her life. Yes, her fear was consuming but so, too, was her anger. Judge could no longer stomach her enslavement, and it was the change in her ownership that pulled the trigger on Judge's fury. She had given everything to the Washingtons. For twelve years she had served her mistress faithfully, and now she was to be discarded like the scraps of material that she cut from Martha Washington's dresses. Any false illusions she had clung to had evaporated, and Judge knew that no matter how obedient or loyal she may have appeared to her owners, she would never be considered fully human. Her fidelity meant nothing to the Washingtons; she was their property, to be sold, mortgaged, or traded with whomever they wished.

The beast that slept in every slave's soul was awakened. Confronting a future with Eliza Law coaxed the hunger for freedom out of the recesses of Judge's mind, and now she was willing to fight for what she clearly believed was her right. Her decision to run was just the beginning of her liberation.

The waiting was difficult. For nearly two weeks, Judge had to calm her nerves and suppress her anger, as allies completed the planning for her escape. She could not raise suspicions, so Judge worked in tandem with the rest of the household, as they made the necessary preparations for a lengthy trip back to Mount Vernon. Judge later stated,

> *Whilst they were packing up to go to Virginia, I was packing to go, I didn't know where; for I knew that if I went back to Virginia, I never should get my liberty.*

Judge kept her plans a secret, making certain not to share information with anyone who lived in the Executive Mansion. She knew that fearful or jealous slaves were often responsible for foiled fugitive escapes; she decided to rely only on the assistance of free blacks who resided outside the walls of the president's home.

Not only did Ona Judge have to pack her things to leave, she also had to determine when she would escape. Although the Executive Mansion possessed more slaves and servants than did most Northern residences, Judge was the first lady's preferred house slave and had to be available at all times for whatever reason. There was only one duty from which she was exempt: meal preparation. The famed Hercules and a kitchen staff prepared all the meals served to the president and the first family. Judge sometimes received a bit of free time during the afternoon meal and the evening supper, as other servants or slaves were assigned to serve the Washingtons. The president often entertained dinner guests, extending the festivities into the evening and inviting guests to retire to the parlor to enjoy a bit of wine and additional conversation. This would be the only moment that Judge could use to her advantage.

And when the moment arrived, she gathered her steely nerves and fled. On Saturday, May 21, 1796, Ona Judge slipped out of the Executive Mansion while the Washingtons ate their supper. She disappeared into the free black community of Philadelphia.

⚜

No one knows exactly when Martha Washington realized that her prized slave was missing. Perhaps dinner ran well into the evening, and Judge's absence went unnoticed until late that night. Or maybe the president and his wife uncovered her escape just minutes after Judge left the Executive Mansion. The details may never be uncovered. But once the Washingtons realized that Judge was gone, they quickly understood that it was highly unlikely that she possessed any intention of returning. Washington was accustomed to slaves running away from Mount Vernon. On occasion, they would return after several days or weeks, but unlike past attempts made by fugitives, Judge's starting point was in the North. And the Washingtons knew time wasn't on their side.

On May 23, 1796, just two days later, Frederick Kitt, the steward for the Executive Mansion, placed an ad in the *Philadelphia Gazette* acknowledging the disappearance of Ona Judge. He placed another ad in *Claypoole's American Daily Advertiser* the next day with additional details about the escape. The language of the runaway ad was similar to others that appeared in eighteenth-century newspapers, describing Ona Judge while simultaneously announcing that she had defied the president:

> *Absconded from the household of the President of the United States on Saturday afternoon, ONEY JUDGE, a light Mulatto girl, much freckled, with very black eyes, and bushy black hair— She is of middle stature, but slender, and delicately made, about 20 years of age.*

Judge's runaway ad went on to describe the possessions that she had packed up. The ad noted that Judge had "many changes of very good clothes of all sorts, but they are not sufficiently recollected to describe."

Frederick Kitt's ads alerted shadowy slave catchers to Judge's probable escape route: the Delaware River. The advertisement warned all who worked on the docks of Philadelphia's busy port that the runaway would take to the open seas,

> *But as she may attempt to escape by water, all matters of vessels are cautioned against admitting her into them, although it*

is probable she will attempt to pass for a free woman, and has,
it is said, wherewithal to pay her passage.

A ten-dollar reward (the cost of a barrel of flour) was offered
for Judge's return—a typical amount proposed by slaveholders trying to reclaim their property. However, wanting to ensure a successful outcome, Judge's owners offered the reward to anyone who
turned her in, no matter their race. Kitt's second and subsequent
ads for Judge's return stated, "Ten dollars will be paid to any person, (white or black) who will bring her home, if taken in the city,
or on board any vessel in the harbor."

Judge knew that the moment she walked out of the President's
Mansion she would become a hunted woman. She would transform
from a trusted house slave for the most powerful American family
to a criminal, guilty of stealing her own body away from her owners.
Now she had to leave the city of Philadelphia as fast as possible and
search for an environment in which she would be safe from the
president's grasp. Although a few scholars suggest that Judge may
have spent some time hiding among the free black community of
Philadelphia, it is highly unlikely. This was a formidable task, as federal law made every state in the nation a danger zone for fugitives.

Word spread about the runaway slave woman, and reports of
supposed sightings trickled back to the president quickly. On June
28, trusted friend Thomas Lee Jr. wrote to Washington about his
female fugitive. Apparently, the president had asked his friend to
inquire about Judge in and around New York. Lee obliged him, and
after a bit of investigation, discovered that the escapee had indeed
made her way to New York. According to Lee, "a free mulattoe
Woman" who served as a cook in one of New York's numerous
boardinghouses reported that "she is well acquained [*sic*] with Oney
& that she has been here" and was supposedly headed to Boston. But

Lee didn't trust her claim. The free woman might have been trying to lead Lee down an errant path with false information. Or maybe she was simply mistaken and was confusing Judge for someone else. Thomas Lee may not have been certain about the supposed sighting of Judge, but he took no chances and notified law-enforcement authorities in New York about the possibility of the fugitive's presence anyway.

Judge would have been warned against spending any time in New York, the place she once called home and where she was recognizable. Free blacks in Philadelphia would have urged her to flee with the most urgent speed and to make no stops along the way to her final destination. Harboring a fugitive was punishable by a fine and/or imprisonment, and to assist the president's slave in her escape would have been even more dangerous. Those who aided Judge pushed for an expeditious departure, knowing the president was prepared to use all of his immense power to recapture his property. Judge needed to leave Philadelphia as fast as possible and looked to the wharves of the Delaware River to make her escape.

In fact, Judge escaped the city by boat. In her 1845 interview, Judge told of her journey to Portsmouth, New Hampshire, on a vessel that was commanded by Captain John Bowles. Judge remained secretive about her escape almost her whole life, only announcing the name of the captain more than a decade after his death, in July of 1837: "I never told his name till after he died, a few years since, lest they should punish him for bringing me away." Ona Judge knew that she owed her life to Bowles.

Like many other eighteenth-century sailors, John Bowles operated a shipping business with a partner, Thomas Leigh. The two ran their freight business along the eastern coast transporting lumber and fish to the port cities of New York and Philadelphia. They sold their items at market and returned with leather goods such as boots, bridles, and saddles to sell in New Hampshire's seaport town. Bowles knew the Atlantic well. He most likely began his relationship with the sea as an apprenticed deckhand, quickly moving up the ranks and eventually commanding his own ship, the *Nancy*. For many years he conducted his business up and down the North Atlantic coast, traveling to the Caribbean and back until the English navy captured his ship in 1800.

In 1796 Bowles was still very active, however. The local Portsmouth newspaper *Oracle of the Day* reported the departures and arrivals of ships and announced the items that would be exported and imported. The Portsmouth Customs House cleared the *Nancy*'s voyage to Philadelphia in early May of 1796. Bowles most likely left the Portsmouth harbor and sailed directly to Philadelphia, a trip that would have taken four to five days, weather permitting. The *Philadelphia Gazette* announced Bowles's arrival in the city on May 10, and while docked in Philadelphia, Bowles advertised his wares for sale as well as reasonably priced freight and passenger rates. The captain lingered in the Philadelphia port, perhaps looking to pick up additional passengers or to sell as much of his cargo as possible. Ona Judge eventually boarded Bowles's ship, a sloop that carried molasses, coffee, potatoes, leather goods, and candles. The *Nancy* slipped out of Philadelphia sometime after Saturday, May 21. If Bowles charged her, she would have paid for it either out of the money shared from the "gifts" the Washingtons doled out, a dollar here and a dollar there, or she was assisted by the free black community who most likely steered Judge toward Bowles and may have aided with her fare.

The commander of the *Nancy* was not publicly known for his

antislavery sentiment, but he must have been a relatively safe bet and not known as hostile to runaways. Judge's fair skin, her clothing, and perhaps her demeanor may have led Bowles to assume that his passenger was a free woman instead of a hunted slave. But while her appearance may not have alerted Bowles, traveling alone as a young woman would have caused most people to raise an eyebrow. In the 1790s, few women (black or white) traveled unaccompanied, as the social norms mandated that women travel with a chaperone, such as a family member or a friend, especially if their travels took them far from home. Young women who traveled by themselves were most likely running from someone or something.

Captain Bowles turned a blind eye to the unusual passenger. He was a man who had traveled the Atlantic and had met many people, and while he might not have known that the young traveler was the president's slave, he could tell that Ona Judge had a reason for wanting to leave the city. Fortunately for Judge, Bowles either didn't care about the young woman's past or was perhaps sympathetic to the plight of black slaves. Grateful for the shipmaster's acceptance, Judge quietly boarded his ship, beginning her life anew, now as a fugitive.

Nine

Slavery and Freedom in New Hampshire

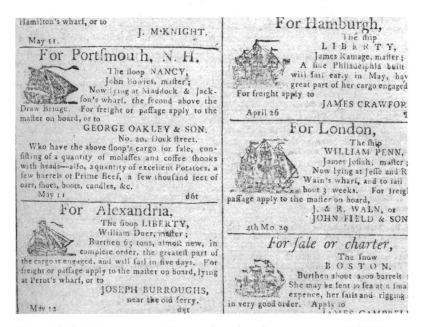

The Philadelphia Gazette & Universal Daily Advertiser, *May 17, 1796.*
Courtesy of the Library Company of Philadelphia.

The crashing waves of the Atlantic Ocean hurled saddles and candles from one side of the storage hold to another. The smell of molasses and coffee was thick, nauseating passengers who were unaccustomed to sailing with Bowles on his frequent trips between Philadelphia, New York, and Portsmouth. Transportation in the eighteenth century was never easy, and traveling by sea could be dangerous. Old and poorly inspected ships slipped in and out of cities with torn sails and weathered caulking, hoping to make it to the next port without incident. Ona Judge had never before sailed on such a ship, a single-masted sloop that could carry up to seventy-five people (depending on the size of the cargo). These vessels were designed to haul freight from one coastal town to the next, but ship captains like Bowles earned extra money by allowing passengers to ride along. Any seafaring voyages that Judge might have taken with the Washingtons would have been close to enjoyable. Short river crossings in relatively luxurious vessels were what Judge had come to know, but she had turned her back on all of it. Now on board the *Nancy*, space was minimal and travelers lodged themselves wherever there was room. Once again, the fugitive found herself sleeping in tight quarters, but this time it was with strangers—some were traveling home to visit with family and friends and others who, like Judge, were leaving behind a difficult past for the possibilities of a new future in Portsmouth.

The unsettled sea likely forced Judge's stomach to turn somersaults, sending her to look for refuge from her nausea above deck. The wind would cool her flushed and sweaty forehead, offering temporary relief from seasickness. Surely other passengers suffered the same way, hanging their bodies over the sides of the sloop, releasing the contents of their stomach into the Atlantic. Every morning when the sun lifted itself above the horizon, Judge would have looked out across the ocean, thankful to have survived another day away from her owners, but still, she was terrified.

For five days, Judge contained her fear. She could not appear too nervous, as passengers were already throwing quick and curious glances toward the light-skinned black woman who traveled alone. She knew that the Washingtons were looking for her and that by now her name and a bounty probably appeared in many of the Philadelphia newspapers. She wondered how much of a reward was attached to her recapture, a thought that sent her eyes to scan the strangers on board. Surely none of Washington's agents had made it to Bowles's ship before it left Dock Street, but she wouldn't know this for certain until the *Nancy* reached New Hampshire.

The beautiful and expensive clothing that she wore to serve the Washingtons was packed away, and instead, Judge would have dressed in inconspicuous clothing, allowing her to hide in plain sight. She was a hunted woman and would try to pass, not for white, but as a free black Northern woman.

During her five-day journey, Judge reviewed her arrival plans over and over again. Her Philadelphia friends had not shared with her the ship's destination or any other details about her journey until Judge was about to set sail. This kind of discretion was necessary to protect the fugitive and all those who helped in her escape, but the lack of information and the not knowing must have fueled her anxiety. Before she departed Philadelphia she was likely told who would help her once she arrived in Portsmouth, and given a description of a chaperone who would meet her near the docks and lead her to relative safety. Everything that Judge knew about her future in New Hampshire was conveyed to her in haste.

Even if Judge had been literate and able to write down her instructions, she would have been warned against doing so. Her Philadelphia friends surely demanded that the escape plan be committed to memory with no existing documentation that could tie her to the free black community. Judge had a lot to think about during her time at sea, most likely worrying about the basics in life such as food, shelter, and safety. How would she take care of herself once she arrived in her new city, and could she remain hidden for the rest of her life? She knew that it was just a matter of time before her owners sent slave catchers to look for her. Judge would have wondered if Portsmouth was far enough away from the Washingtons to ever allow her peace of mind, and perhaps she second-guessed her decision to run away. But there was no turning back.

Weak from a difficult journey and filled with fear, Judge nevertheless placed one foot in front of another and disembarked. Perhaps she offered her thanks to John Bowles, but more than likely, she quickly left the wharf, just in case there were slave catchers on the prowl. Ona Judge's friends in Philadelphia must have thought that Portsmouth would be a relatively safe location for her to live in anonymity. Although the black population was small, the hope was that Judge could find a way to secretly integrate into a new community more than three hundred miles away from Philadelphia.

⸎

Portsmouth was unlike any place Ona Judge had ever lived. Different from the bustling environs of a Philadelphia or a New York, Portsmouth was a growing port city with a developing eighteenth-century shipping industry. But compared to Philadelphia, the city was tiny, counting close to five thousand residents. Judge was accustomed to moving, making new friends, and learning the new sights and smells of a city. But this was the first time that Judge moved without the comfort of family or friends. She didn't have the reliability of her older brother, nor did she have the advice of the enslaved Moll to help direct her. Judge didn't know a soul in Portsmouth. She was completely alone.

It wouldn't take long for Judge to realize the differences between Portsmouth and Philadelphia, but one of the most startling contrasts was that her new city counted very few black people. At the time of Judge's arrival, there were fewer than eight hundred black men and women living in New Hampshire, and fewer than two hundred of them were enslaved. Similar to the rest of New England, three out of every four citizens who lived there at the end of the eighteenth century were of English, Scottish, or Irish ancestry. Judge's new community of black men and women in Portsmouth never climbed above 2 or 3 percent of the population, and the majority of them lived and worked along the sea and the rivers. It wouldn't take long for Judge to become acquainted with her new community; there were fewer black people in the entire city of Portsmouth than there were slaves living at Mount Vernon.

Judge's first priority was to find a place to live, no easy task for a single black woman with limited resources. Once again, she would have to rely on a network of free blacks, this time in Portsmouth. They undoubtedly were prepared for the fugitive's arrival, directing Judge to her new temporary home, where she "lodged at a Free-Negroes." Free blacks in Portsmouth were accustomed to helping fugitive slaves.

With the question of temporary housing settled, Judge set about to find work. She would need to locate an employment opportunity quickly, one that would allow her to support herself. Grateful for the roof over her head, Judge would have wanted to prove to her hosts that she was ambitious and determined to be independent. If she took too long locating employment, her hosts might tire of her, or worse, feel resentful. Judge was a superior seamstress and was capable of making the most beautiful clothing (as she had done for the Washingtons). But this kind of work would be hard for a fugitive to find. She had no references and no sample work.

Domestic labor was the only opportunity that Judge had to carve out a meager living, and she grabbed it, quickly finding a position in a local home. Most black women, no matter their status as enslaved or free, engaged in backbreaking domestic labor that proved cruel to the human body. They toiled in the homes of

New England's white residents, cooking, cleaning, and tending to the personal needs of their employers. Although Judge was accustomed to being on call in a domestic capacity for Martha Washington, she did not do the heaviest and most physically taxing labor required in an eighteenth-century home. The Washingtons' large staff allowed for white servants and male slaves to provide assistance with difficult domestic chores, freeing Judge to tend to the delicate and intimate needs of her owner. In New Hampshire, she could not be so selective.

Black domestics scrubbed floors, washed laundry, cooked meals, and cleaned the homes of their employers, difficult chores in the snowy winters of New England. Judge and other women, both black and white, tore muscles and broke bones as they strained to carry large loads of laundry, assisted in the fields of rural New Hampshire, and toted heavy cauldrons of water for meal preparation and bathing. Arguably, one of the most physically taxing responsibilities of a domestic was the preparation of the wash. Enslaved and free domestics began their days carrying ten- and twenty-gallon containers of water from the pump back to the home. It could take upward of one hundred gallons of water per day to complete all the washing and cooking required for a single family. This necessity could send black women to and from the pump up to five times per day. Arm strength alone was not sufficient, prompting black women to reach back to their ancestral traditions. Black domestics often carried large containers of water upon their heads, an age-old method used in Africa, but one that could lead to curved spines and skull fractures. More than taxing, icy and snow-covered footpaths could make the difficult task of water retrieval a dangerous journey.

In addition to water retrieval, domestics and laundresses also built the fire necessary for washing, bending their backs over hot wooden tubs for hours at a time. Before the washing process began, Judge and other domestics would have made soap by hand from lye and animal fat, using wood ashes, dung, or hemlock to remove stains. Once the water was collected and brought to the house, the arduous labor of washing the clothes began. Judge stirred the clothes in boiling water and then had to wring each article of clothing or linen by hand and hang them to dry. After thorough drying, clothing and bed linens would need to be ironed, another time-consuming and often dangerous and terribly hot task.

Food preparation also required countless hours of dedicated work and consumed much of the day. Ona Judge had never been charged with feeding her owners or herself. Hercules and a kitchen staff prepared each meal for the first family and their slaves and servants. Judge would now have to learn how to cook, and to cook well. Surely she had watched the slaves at Mount Vernon make hoecakes and prepare fish stew, but there was a difference between watching and doing. Her new black friends in Portsmouth would have provided recipes and culinary tips suitable to Northern palates. Presenting as a bad cook could earn any domestic a swift dismissal.

Black domestics, both enslaved and free, would rise early in the morning to prepare the breakfast meal. The kneading of dough and the baking of bread, in addition to the plucking of chickens and cutting of vegetables promoted early signs of arthritis in the fingers and hands of domestics. Torn and fatigued muscles received little care as enslaved women and live-in domestics were often allotted living spaces in the coldest and least-insulated locations of the household. Forced to sleep in cellars or attics, slaves were contained in the most out-of-the-way spaces. Attics contained very little to no ventilation, promising unbearably cold conditions in the winter and stifling heat during the summers. The conditions of slavery and servitude wore on the black female body, ensuring

that the majority of black women in New England did not live
beyond the age of forty. Yet Judge had few choices but to become
a domestic and a laundress, choosing to endure physically punishing work in New Hampshire, rather than accept her life as a slave.
That Judge elected to become a domestic, that she chose to endure
physically punishing work in New Hampshire, rather than remain
a slave, says everything we need know about how much she valued
freedom.

Human bondage had existed in New England for more than 150
years. African slavery was first legalized in Massachusetts in 1641,
unleashing the traffic in human souls to spread quickly throughout
the rest of the Northern colonies. Black men and women lived and
worked in the seaport of Portsmouth as early as 1645, when the
earliest-known African first arrived. Slave trader Captain Smith
arrived in New England with a handful of bound laborers who
had survived the long and horrific Middle Passage. Smith sold one
human to a "Mr. Williams of Piscataquak." No name or details
remain about the captive who arrived in New England; however,
he probably spent his life toiling against his will for Mr. Williams
in some capacity.

New Hampshire watched the town of Portsmouth develop
with the assistance of slave labor, and while it didn't grow a cash
crop such as tobacco or rice, it had its own list of hazards for Africans. The journey to New England was long, forcing Africans to
endure the unconceivable atrocities of the Middle Passage beyond
the shores of West Africa or the islands of the Caribbean. Many
perished before stepping foot onto the New England colonies, a
reality confronted by slave owner William Pepperell of Kittery
Point, Maine. In 1719 Pepperell purchased five enslaved Africans

from the island of Antigua, and only one of his bound laborers, a woman, survived the journey. After only three weeks in New England, she, too, succumbed to illness. The extreme cold and acclimation to life in New England found slave owners like Pepperell in jeopardy of losing a great deal of wealth in the risky business of slave trading.

But when Ona Judge arrived in New Hampshire, she encountered a state that was on its way to ending the institution of slavery. Since the Fugitive Slave Law of 1793 allowed slave owners to cross state lines to retrieve their human property, it was important for runaways to find communities that were at the very least rethinking the institution of human bondage. After Judge stepped onto the shores of Portsmouth, she would eventually meet and come to know many, if not all, of the town's black residents, whether free or enslaved. These men and women of Portsmouth cautiously watched the change in state laws that appeared to welcome additional sources of labor.

New Hampshire began to wrestle with the issue of slavery in the decade prior to Judge's arrival, joining Pennsylvania, Massachusetts, Connecticut, and Rhode Island in its reconsideration of human bondage. Although a bill of rights promised equality and liberty to the citizens of New Hampshire, slavery continued for decades. A revised tax code of 1789 lifted the hopes of men and women held in bondage, as new wording stated, "Slaves cease to be known and held as property." But the optimism of the enslaved was dashed as the majority of slave owners in New Hampshire did not move to emancipate their slaves but instead read the new code as a tax relief that exempted their human bondage as a tax liability.

The slow process of gradual emancipation moved in fits and starts across New England, but in Judge's new home of Portsmouth, human bondage disappeared by 1805. Similar to other

urban or coastal cities and towns, Portsmouth ended its relationship with slavery before the rest of the state. While slave owners
in Portsmouth transitioned to a free wage labor system, the rest of
New Hampshire lagged behind: it wouldn't be until 1857 that the
New Hampshire legislature took the final step of abolishing slavery
altogether.

Black men and women privately celebrated the gradual steps
of emancipation but took a cautious and skeptical approach to
the promises of freedom, as they still encountered daily indigni-
ties, violence, and a lack of citizenship or equal protection under
the law. The black community of Portsmouth would pass on local
history and information about the law to newcomers like Judge.
Just as she had done in New York and Philadelphia, she listened,
realizing that the decision to relocate to Portsmouth had been
the most strategic of moves. Judge had her Philadelphia friends
to thank for that.

Ten

A Close Call

"Governor Langdon's Mansion."

Early each morning, Ona Judge would rise from fitful sleep. Her mind refused to give her body the deep slumber that it needed as it revisited the images of her siblings and nieces left behind at Mount Vernon. Awakened by nightmares, Judge would have to train her mind to believe that she was safe from harm. The only cure for what must have been acute insomnia was the body-stiffening domestic labor that threw most black women into almost instant sleep at the end of their evenings.

As the days transitioned into weeks, and then months, the fugitive fell into the rhythm of domestic work and life. The sun rose early during the summer in New England, a gift to Judge and the other domestics who depended upon its light for breakfast preparation and early-morning chores. Each day, as Judge walked to her new job, one that paid her wages, she would welcome the hard work that lay ahead. The work was difficult, and perhaps, to her mind, demeaning, but it was hard and honest labor that allowed her to survive in Portsmouth.

Though she spent the entirety of her day in service, her work required trips to local shops to fetch needed household items. Judge moved about her new city without the surveillance of an owner and over time, grew accustomed to this new freedom. She could visit the marketplace to purchase turnips and striped bass, dinner items that she could present to her hosts as symbols of her deep appreciation. When she received her wages, she might even be able to surprise them with additional quantities of tea, and maybe even sugar.

The long days of summer offered the fugitive a bit of extra daylight when she returned home from work. After helping her hosts with their own domestic chores, she could refresh herself on the art of sewing, remembering what an excellent seamstress she had been. Perhaps she would start with something simple, such as a linen shift for the lady of the house. Poor women could afford only one or two of these essential items, which they wore under their clothes every day. It would make a perfectly practical gift for any free black woman struggling to survive in New Hampshire.

If Judge could save enough from her modest wages, she could purchase material, ribbons, and buttons, allowing her to create sample clothing for the residents of Portsmouth to examine. Over time, she might be able to earn a reputation as an esteemed seamstress, earning enough money to leave the domestic work and laundering behind. The skills that she perfected back at Mount Vernon and in the Executive Mansion might allow her to find a way out from underneath crippling poverty. Judge knew that in order for this to be a possibility, she would have to be patient, work hard, and save her money, all the while, and most importantly, remain undetected in her new city.

While her walks about town were a reminder of her newfound freedom, they were always accompanied by the concerns of recapture. Judge never forgot that she was a hunted woman. Ever vigilant and alert, she knew she'd be a fool to dawdle in the narrow streets of her new city, for she might be asked to present freedom papers. Black men and women needed to walk with purpose in Portsmouth, lest they be questioned about their business, attracting unwanted or perhaps hostile attention from their white neighbors. Evening curfews were strictly enforced for Portsmouth's black residents, and Judge would have made it a priority to be safely indoors and away from prying eyes and officials with invasive questions before nightfall. In the streets, allies could be hard to distinguish from enemies, and in many ways the family that could harm her the most was also the most prominent family in New Hampshire, the Langdon family.

Senator Langdon and his family were probably the most respected family in New Hampshire and close friends of the Washingtons. A native of Portsmouth, John Langdon was born in 1741, and unlike many young men of his class, he bypassed an elite education and opted for a lucrative career in trade. Quickly learning the Atlantic trade routes, Langdon became a successful ship captain, transporting and selling goods and eventually purchasing his own vessels. It was only thanks to the restrictions of British trade policies that Langdon found himself thrust into the politics of the American revolutionary era. Langdon led a successful charge against a British military installation, cementing his position as a Revolutionary War hero and political leader in New Hampshire. Serving as a delegate to the Second Continental Congress, speaker of the New Hampshire House of Representatives, and a delegate to the Constitutional Convention, John Langdon became one of the most powerful men in the nation, eventually elected the first president of the United States Senate, the most powerful position in the country until George Washington was elected to the presidency. It was Langdon who sent word to Mount Vernon via messenger that Washington was the unanimous choice to lead the nation. After the election of George Washington, Langdon continued his political career, serving as a senator and a governor of New Hampshire.

Langdon met and worked with George Washington on many occasions. In November of 1789, Washington described a visit to New Hampshire in his diary, writing, "Portsmouth, it is said, contains about 5,000 inhabitants. There are some good houses, (among which Col. Langdon's may be esteemed the first)." Washington did not stay with Langdon in his home (the president preferred to stay in nearby inns, never wanting to impose upon his friends and political acquaintances), but he did enjoy tea in the Langdon parlor and shared a few meals with the Langdon family during the trip. The senator and his wife, Elizabeth Sherburne Langdon, often referred to as Betsy, had two children, Elizabeth and John, who died as an infant. As the Langdons became friendly with the Washingtons, Elizabeth developed a friendship with the president's granddaughter, Nelly.

During the 1790s, the two young girls visited with one another at the Executive Mansion in Philadelphia. One can imagine them taking long walks and talking incessantly about their lives. Elizabeth and Nelly represented the new version of American royalty, one the daughter of a senator, the other, the granddaughter of the president of the United States. Both girls understood the pressures that came along with elevated status, as well as its privileges. Ona Judge watched these two young girls grow up in the spotlight of early American politics.

Judge remembered the times in Philadelphia when Moll was overburdened with caring for the Washington grandchildren, and she had stepped in to help. She may well have served the senator's daughter tea or acted as a chaperone or caregiver for the two young girls. Elizabeth Langdon and Ona Judge knew each other, a liability that the fugitive must have contemplated after she arrived in New Hampshire.

Liabilities and all, Judge came to appreciate if not love her new city. During the summer months following her escape, Judge carefully explored her surroundings and began piecing together a new life. She carried herself as if she had never been enslaved, an important performance for all fugitives, but one that began to feel more and more natural. That is, until Judge came face-to-face with her past.

As she walked through the narrow streets of Portsmouth, perhaps on an errand or on her way to do a bit of shopping, a familiar sight ignited terror in the fugitive's chest. There, in front of Judge, was the young girl she had served in the Executive Mansion. Elizabeth Langdon, now eighteen years old, walked directly toward the frightened fugitive. The moment that Judge had feared had finally come.

The speed of her pulse quickened as Judge's eyes focused upon the woman she had gotten to know in Philadelphia. Her first priority would be to flee, to leave the street and to hope that the senator's daughter had not recognized her freckled face. Judge's stiffened body, newly worn by the tyranny of domestic work, readied itself to run, to bolt from Portsmouth's city streets and to look for refuge. Quaint and intimate, the small streets of her new city presented no safe space for the fugitive to hide. But within a few seconds she would have realized that running would be the worst possible reaction. If she fled, she would draw attention to herself, something no fugitive could risk.

She had only a matter of seconds to figure out what she should do to safeguard her new life. For most of her life as a slave, Ona Judge had to hide her feelings. She was accustomed to erasing anger from a furrowed brow or holding back tears in sorrow filled eyes, and now, she steadied herself and tucked her fear away. Lowering her head in an attempt to avoid eye contact with her owners' family friend, Judge kept walking. Elizabeth Langdon paused, expecting a cordial greeting from the familiar face, but she received no such acknowledgment.

Flashes of enslavement back at Mount Vernon might have quickly pushed their way to the front of Ona Judge's mind. She would have remembered the stories of enslaved people who had unsuccessfully attempted escape back at her Virginia birthplace. Some of these men and women were punished, and sold. Her purposeful walk quickened to a trot as the fugitive swiftly dodged the dangerous confrontation. But where could she go? Where would she hide? A return to her new home would have been risky. She couldn't chance being followed by Langdon, as it would put her host family in danger, or place them in a position of being charged with breaking federal laws for harboring a fugitive slave. She'd have to wait until nightfall to try to outwit any would-be captors.

When Judge finally returned home, she most likely looked to her hosts for advice and strategy, as any semblance of a normal routine that she had cobbled together over the summer had been destroyed when she came face-to-face with Elizabeth Langdon. If for some miraculous reason Langdon had not seen her, it was just a matter of time before one of the Washingtons' friends, or perhaps a family member of Portsmouth native Tobias Lear, discovered her.

~~~~~

Elizabeth Langdon rarely took notice of common folk as she walked about Portsmouth. As the senator's daughter, she was accustomed to staring eyes and false-pretense situations that could be avoided by offering little to no direct eye contact. But she couldn't stop thinking about the woman she had seen in the street. The face of the young black woman looked hauntingly familiar to Elizabeth. And there was something about those eyes. She was certain that she'd seen them before. But where? And then, it dawned on her: the Executive Mansion.

But what on earth was Judge doing in Portsmouth, and where was Mrs. Washington? Surely she would have known if the president and his family were in town on official business or for a quick visit. For a moment, the senator's daughter second-guessed herself. The only other alternative for the slave woman's presence in Portsmouth was completely unimaginable. Yet, on the off chance that it was Ona Judge, she must alert her father immediately.

Once Elizabeth Langdon conferred with her parents, the situation became quite clear. The senator's daughter had spotted the Washingtons' fugitive. Still in shock, Langdon probably found herself wondering about Judge's escape from her owners. But perhaps more curious to her was Judge's reason for wanting to leave the Washingtons in the first place. For the slaveholding elite, it was difficult to accept the agency of black thought or the desire and risk involved in escape. The Langdons had participated in the buying and selling of slaves from the late 1600s up until the eve of the Revolution, and just like the Washingtons, they considered themselves to be benevolent masters, affording their slaves more than the bare necessities of life. They fashioned themselves as different from those hardened slave owners, notorious for the use of the lash and for cruel and demonic torture. In their minds, they had been noble slave owners who provided food and shelter for their slaves, whom they believed to be incapable of caring for themselves.

The Langdons would have known that the president offered pocket money to his slaves, allowed them to attend the theater, and even negotiated with them, allowing slaves to keep their families together. In their estimation, he was a good owner, paternalistic, and adhered to the rules of Southern gentility. Why would any of the Washingtons' slaves run away, especially Ona Judge? Hadn't she been treated well, clothed, and fed?

What the New Hampshire family could not envision was the suffocation felt by house slaves who controlled very little of their time. Under the constant and watchful eye of her mistress, Judge withstood her teenage years under Martha Washington's scrutiny. She spent most of her days and nights in proximity to the Washington family, and without designated slave quarters, there was no place to breathe, no place to reconnect with friends or family, and no place to release the frustration and depression that came tied to the institution of slavery. Judge chose to take her chances on a risky escape rather than live a life trapped in human bondage, and her fierce insistence upon freedom was almost incomprehensible to most white people, the Langdons included.

Even though John Langdon was no longer a slaveholder, he knew what must be done. Not only were the Washingtons family friends, but as a senator of the United States, he was obligated to follow the law. Ona Judge was a fugitive and the Washingtons were entitled to their property.

On August 21, the Washingtons returned to Philadelphia from their extended visit at Mount Vernon and knew exactly where to find their slave woman.

Eleven

The Negotiator

Market Square, Portsmouth, New Hampshire, from Gleason's Pictorial Drawing Room Companion, *1853. Courtesy of the Library Company of Philadelphia.*

There were many pressing matters for the president to address during the late summer of 1796, but his decision to step down as president took center stage. Ignoring the fervent wishes of his party members who wanted Washington to remain in office, he was steadfast in his resolve to retire. The president was exhausted and wanted to return to life as a civilian farmer, a simpler life that would not wear on his aging body. He made it very clear that nothing short of a national emergency would change his mind about retirement. Washington was ready to go back to Virginia.

With an election fast approaching, the president chose to

announce his intentions quickly. His farewell address, created in most part by Alexander Hamilton, was complete, so he sent Tobias Lear to fetch David Claypoole, publisher of the Philadelphia newspaper *Claypoole's American Daily Advertiser*. Washington wanted his farewell address to appear in David Claypoole's paper, the same newspaper that four months earlier printed an advertisement with a ten-dollar reward for the return of Ona Judge. On September 19 Washington's "Farewell Address" was publicly released in Philadelphia, leaving the American people with the task of selecting a new commander in chief.

In the midst of planning for retirement, however, the president took up the work of slave catching. Ona Judge had placed her owners in a very difficult situation. The Washingtons were now faced with the politically tricky task of attempting to reclaim a slave in the state of New Hampshire, which was not as committed to African slavery as was their beloved Virginia. They would need to devise a plan to recover her, one that was swift and discreet.

The Washingtons were perplexed about Judge's motivations, associates, and her desired destination. For a second time in one year, they were feeling their way through a disturbing situation that had caught them off guard. First, their granddaughter Eliza Custis's marriage and now in a reversal of roles, Ona Judge was the cause of surprise and uncertainty for the Washingtons. But any confusion that the president possessed had given way to anger—Judge had finally interrupted his slave-rotation plan. The president knew that if he pursued the fugitive, even with the law on his side, he might have a public relations problem, a dilemma he had managed to avoid throughout his residency in Philadelphia.

Runaways reminded Americans who were sorting out their feelings about human bondage that slaves were people, not simply property. Judge's escape made a new case for a growing number of Northerners who bristled at the thought of African slavery: it mattered not if a slave was well dressed and offered small tokens of kindness, worked in luxurious settings or in the blistering heat. Enslavement was never preferable over freedom for any human being, and if given the opportunity, a slave, even the president's slave, preferred freedom.

Ona Judge's escape set a bad precedent for the slaves who worked in the Executive Mansion. As such, Washington was selective about who he brought back to Philadelphia after his trip home to Virginia had come to an end. Only Moll and Joe Richardson had been allowed to return to the capital for the president's final year in office. Shaken up by Judge's escape, the Washingtons made do with Northern white servants, fearful that the fugitive had started a trend. Immediately after he settled his new staff, both enslaved and wage-earning, Martha Washington gave the president his marching orders: Retrieve Ona. The fugitive belonged to the first lady, after all, and Judge had already been promised to her granddaughter. The president would need to work quickly to capture the fugitive, or he would have to deal with the displeasure of his wife, not to mention reimburse the Custis estate for the loss of its property.

Weighing all of his options carefully, and placing discretion above all else, the president decided to enlist the services of the federal government to quietly recapture the fugitive. He approached Secretary of the Treasury Oliver Wolcott Jr. The secretary must have listened to Washington's request for assistance with his normal deference, and of course, he offered to help the president with his problem. Following their conversation, the next day the president sat down to write the first of six letters that would change hands between the president and his slave-catching agents.

On September first, the president began his letter writing to Wolcott. Several months had passed since Judge's escape, but Washington was still angry, and the more he wrote, the angrier he felt. To his mind, the slave woman had been treated well, more like a family member than a slave, and this was how she repaid her kind masters. And of course, she couldn't have chosen a more inopportune time. The last thing Washington wanted to deal with during his final months in office was the recapture of a fugitive. He had many more pressing matters to attend, a thought that stirred his anger and commanded his thoughts.

Martha Washington's slave, a woman who did her best not to be seen or heard, was now at the forefront of the president's mind. As he sat at his desk, he thought long and hard about Judge, remembering how in 1784, a freckle-faced ten-year-old joined the team of house slaves at the Mansion House. She began her new assignment just as the president returned from the war, perhaps a memory that prompted Washington to realize that both he and Judge had acclimated to a new way of life at the very same time. He thought about the seven years that Judge had spent with his family in New York and Philadelphia and how she knew the most intimate details of the Washingtons' lives. His reminiscing added fuel to the fire.

As he wrote his lengthy three-page letter about the fugitive, Judge's face reappeared over and over again in his mind. But oddly enough, Washington never offered a physical description of her. Perhaps he had shared this information during his conversation with Wolcott, but it was more likely that the secretary was familiar with Ona Judge from his frequent visits with the president. And of course, the runaway slave advertisements that appeared in the *Philadelphia Gazette* could serve as a helpful guide.

One strand of hearsay that Washington addressed in his letter was that a male suitor had put Ona Judge up to the business of escape. In Washington's mind, there was no possible way that Judge could or would have engineered her own escape under the watchful eyes of her owners. Someone else must have lured her away and planned her escape, for as Washington wrote to Wolcott, "not the least suspicion was entertained of her going, or having formed a connexion with any one who could induce her to such an Act."

Over time, Washington grew adamant that a boyfriend was at the center of Judge's getaway. The president believed that a known acquaintance of the first family, a "Frenchman" to be exact, was involved in Judge's escape. This man (who Washington never named but suggested was mentally unstable) had not been seen since the fugitive left the president's house. Subsequent conversations with Washington's sources reported that this French boyfriend abandoned Ona Judge, leaving her destitute and dependent upon earning wages as a seamstress and begging for domestic work.

Believing that Judge had been beguiled into running away, Washington asked Wolcott to contact Portsmouth's customs officer Thomas Whipple, which, to his mind, was a completely appropriate request. It was the president's residency in Philadelphia—a matter of state business—that allowed for Judge to take flight in the first place, therefore the use of governmental resources in his slave catching was justifiable. Washington believed the customs collector could play a crucial role in recovering his slave woman, serving as the president's eyes and ears on the ground in Portsmouth.

The president offered suggestions about recapturing the fugitive, and all of them were clear violations of the law. Washington understood the Fugitive Slave Act of 1793, after all, he had signed the bill. His advice for the customs collector conveniently sidestepped all of the regulations that were in place to appropriately return a runaway to his or her owner. The law stated that anyone who captured a fugitive must bring him or her in front of a judge or magistrate and provide proof of ownership before leaving the state with their human property. The president had no intention of involving judges or magistrates in the handling of this dilemma, but he did suggest that Elizabeth Langdon or her mother could offer a formal identification of the runaway if "positive proof [was] required." Washington hoped that such an identification would be unnecessary, but the appropriate people were in place, if needed. Once captured, Whipple should "put her on board a Vessel bound immediately to this place,—or to Alexandria which I should like better."

Always cash-strapped, the president believed his suggestions for Judge's recovery would prove "the safest & least expensive." For his troubles, Whipple would be compensated for any and all costs associated with the capture and return of his fugitive slave, and of course, the president would be thankful for his assistance. For many who served the young nation in any kind of authoritative role, the appreciation of the president was most welcome, for who wouldn't want to be in the good graces of the president of the United States? Given Washington's stature, one would assume Whipple would have completed the task with enthusiasm.

Though Washington closed his letter with an apology to Oliver Wolcott, writing, "I am sorry to give you, or any one else trouble on such a trifling occasion," his annoyance with Ona Judge was evident. "The ingratitude of the girl, who was brought up & treated more like a child than a Servant (& M^rs· Washington's desire to recover her) ought not to escape with impunity if it can be avoided." His pride, in addition to his wife's anger and strong desire to have her bondwoman back in her possession, moved the president to pursue Judge, no matter the law.

On behalf of the president, Secretary Wolcott contacted Portsmouth's collector of customs, Joseph Whipple. He responded to

Wolcott by letter on September tenth, acknowledging that he would "with great pleasure execute the Presidents [*sic*] wishes in the matter to which it relates."

Joseph Whipple, born sometime around 1737, was the son of Captain William Whipple Sr. and Mary Cutt Whipple from Kittery, Maine. The Whipples raised five children, but it was Joseph's brother, General William Whipple, who elevated the family name. William Whipple Jr., a soldier in the American Revolution, and an associate justice of the New Hampshire Superior Court, signed the Declaration of Independence. In addition to all of his political contributions, he was an entrepreneur who ran a mercantile business with his brother Joseph in Portsmouth until the beginning of the Revolution. While the customs collector was an important man in Portsmouth, he would never be as well-known or respected as William. He lived in his brother's shadow.

The Whipples were not unfamiliar with bound labor, for the family had held Africans in bondage. However, by the 1780s the Whipples began to emancipate their slaves, in particular, those who had fought in the Revolution. Their slave, the famed Prince Whipple, who gave his service to the American troops, was rewarded for his service with freedom. Previously owned by William Whipple Jr., Prince Whipple's name became well known after he was erroneously labeled as the black soldier in the famous painting of Washington crossing the Delaware.

Joseph Whipple was an educated businessman who happened to be friends with Senator Langdon. In August of 1789 (following a recommendation from his friend), Washington formally appointed Whipple as Portsmouth's customs collector. Whipple held this position throughout Washington's two terms in office, eventually leaving his post during the Adams administration, as his political sentiments became heavily anti-federalist. (Whipple found his way back to his post when the Republican Thomas Jefferson became president in 1800.) The Customs office was small and adjoined the home he made with his wife, Hannah Billings of Boston. While it would be more than presumptuous to label Whipple an abolitionist, it was clear that his views on slavery were in line with many of the residents of Portsmouth. With the Whipples having emancipated their own slaves and with Joseph Whipple rethinking his own Federalist feelings during the last year of Washington's term in office, the request from the president placed Whipple in a difficult position. Although he accepted the assignment from Washington with a professed eagerness and due respect, he planned to investigate the claims about Ona Judge and come to his own conclusions about her escape.

⁘

Whipple spent the next several weeks searching for the president's fugitive. He would have started his investigation down by the Portsmouth docks, asking ship captains and dockworkers, merchant friends and small shopkeepers if they had seen a young woman with freckles and bushy hair. He would have been discreet, mentioning nothing about her status as a runaway nor her connection to the president.

Like Washington, Whipple came up with subterfuge to lure Judge into his sights. He told his acquaintances that he was looking for a good servant, a woman, who would be able to help his wife, Hannah, with traditional domestic work, knowing that the grapevine would spread the word. If he were smart, just to be sure, he would have asked free blacks—those who served as maids and waiters to his friends—if they knew of anyone who needed work.

Ona Judge learned that the customs collector was in need of a domestic, and was immediately intrigued. Friends would have told her about Whipple and his relatively famous family, prompting Judge to remember that this kind of work was something to which she was accustomed. She certainly knew how to serve the rich and famous. The job would most likely be permanent, not a temporary position that always left black domestics vulnerable once their pay was discontinued with little to no notice. Most important, Judge's friends would have told her that Whipple did not own slaves, another promising attribute about her potential employer. She knew enough after her three-month stay in Portsmouth that this might be the opportunity she so desperately needed: stable and solid employment.

With a mixture of optimism and caution, Judge agreed to meet with Whipple to discuss the position. Never forgetting her fugitive status, Judge was inevitably both reserved and alert, sizing up her potential employer as he asked questions about her cooking and sewing skills. She desperately needed this kind of work, but something seemed off about the customs collector—in fact, he was too nice to her. Whipple began to ask about her personal life, fair game for any white employer in eighteenth-century Portsmouth, but Whipple appeared to know more about Judge's life than was appropriate. This, after all, was their first meeting. Whipple asked if she had a husband and then began to ask curious questions about her love life, odd questions that would make any young woman uncomfortable. The customs collector tried desperately to verify Judge's identity without tipping her off, but he failed. Whipple's charade quickly unraveled once he asked the fugitive about a French suitor. She denied a relationship with anyone, and it dawned on her that she'd been tricked. Readying her feet for a quick departure, Ona Judge grew quiet, and waited.

The moment she had dreaded was finally in front of her. Judge had been informed upon and now she stood before one of the president's appointed officials, a white man, wondering how long it would take before she was sent back to slavery. But there was something that soothed her tightly wound nerves. To Judge, Whipple seemed like a nice enough man; that is, he hadn't yet called for the constable to have her arrested.

Realizing that he had given away his own intentions, Whipple sensed the fugitive's fear. He had no choice but to come clean with Judge and to convince her that he was an ally, not an enemy. Yes, he had been given a mandate by Washington, but he had his own solution to her dilemma. Rather than tell her what to do, Whipple consulted with her, asked her why she had run away, and discussed possible alternatives to a life of enslavement back in Virginia or elsewhere. During their discussion, the fugitive realized that the customs collector would not use brute force to capture her. Rather, he wanted to talk to her, to *reason* with her; he gave Judge the courage to speak her mind.

Her language shifted from sugary deference to proclamations of righteous indignation. The kind words she offered about the Washingtons toward the beginning of their conversation transformed into declarations of intent. She told Whipple that under no circumstances would she return to slavery, where she could be "sold or given to any person." She would rather die than return.

At an impasse, Whipple thought that compromise was the only way forward and assured the fugitive that he could negotiate with the president on her behalf. Washington might agree to arrange for Judge's freedom in the future, once he and Mrs. Washington were deceased. This compromise would allow for Judge to return to her family, the relative luxurious conditions she had come to know, and end her shadowy life as a fugitive. All she had to do was trust him, a tall order for any black fugitive to contemplate.

Judge realized the tables had turned and the customs collector was now negotiating with the fugitive, asking her to listen to his advice and imploring her to travel voluntarily back to Philadelphia. Judge realized that she simply needed to leave. Her resolve was as solid as the granite found throughout the earth in her new state. She told Whipple what he wanted to hear, agreed to return to her owners, and left his presence with no intention of ever keeping her word. Whipple told Judge that he would arrange passage for her on a ship, promising her a smooth transition back to the Washington household and to life as a slave.

Judge politely agreed to meet the ship when it was scheduled to depart. She left the customs collector, most likely returning home to her hosts. If the president wanted to claim his fugitive, he would have to do it by force. She would never return to the Washingtons, not if she could help it.

Whipple's plan to return the fugitive was delayed as bad weather prevented ships from leaving Portsmouth. After a few days, the sea settled itself, finally allowing vessels to safely leave port. The customs collector sent word to Judge, giving her a time to meet for her departure and eventual reunion with the Washingtons. It was Whipple's duty to see the fugitive off, so he most likely paced the docks, awaiting her arrival. Repeatedly checking his timepiece, he grew anxious as the minutes turned into hours. Whipple probably convinced himself that there was some kind of miscommunication, perhaps asking the ship's captain to wait a bit longer before leaving port. But then, everything became crystal clear. Just as Whipple had lured Ona Judge to his home with a false employment opportunity, she in turn, sent him on a fool's mission. The fugitive never had any intentions of leaving Portsmouth. Two could play at subterfuge.

If Judge ever wavered in her conviction, the small black community of Portsmouth made it their priority to buttress her resolve. Once her friends caught wind of the concocted compromise, they worked in earnest to convince her to remain in Portsmouth. Judge was "dissuaded from returning and the Vessel sailed without her." The bondwoman avoided the empty promises of Washington's associate who'd been tasked with the uncomfortable business of hunting fugitives. Whipple was left empty-handed.

Even though the fugitive had misled Whipple, he wasn't angry with her. He knew that his failed attempt at slave catching would prove thorny with the president, but he couldn't blame Judge for her response. How could anyone want to return to a life of slavery? Instead of worrying about Judge, he turned his attention to the next task at hand—informing Secretary Wolcott that he was unsuccessful at apprehending the runaway. As he sat down to pen the difficult letter, he understood the need for diplomacy. Whipple needed to demonstrate that his attempt at capturing Ona Judge simply fell short and, under no circumstances, let on that he wasn't unhappy about his failure. His tone was apologetic, explaining that he had found Judge, investigated the situation, and had uncovered several important details. He wrote,

> After a cautious examination it appeared to me that she had not been decoyed away as had been apprehended, but that a thirst for compleat freedom which she was informed would take place on her arrival here or Boston had been her only motive for absconding.

The customs collector knew that this information, as well as the rest of his letter, would trouble Wolcott and the president, so he tried to disengage the bomb that he knew was about to explode. He spoke well of Ona Judge, and made note of how respectful she was of the first family. According to Whipple, Judge was kind with her words and affectionate toward the president and his wife:

> she expressed great affection & Reverence for her Master & Mistress, and without hesitation declared her willingness to return & to serve with fidelity during the lives of the President & his Lady if she could be freed on their decease, should she outlive them.

The only way Whipple could see Ona Judge returning was if she were eventually set free, and he went so far as to negotiate on her behalf. Audaciously, Whipple told Wolcott and thus the president, that gradual emancipation was the best route to follow. The customs collector dared to tell the first president of the United States that he should consider abandoning slavery, and that he should begin with Ona Judge.

Whipple may have suspected what was sure to follow the receipt of his letter—an escalated attempt to reclaim the fugitive, which he thought was a pointless task, though he didn't say so in such direct terms. Instead, he reminded Wolcott of the changing attitudes in New Hampshire, attitudes that were no longer congruent with the institution of slavery. Not only were whites in New Hampshire unlikely to support the covert actions of the president, but blacks would also do their best to shield fugitives from a return to slavery. Whipple wrote,

> I am informed that many Slaves from the Southern States have come to Massachusetts & some to New Hampshire, either of which States they consider as an Asylum; the popular opinion

here in favor of universal freedom has rendered it difficult to get them back to their masters.

Careful not to explicitly state his own feelings about slavery, Whipple pointed the Secretary in a new direction, one that would take this matter out of the hands of the customs collector and place it in the control of different authorities. Whipple told Wolcott that Ona Judge was immovable and would not be convinced to return of her own free will. Given the circumstances, the customs collector felt it best for the president to hire a lawyer and that all future inquiries "should come from an Officer of the President's Household to the Attorney of the United States in New Hampshire."

Whipple wanted out. He knew that the situation was a hornet's nest, and once it became clear that Ona Judge could not be whisked away in the middle of the night, he backed away from the messy business of slave catching. Whipple concluded his letter ending his direct involvement with the messy affair. He wrote, "It is with regret that I give up the prospect of executing the business in the favourable manner that I at first flattered myself it would be done."

If Washington wanted his slave woman back, he would have to follow the law and consequently expose himself to the growing antislavery sentiment in New Hampshire and across New England.

⁓⟨☙⟩⁓

Oliver Wolcott informed the president of Whipple's botched attempt at reclaiming the runaway slave. In a moment of anger and frustration, Washington released Wolcott from his slave-catching duties and on November 28, 1796, wrote directly to Joseph Whipple. He addressed Whipple's suggestions about emancipation, stating, "To enter into such a compromise with *her*, . . . is totally inadmissible." The president was offended by the simple thought of negotiating with one of his slaves. He found Judge's conduct reprehensible, and refused to reward bad behavior with the promise of freedom. Perhaps in an attempt to massage the moral beliefs of Whipple, Washington went on to hint at his own misgivings about slavery, stating,

> *for however well disposed I might be to gradual abolition, or even to an entire emancipation of that description of People (if the latter was in itself practicable at this moment) it would neither be politic or just to reward unfaithfulness with a premature preference.*

The president's attitudes regarding African slavery did soften during the latter years of his life; by the 1780s, years before Judge ran away, he discussed his growing unease with lifelong enslavement with close friends such as Tobias Lear and the French military officer and Revolutionary comrade the Marquis de Lafayette. But Washington was not willing to entertain a life without bound labor and was certainly unwilling to offer Judge anything but a return voyage home to Virginia. The president explained that he would offer fairness to his runaway; however, he could do no more, as her actions were impudent and unacceptable.

Although Washington leveled subtle accusations of mishandling the situation, he refused to allow the customs collector to back out of his assignment. That was simply not a choice that the president was willing to offer to his appointed official. He directed Whipple to assure the fugitive that she would not be punished for her momentary lack of good judgment. The president wrote that Judge "will be forgiven by her Mistress, and she will meet with the same treatment from me that all the rest of her family (which is a very numerous one) shall receive." This apparent olive branch to Judge was in actuality a thinly veiled threat. Fugitive slaves knew all too well about the risk of reprisals that often affected family members, and the casual mention of Judge's family served as a reminder to Judge that the punishment for her escape could land squarely on the shoulders of her immediate family. This was the only way in which the president would negotiate with his slave woman; he demanded that Judge come back into his possession or face the knowledge that her actions could cause pain and suffering for her family members.

If Judge decided not to return voluntarily, Whipple was instructed to place the bondwoman on a vessel bound for Alexandria or the Federal City, directly back into the jaws of slavery. Washington made it clear that he did not want Whipple to use extreme force with Judge, for he knew that this could cause a public disturbance or "would excite a mob or riot," something that Washington did not want to confront during the last few months of his presidency.

The president reminded Whipple to use discretion and not to show his cards as he had on his first encounter with the fugitive. As a Revolutionary War hero, Washington understood the importance of strategy, and he knew surprise was sometimes the best weapon in battle. The act of capture would only work with discretion, and if done properly, Judge could be returned home with relative speed, something that the president wished for the benefit of Mrs. Washington, who was "desirous of receiving her again." Yet it was the last few sentences in Washington's letter that revealed another motive for the speedy return of his property:

We had vastly rather she should be sent to Virginia than brought to this place [Philadelphia], as our stay here will be

but short; and it is not unlikely that she may, from the circum-
stances I have mentioned, be in a state of pregnancy.

So now the president believed that Ona Judge was pregnant. If this was true, the First Family's property had increased, and the president was now hunting Ona Judge and her unborn child.

Almost an entire month passed before Whipple returned Washington's letter. The customs collector may have been unusually busy, but it's more likely he was at a loss for words and worried about the repercussions of failing to collect and retrieve the president's slave. It wasn't until December 22 that Whipple sat down to write to the president. With only three months left to Washington's term in office, Whipple was careful in his tone, apologizing to the first lady for his inability to apprehend Judge:

I sincerely Lament the ill success of my endeavours to restore
to your Lady her servant on the request of Mr Wolcott—It had
indeed become a subject of Anxiety to me on an Idea that her
services were very valuable to her mistress and not readily to
be replaced.

Whipple responded to some of the claims leveled by the president in their last correspondence, making certain Washington understood that he was not at fault. If anything, Whipple was insulted that the president didn't understand the extent to which he had even tried to protect Washington's reputation among the men and women of New Hampshire. In his estimation, he had worked in the best interests of the president.

Still, no appointed official wanted to raise the ire of the president, so Whipple halfheartedly agreed to do all that was possible to continue with the plans of returning Judge. He made it clear that he would continue to pursue her as long as there was no public cry of outrage. Whipple made no promises, stating that he would need to decide for himself if the conditions were suitable for the return of a fugitive.

Whipple ended his letter with a promise to help in whatever way possible, but not before offering a piece of political advice. Although the president was on his way out of office, Whipple, for the moment, had the president's ear, and suggested that gradual emancipation would be the only way to stem the tide of fugitives who would cause disruption for white Northerners, Southern slave-holders, and for the runaways themselves. Slave owners (such as the president) could "prevent this growing evil" and menace of fugitive slaves—all they had to do was let go of human bondage.

Perhaps Whipple was compelled by his own feelings and concerns regarding slavery, but more likely, his inability and unwillingness to serve the president was linked to his changing political allegiance. Both he and his friend John Langdon had shifted away from the Federalist Party, prompting Whipple to feel no real obligation to serve the outgoing president. While he never articulated a personal reservation about the moral bankruptcy of the institution of slavery, Whipple expressed support for gradual abolition, a strategy that would honor the financial investments of slaveholders and that would allow for emancipated men and women to remain in their own states. A prolonged ending of slavery might reverse the trend of fugitives heading North, disentangling the residents of New Hampshire and all of New England from the knot of Southern slavery. Whipple's letter made one thing clear: Washington could not depend on the help of appointed or elected officers in New Hampshire to get Judge back to Virginia.

The president never wrote back to Whipple about Ona Judge, accepting that his influence over the customs collector was far less than he had anticipated. He realized that he wouldn't be able to recapture the fugitive, at least not immediately. Martha Washington would need to be patient and select a different slave to serve their newly married granddaughter, a task that shouldn't prove difficult given the hundreds of available slaves at Mount Vernon. Instead, Washington would turn his attention to the transfer of power to John Adams, his Massachusetts-born vice president, who had just weeks before narrowly won the first contested American presidential election. Washington needed to focus on a seamless administrative transition and a permanent relocation back to his beloved Mount Vernon. Tracking down a fugitive slave would not make its way onto the president's list of priorities.

Ona Judge was safe, for now.

Twelve

Mrs. Staines

PORTSMOUTH, *Jan.* 14.

MARRIED]—*At Haverhill, (N. H.)*
Thomas Thompſon, Eſq. Attorney at Law,
to the amiable Miſs Eliza Porter, daughter
to Col. Aſa Porter, of ſaid place.
In this town, Mr. John Stanes, to Miſs
Oney Gudge.

New-Hampshire Gazette, *January 14, 1797. Courtesy of the New Hampshire*
Historical Society.

Three days after Whipple penned his December letter to the president, Judge celebrated her first Christmas away from the Washingtons. Her meager wages would not have allowed Judge to purchase gifts for her new friends in Portsmouth, but she may have presented them with nuts or a small amount of chocolate, token offers of appreciation for all that they had done for her. The year that had passed had been dizzying. And while she was grateful for the freedom that she had stolen from the Washingtons, her joy would always be tempered. Her loved ones remained enslaved back at Mount Vernon, and the guilt of her successful escape must have weighed constantly on her heart. Most fugitives coaxed their minds into temporary amnesia, creating an emotional distance from the memory of their pasts. Judge pushed her pain and sadness deep into the recesses of her soul—it would be the only way for her to move forward with a new life.

And move forward she did. News of the single young woman would have spread quickly through the small black community, and eligible bachelors would have taken notice of the newcomer, even with her complicated fugitive status. It was Jack Staines who caught her attention.

Judge was a quick study and soon understood that she needed to find a husband. In eighteenth-century America, a woman (white or black) needed a spouse for protection and survival. Independent living was no easy task for Judge, and although she was able to pick up low-paying domestic work, black women knew that two incomes were almost always necessary. Although free black men were constantly disrespected and trapped in the web of racial discrimination, they carried some power in their male bodies, power that would allow Ona Judge to have a chance for security and maybe even prosperity.

Eliza Custis Law would not be the only one to select a husband and marry quickly. Ona Judge and Jack Staines would celebrate the Christmas of 1796 together, completely aware that the president might try to reclaim Judge at any moment. And by January of 1797, the two chose to marry one another. For Judge, this was another example of freedom's possibilities.

Before the romantic notions of marriage became the established norm, men and women across the new nation married for reasons other than love, more specifically, for survival. Male farmers married young women with modest dowries and the physical capabilities to complete the hard domestic duties and fieldwork that often accompanied life on a small farm. Aside from a dowry, a woman could bring many things to a marriage, but children were the most-valued prizes of all. Ensuring that the family name would live on, children, male children in particular, offered small farmers an important nuclear family during an age in which subsistence farming was still the modus operandi for many. Children would grow into strong young men and women, capable of assisting fathers and mothers in the fields, the house, and the blacksmithing shops across the country.

Judge, of course, had no dowry to offer, but she was young and healthy. It was almost impossible to make a life for oneself without a family network, and Judge found a remedy to the ailment of poverty and isolation in a free black man. Whether it was a marriage of convenience or a true love affair that brought the two together, Ona Judge would begin the New Year with a legal marriage to a free black man—that she chose. The institution of slavery prohibited the legal marriages of enslaved men and women, and had Judge remained under the ownership of the Washington-Custis family, she may never have experienced the autonomy that came along with the selection of a spouse.

Like many other free black men who lived along the Northeast Seaboard, Jack Staines spent long periods of time working at sea. Black men who followed this employment path were known as "black jacks," and although seafaring was viewed as an unstable and unseemly occupation for whites, it offered opportunity to black men incapable of finding decent wages elsewhere. While out at sea, black jacks suffered racial discrimination from their crew and sea captains, but the open seas also offered protection from corrupt slave catchers and kidnappers who lurked in the streets and alleys of Northern cities. Barred from jobs of distinction or respectability, black sailors were often catapulted into positions of honor in early free black communities. More, the lump sum payouts (which were on par with what white men received) that Jack Staines and other black seafaring men received at the end of their journeys were often applied to the purchase of land or a home, an unreachable goal for most black men at the turn of the nineteenth century.

Of course, there were risks: journeys to the South or to the Caribbean were dangerous. By the beginning decades of the nineteenth century, some Southern states imprisoned free black sailors. South Carolina's 1822 Negro Seamen Act followed the foiled slave insurrection plotted by Denmark Vesey, a former slave and sailor. Free men such as Staines who sailed into the Charleston port of call were imprisoned during their stay, and the captains of vessels who used free black crewmembers were forced to pay for the prison lodging of their sailors until they departed. On longer voyages to places such as Jamaica and Barbados, free black sailors not only encountered the expected dangers of pirating, shipwrecks, and illness, but they also faced the fear of unlawful enslavement. Who would come to the rescue of Jack Staines if he were imprisoned and sold into Caribbean slavery? Although the risks were great and the pay was minimal, black sailors gambled with their lives to provide for themselves and their families.

Marriage would not free Judge from hard domestic labor; she would have to work, too. Judge was in the same position as many other married free black women of the era: her income was necessary. Whatever meager earnings she could collect from domestic work, laundering, or sewing would help the family survive between the long periods of time that spanned Jack Staines's pay days. Ona Judge knew that being married to a black sailor would be filled with opportunities; in Staines she found a husband who was employable and who could provide for her and whatever children they might have. Yet she knew that marriage to a sailor would also mean a life of long absences and weeks of solitude. Judge would spend many months waiting for Jack Staines's ship to appear in port, and while she waited, she would be left alone to fend off any would-be slave catchers.

News of the Staineses' marriage engagement traveled around Portsmouth, even finding its way to the information-hungry Whipple, who had, reluctantly, agreed to continue to help Washington. He learned that Jack Staines and Ona Judge celebrated the Christmas season by carefully planning their impending matrimony. The couple visited the county clerk in Portsmouth and applied for a marriage certificate, careful to follow the law and make certain that their marriage was legally recognized by the state. The document that certified the union between Jack Staines and Ona Judge was not only a symbol of choice, but also one that was legally binding. If something happened to Jack during one of his long voyages out at sea, Judge would be the legal beneficiary of any owed wages or land that had been purchased by her husband. Legal proof of marriage was not simply a luxury for the fugitive; it was another form of protection.

Once Whipple caught wind of the couple's application for a marriage certificate, he felt compelled to communicate with Portsmouth's clerk. Although he was uncomfortable with his involvement in Washington's slave catching, Whipple confided in the clerk, probably telling him about the bride-to-be, her powerful owners, and their deep desire to reclaim their property. Whatever words were shared between the clerk and the customs collector resulted in delayed paperwork, and the couple would soon learn that claiming a marriage certificate in Portsmouth would be next to impossible.

This roadblock was disappointing to the young couple, but Jack Staines and Ona Judge would not give up on their dream of a legal marriage. They simply couldn't. The two must have spoken with friends, collected advice, and planned their next strategic move, deciding to bypass the clerk in Portsmouth altogether.

Staines and Judge traveled to nearby Greenland, a few miles outside the city, where county clerk Thomas Philbrook provided the
couple with the required documents. On the very same page of the
New-Hampshire Gazette that reported George Washington's words
of appreciation to the nation, the newlyweds announced their
marriage to the New Hampshire community. The small section of
the paper that announced recent marriages listed only two couples
on January 14, 1797. Attorney Thomas Thompson announced his
nuptials to Miss Eliza Porter in Haverhill, New Hampshire, and
listed directly below them was the fugitive and her new free husband. A simple ten words publicly announced their union: "In this
town, Mr. John Stanes, to Miss Oney Gudge [*sic*]." Samuel Haven,
reverend of Portsmouth's South Church, married them.

With no extra money to purchase a new wedding dress, Judge
would have selected to wear something from her existing wardrobe. For months, the fugitive dressed inconspicuously, wearing
plain clothing appropriate for a domestic. But on her wedding
day she would have pulled out one of her nicer dresses, one that
she used to wear while serving the Washingtons. Many women
placed small flowers in their hair to mark the special occasion,
but January's heavy snow left Ona Judge with no such embellish-
ments. Perhaps she attached a few scraps of lace to her wedding
attire, but a veil would have been too costly and impractical. Jack
Staines probably dressed in a tailcoat and his nicest pair of trousers
(typical pants for sailors and working men) instead of costly knee-
length silk breeches. There would be no expensive wedding bands
or elaborate celebratory meals, but instead the newlyweds probably shared a simple dinner of fish or oyster stew, brown bread, and
maybe a bit of Indian pudding for dessert.

The couple spent their first year together settling in, secur-
ing work, and trying to forge ahead. As was custom, Ona Judge

adopted her husband's last name, becoming Ona Staines, and continued to acclimate to her new life. With her husband's sailing income and her wages from domestic work, the two were able to move into their own home. The census listed Jack Staines (who also used the first name John) as the head of household, along with three other people in the Staines home. No slaves were recorded in their dwelling, a reminder that the fugitive Mrs. Staines passed as a free woman. Early census records offered much more detail for white families, such as the gender and age of all household occupants. Records concerning people of color were far less descriptive, simply noting the free status of an individual and the number of people who belonged to a specific household. Many black women who served as domestics lived with their employers, but Staines did not fall into this category. Not only did she live in a separate space from her employer, she lived with her husband and two other people.

One of these roommates might have been someone in need, a boarder who couldn't afford to live alone, who appealed to the young black family for help. It was likely that this person could share in a few household expenses, easing the financial responsibilities that continued to grow in the Staines household. Plus a boarder provided her the opportunity to give back. A family had taken her in during her time of need; now it was her turn to reciprocate. Extra money was always welcome, especially once Ona Staines told her husband the exciting news: she was expecting a child.

Her pregnancy would cement the young couple's relationship, reminding Jack and Ona Staines that they had more than themselves to think about. She continued with her domestic work, though that became more difficult as the months elapsed and her belly swelled. Scrubbing floors and lifting heavy containers of water became almost impossible as she approached the end of her pregnancy, but she did not have the luxury of unemployment. An aching back and swollen feet were symptoms that simply couldn't interfere with the collection of wages, so Ona Staines most likely relied upon home remedies to ease her discomfort. A vinegar and rosewater solution was believed to reduce the inflammation of feet and ankles, and swathing bands were tied around the bottom of the abdomen and the back of the neck to offer back support. She grew up watching enslaved women in Virginia remain in the fields up until the delivery of their babies. These women returned to their work assignments shortly after giving birth, never giving their bodies time to heal from the trauma of birth. She'd have to do the same.

When the time came, Ona Staines would have relied upon her small circle of friends for help with delivering her baby. Labor was usually long and dangerous, often taking the lives of both mother and child. Perhaps she had saved enough money to pay for a midwife, someone who would guide Mrs. Staines through delivery as friends and neighbors supported her on a birthing stool. Although we do not know that exact date, sometime in 1798, Ona Staines delivered a healthy baby girl. They would name her Eliza.

The birth of this child served as another marker of freedom. Ona Staines reared Eliza according to her own will—and, with the help of her husband, the young family directed its own future. Yet Staines had to temper her happiness with a realistic fear. She could never lay her worries about capture to bed. Every day and every night, Staines knew that her world could be turned upside down by a forced return to her legal master. Now the stakes were higher; she had to think about her baby daughter, Eliza, as well. Staines had passed the disease of slavery to her daughter. Even though she was born in Portsmouth, Eliza was the legal property of the Custis estate. Jack Staines's status as a free man made no difference when it came to the condition of his daughter.

~~~✦~~~

Some five hundred miles away, the Washingtons were becoming reacquainted with their beloved Mount Vernon. John Adams became the second president to lead the nation, and George Washington retired to a life as a private citizen. When Martha Washington made her final return home in May of 1797, she was elated to leave public life and to reconnect with her family. The past fifteen months had been nothing short of a whirlwind, a period that began with the news of the impetuous engagement and marriage of Eliza Parke Custis and was followed by her bondwoman's escape.

After the excitement of the presidential election, the Washingtons prepared for additional life-changing news. Now married, granddaughter Elizabeth Parke Custis Law prepared to give birth to her first child, the first Custis-Washington great-grandchild who would survive childhood. On January 19, 1797, little Eliza was born, marking a new era in the Washington family. Thomas and Elizabeth Law's fast and furious nuptials were now strengthened by the birth of a child. Coincidentally, both Ona Staines and Elizabeth Custis Law began their lives as newly married women with daughters named Eliza.

~~~✦~~~

For the first few years of the Staineses' life in New Hampshire, the young family found a way to survive and to avoid money-hungry slave catchers. But the president's interest in reclaiming Staines reemerged with a vengeance in a relatively short time. By July of 1799, Washington had occupied the space of private citizen for a little more than two years and decided that it was time to pursue his runaway property again. During a visit with Martha Washington's nephew, Burwell Bassett Jr., the president rekindled the search for Staines, this time relying upon his nephew to handle this very personal and discreet piece of family business.

In the president's mind, Burwell Bassett Jr. was the perfect person to negotiate the return of the family's slave woman. As a member of the Virginia Senate, Bassett Jr. could travel to New Hampshire on business and while there, find an opportunity to interact with Senator John Langdon, the former ally and friend of the president.

As the final preparations for the trip were made, the president gave Bassett a letter in which he made clear that Martha Washington was still in need of her "body servant" and he offered his nephew additional details about Staines's escape. Not that he used or ever would use her married name. Three years later, and despite Whipple's report to the contrary, the president still maintained that Mrs. Staines had been "enticed away by a Frenchman" and that she had considered returning to the Washingtons but decided to remain in New Hampshire when her demand for freedom was denied. Washington's views had not changed. Under no circumstances would he allow Mrs. Staines to negotiate for her own freedom, stating that it would set an impolitic "& dangerous precedent."

Burwell Bassett set out for New Hampshire, where he lodged with Senator John Langdon, the father of Elizabeth Langdon, the first person to notify the Washingtons of their fugitive's presence in New Hampshire. While Langdon did not count himself among the early antislavery agitators, he had shifted his position regarding many issues since the beginning of his relationship with the president. Although he began his career in politics in the new republic, his political beliefs and alliances had changed by the time Washington left office. No longer a staunch Federalist, Langdon switched parties, and during the Adams presidency he labeled himself a

Democratic Republican. Even though the Langdon family had a long history of slave ownership, the senator expressed reservations about the inclusion of slavery in the United States Constitution and suggested that the transatlantic slave trade be abolished earlier than 1808. Slaves who were previously owned by the Langdon family were emancipated and rehired as paid laborers, yet Senator Langdon did not refer to himself as an abolitionist. Burwell Bassett Jr., therefore, assumed that he could rely upon the senator for help and advice during his travels to Portsmouth. By all accounts, his trip should have been a quick one. After all, he already knew where she lived. There would be no time wasted searching for the runaway.

Now twenty-five years old, Ona Staines heard a knock at the door and unknowingly opened her home to her worst nightmare. Standing in front of her was a familiar face from the past, one that she had never wanted to see again. She must have felt the blood drain from her head and neck as familiar stomach-turning fear temporarily stopped her in her tracks. Baby Eliza, now about one year old, would have been close by, probably teetering around the Staines home with unsteady legs and an unrelenting curiosity to touch anything within sight. She would have looked at Bassett without fear, for she had no idea just how dangerous this smooth-talking visitor really was. A mother's instinct would have prompted Mrs. Staines to scoop her baby up into her arms, holding Eliza tight as she faced Washington's nephew for what would be the battle of her life. She couldn't run and hide—Staines had to confront the slave catcher. How she wished she hadn't answered the door.

The timing couldn't have been worse, as Bassett's visit coincided with one of Jack Staines's lengthy voyages at sea, leaving the fugitive to take care of herself and their small child. Her husband's absences were always difficult, but the appearance of Washington's slave catcher reminded Mrs. Staines that she would always have to rely upon her own abilities and the resourcefulness and kindness of friends to elude her owners' grasp.

Bassett followed the advice offered to him before leaving Mount Vernon; that is, he tried to convince the fugitive that she would face no retaliation if she voluntarily returned to Virginia. He was not abusive or rough in his tone, a tactic used to show the runaway that she could return to Virginia with little reason to worry. But Mrs. Staines knew that the Washington family slave catcher offered nothing but falsehoods and that his words were empty promises. Even if Bassett spoke the truth, Mrs. Staines had no intentions of marching her baby into the death trap of slavery while leaving her husband behind in Portsmouth. Staines told Bassett she would not go with him. She simply refused.

As a Virginian, it must have been abnormal if not offensive for Bassett to have to negotiate with the slave. Yet it became apparent that the fugitive would not cower. Bassett sweetened the deal, promising that the Washingtons "would set her free when she arrived at Mount Vernon," but Mrs. Staines saw right through the slave catcher's threadbare lies as he continued with saccharine-sweet language and promises for a gentle return to Virginia. Perhaps he tugged on her heartstrings, reminding Staines of the family that she had left behind at Mount Vernon, or maybe he described a devastated Martha Washington who simply couldn't find another person to take the fugitive's place. But as Bassett prattled on, the fugitive found her resolve. Ona Staines looked the president's nephew in his eyes. Righteous indignation and a belief in her right to be free prompted her final and fierce response to Bassett, telling him, "I am free now and choose to remain so."

According to federal law, Staines was not free, and could be captured and returned to her owner, but Bassett knew that he had to tread lightly in a region where slavery was being reconsidered. The president had most likely warned his nephew of the difficulties he encountered when he tried to reclaim the fugitive three years prior. The Washington family must have felt as though the three years that had passed had diminished the chances of a public scandal, or that Mrs. Staines would be in such dire straits that she would want to return on her own volition. In very little time, however, Bassett Jr. realized that Mrs. Staines's removal would be more difficult, not less. Three years of independent living had prepared her for the battle of her life.

Stunned by her refusal, Bassett walked away from the Staines home having failed to complete the familial obligation of returning Mrs. Washington's body servant. He understood that Northern sentiment was different, but his Southern sensibilities were stoked by the fugitive's stubbornness. Black slaves might be able to speak disrespectfully to white men in New Hampshire, but in Virginia, this simply didn't happen, at least not without swift correction. Bassett's display of Southern gentility began to evaporate. Kind words and offers of freedom in Virginia had failed miserably, so he would need to regroup, contact his uncle, and wait for further instruction.

When Bassett returned to the Langdon home after his unsuccessful attempt to claim Staines, he made clear to his host that he would not leave the fugitive in Portsmouth and that he would take her by force if necessary.

The senator was in a difficult position. As an elected official, Langdon was to follow the laws of the land, and that included the returning of fugitives across state lines. But this was a delicate situation, one that required the senator to walk the line between federal law and the sensibilities of his state's citizens. Langdon listened to the Virginian's plans, and this sensitive information was relayed to Mrs. Staines. Perhaps the senator sent word to the fugitive, but it is more likely that one of the free black domestics working within the walls of the Langdon home, sent along this crucial warning. The young fugitive was told that her life was in danger.

Something seemed amiss to the president's nephew once he finally returned to the Staines home. He had come for the fugitive, and this time there would be no considerate persuasion. If necessary, he would take her by force. Perhaps Bassett notified a few discreet friends, men who could help contain the fugitive and her child if she resisted. He might need to tie her arms and legs and forcibly place her in the back of a wagon, a scene that he hoped to avoid but was willing to entertain if necessary. It's almost certain that a ship was stationed in port and ready to sail directly to Alexandria, Virginia. All he needed to do was apprehend the fugitive.

He knocked at the door, probably politely at first, and then more angrily, eventually forcing his way into the home. What he found was a lived-in residence that was empty of its occupants. Perhaps he frantically asked neighbors and townspeople if they had seen the fugitive, or maybe he put together a small search team. Whatever his response, it was too late. The Washingtons' slave woman had disappeared.

Yet the fugitive outmaneuvered the president and his agents once again. When she learned of Bassett's plans to forcibly return her to Virginia, Ona Staines collected her baby girl, hired a stable boy to commandeer a horse and carriage, and made haste for Greenland, the town eight miles away from Portsmouth that had issued her marriage papers after Portsmouth officials had refused to do so. The carriage moved as quickly as possible, transporting

Ona and Eliza Staines to the care of a free black family, the Jacks, who willingly agreed to harbor the fugitives.

⁘

Bassett returned to Virginia in October of 1799, and had to deliver the unfortunate news to his aunt and uncle. He had been unsuccessful in capturing their human property. Bassett must have also informed the Washingtons that several of their beliefs about the runaway were unfounded. They now knew that their slave woman was not in the possession of a Frenchman, but that she was married with a new baby. If they found that surprising, they would have been shocked to learn that the fugitive was neither destitute nor was she willing to return to her former owners. She considered herself a free woman, and although the laws of the nation stated otherwise, she moved about her life as though her status had never been that of a slave.

Staines's evasion of Bassett must have angered the Washingtons, but it also reminded them of several important facts. Now that George Washington was no longer the president, they could not count upon the assistance of past friends and allies. Even close friends such as Senator Langdon could no longer be considered helpful in an attempt to capture Ona Staines. The former president and his wife would have to devise a new plan; they simply needed a bit of time to figure out the details.

Thirteen

The Survivor

Thomas H. Archibald, "Washington's Runaway Slave," Granite Freeman, May 22, 1845. Courtesy of the New Hampshire Historical Society.

On December 12, 1799, the president took what was a routine horseback ride across the farms of Mount Vernon. Washington was extremely involved in the managing of farm activities, and he spent much of the day in the outdoors suffering through the changing weather that brought snow, hail, and rain. Returning home close to the dinner hour, Washington neglected to change out of his wet riding clothes. He was always a punctual man, so he chose to stay dressed in his damp clothing throughout dinner rather than take time to get more comfortable as snow continued to accumulate through the night. The president complained of a sore throat, which grew worse, eventually causing swelling around his vocal cords and a raspy voice. As the evening drew on, his throat became so inflamed that he was unable to finish his evening ritual of newspaper reading with secretary Tobias Lear. His beloved wife had to ask Lear to complete the reading on her husband's behalf before he retired to bed.

The president failed to sleep much as the discomfort from his throat awakened him in the early hours of the morning. Although Martha Washington wished to send for assistance, the president refused, and instead, waited until their house slave Caroline appeared to light the fireplace at daybreak before he solicited help. They sent for Tobias Lear, who discovered Washington extremely ill, struggling to breathe, and in desperate need of medical attention. Trusted friend and overseer George Rawlins arrived at the president's bed and bled him before Dr. James Craik, a physician and longtime friend, was sent for from Alexandria. As they waited for the arrival of the doctor, family members and staff attempted to alleviate Washington's suffering. A concoction of molasses, butter, and vinegar was given to the president to soothe his throat, but the thick mixture was almost impossible for Washington to swallow. Home remedies worsened his state, throwing him into convulsions and near suffocation.

When Dr. Craik arrived, he bled Washington a second time and ordered a mixture of vinegar and sage tea to be administered for gargling. Dr. Craik must have sensed urgency in the president's condition, for he sent for at least two additional physicians to assist him. A series of uncomfortable therapies was used on the president, from enemas to emetics to induce vomiting. Washington was bled one final time before everyone in his presence acknowledged that the situation was grave. He called for his wife, Martha, to come to his bedside and to bring with her two wills that were housed in his study. Washington reviewed his wills and selected the document that would define his final wishes. The president directed his wife to burn the second version of his will and then he called for Tobias Lear. Still able to speak, Washington told his faithful secretary, "I find I am going, my breath cannot last long. I believed from the first that the disorder would prove fatal. Do you arrange and record all my late military letters and papers. Arrange my accounts and settle my books, as you know more about them than anyone else, and let Mr. Rawlins finish recording my other letters which he has begun." Late in the evening on December 14, 1799, George Washington took his last breath. Surrounding him were Martha Washington, his friends and doctors, and four slaves.

The major life events of white slave owners always directly impacted their slaves. Often, the death of an owner meant the sale or transfer of bondmen and bondwomen, an act that broke apart families. But with the death of George Washington, 123 slaves who lived and toiled at Mount Vernon learned that Washington's final will would eventually emancipate them from bondage, an indication that the president had indeed struggled with the concept of slavery. His will produced a most welcomed surprise for the slaves who belonged to the Washington estate. The president had once considered the immediate emancipation of his slaves upon his demise, but later reversed his thinking. He offered several reasons why this could not happen, but he focused on the trauma that would be inflicted upon slave families at Mount Vernon. To Washington, freedom would break apart families, as more than half of the slaves on his estate were the legal property of the heirs of Daniel Parke Custis, Martha Washington's first husband. Many of the slaves on the Mount Vernon farms had intermarried and according to the president, the immediate release of his slaves would cause "disagreeable consequences" among slave families. In essence, Washington's slaves would be forced to leave Mount Vernon once they were set free, leaving behind wives, husbands, and children who were owned by the Custis estate and still trapped in lifelong enslavement.

The president stipulated in his will that aged slaves, those who were unable to work or support themselves, receive assistance and that they be "comfortably clothed and fed" by the Washington heirs after their liberation took effect. Washington also mandated that younger slaves whose parents were deceased be bound out as servants until the age of twenty-five. During their servitude, they were "to be taught to read & write: and to be brought up to some useful occupation."

The only slave immediately emancipated in Washington's will was the president's faithful valet. Poor health and physical disabilities had removed William Lee from the position as a valued house slave, but a close, lengthy relationship with his owner resulted in his freedom. Washington fixated on the difficulties that could come along with immediate freedom, especially for aged slaves who were disabled, or the very young. The president gave William Lee the option of remaining enslaved at Mount Vernon, to relieve Lee of the responsibilities of independence. Washington made certain that Lee would make this important decision on his own and that in either situation, his trusted valet would have some kind of security. He offered Lee compensation, noting, "I allow him an annuity of thirty dollars during his natural life, whic[h] shall be independent of the victuals and cloaths he has been accustomed to receive." In explaining why William Lee received something that no other slave at Mount Vernon was afforded, Washington wrote, "& this I give him as a test[im]ony of my sense of his attachment to me, and for his faithful services during the Revolutionary War." Lee chose to remain at Mount Vernon and received his annuity on a quarterly basis, but his debilitating knee pain drove him to drink excessively. William Lee died in the winter of 1810 and was laid to rest in the slave burial ground at Mount Vernon.

The eventual release of the rest of the president's slaves depended upon one thing: the life of his dear wife, Martha. Washington's bondmen and bondwomen were to be released only upon the death of their mistress, a clear indication of Washington's desire to care for his wife even after his death. Yet the pending emancipation of Washington's slaves made Martha Washington uneasy. The grieving widow knew that the only thing standing in the way of the freedom of more than one hundred people was her life. In conversations with relatives and friends, Mrs. Washington commented upon her uneasiness, stating that she was "unhappy by the talk in the quarters of the good time coming to the ones to be freed as soon as she died." The former first lady confided in her friend Abigail Adams, who wrote, "She did not feel as tho her Life was safe in their Hands," for she feared that the enslaved, "would be told that it was [in] their interest to get rid of her." A series of suspicious events, including a fire at Mount Vernon, prompted Mrs. Washington to amend her husband's wishes. Although he wanted to provide for his wife via the use of slave labor, Martha Washington had her own slaves, dower slaves that were greater in number and completely capable of caring for her and the estate. So the second-time widow decided that it would be best to emancipate her late husband's slaves as soon as possible, and in December of 1800, she signed a deed of manumission to finalize her husband's wishes. On January 1, 1801, George Washington's slaves were set free.

While there must have been great jubilation among the president's slaves, the bondmen and bondwomen belonging to the Daniel Parke Custis estate were reminded of their own fate. The "dower slaves" at Mount Vernon, close to two hundred of them at the time of Washington's death, were untouched by the president's will, and could not be emancipated by George or Martha Washington. Indeed, upon her death the slaves of the Custis estate were to be divided among Mrs. Washington's grandchildren.

The newspaper reports and tributes to the life of the first president of the United States most certainly alerted the fugitive about the death of her master, but Mrs. Staines understood that this news was not a siren of freedom for her. She knew her lineage, and understood that the president's death changed nothing about her own status. Although she had successfully escaped and lived some five hundred miles away, Mrs. Staines was still a fugitive and in some ways, a bit more vulnerable.

With Washington gone, the heirs of the Parke Custis estate were now in charge of the dower slaves, and that could include an attempt at kidnapping the fugitive and returning her to Virginia. Even if Mrs. Washington contemplated following her husband's example by emancipating the remaining slaves at Mount Vernon, she simply couldn't. The reality was that Martha Washington had inherited only one third of her first husband's estate; the remaining two thirds were to be passed down to her surviving grandchildren. The remaining slaves at Mount Vernon weren't legally hers to liberate, even if she had been so inclined.

In any case, the dower slaves would not have long to ponder their fate, as Martha Washington struggled with illness and lived only a few years beyond her second husband. In May of 1802, Martha Washington died, transferring the majority of her estate to her heirs. Mrs. Washington's wishes included the sale of the majority of her property, the proceeds of which would be divided among her grandchildren. None of the dower slaves at Mount Vernon were offered their freedom. Instead, they were relocated to different farms and endured the dismantling of their fragile families. The transfer of the dower slaves to her grandchildren was not simply done out of obligation or a legal requirement, but because of the first lady's commitment to the institution of slavery. Unlike her husband, Martha Washington left no suggestion that she was ambivalent about slavery. At the end of her life, Martha Washington held only one slave who was not a part of the dower inheritance—a man named Elish. She could have emancipated Elish upon her death, but she chose not to. Instead, Elish was willed to her grandson George Washington Parke Custis.

⸺⟨⟡⟩⸺

The deaths of George and Martha Washington meant very little to the day-to-day actions of Ona Staines and her growing family. She continued to navigate her way through the joys of parenthood, marriage, and life outside the confines of slavery. By the turn of the nineteenth century, Ona Staines and her husband lived with their children in their own home. The fugitive and her husband became members of Portsmouth's free black community, although her name and complete address were never recorded. While no deed or probate record exists under the name of Jack Staines, it is quite possible that the young family rented their home from an employer. Perhaps her employers rented her a small home on the fringes of their property, as was the custom with many free blacks across the North. They found lodging and employment wherever and however they could.

When asked about her life in 1847, Mrs. Staines told a reporter from the *Liberator* that she had three children. Inaccurate record keeping of the early nineteenth century leaves sketchy documentation about the lives of the Staines children, but existing records suggest that four years after the birth of Eliza Staines, the family welcomed little Nancy to their growing household, perhaps named after the ship that brought the fugitive to New Hampshire. The Staineses' third child left behind a more mysterious trail of documentation. No death certificate or record of birth exists for the Staineses' third child, her only son.

It is possible that the third child of the Staines family was William Staines. As an adult, William Staines registered for a Seaman's Protection Certificate in the government office in New York and Portland, Maine. Beginning in 1796, the Congress began to issue these certificates in order to protect American seamen from impressment on British ships. This certificate provided proof of American citizenship and offered physical descriptions of the seamen. In December of 1819, "William Stains" was nineteen years old and was prepared to sail out of New York City. The seaman was described by governmental authorities as five nine and three-quarters in height with a "light complexion." Physical characteristics such as racial complexions included light, dark, brown, yellow, and mulatto, though this as well as other descriptive characteristics were left to the discretion of governmental authorities. In March of 1823, another description of a William Staines appeared among the Seaman's Protection Certificates in Portland, Maine, where officials recorded him as five ten in height with a "dark dark" complexion. Both certificates in New York and Maine list the sailor's birthplace as Portsmouth, New Hampshire, with a birth date around 1800. The only Portsmouth family with the surname of Staines belonged to Ona and her husband Jack, connecting William to the family, or at least to the patriarch. So, it's more than likely that this young William was hers and that he was following in the shoes of his father and many other black men from northeastern seaport towns, taking to the open seas for a sustainable form of employment. And if William Staines knew the story of his mother's escape, then he also understood that he was technically an enslaved person, a fugitive who belonged to the Parke Custis estate. It is understandable that William Staines would have purposely avoided being "counted" during the course of his lifetime and that he chose the profession of seafaring, which frequently took him to faraway places.

Like their free counterparts, the family worked hard to scratch out a living with Jack Staines constantly at sea and Ona Staines most likely picking up domestic work while she cared for their small children. Their family was fragile as free blacks across the new nation found themselves only a few steps removed from slavery and poverty. Illness or the death of a loved one could completely change the life circumstances of a family teetering on the brink of survival. For women, the situation became even bleaker in the wake of the loss of a husband or son. And indeed, Ona Staines confronted this reality when Jack passed away.

Seafaring men risked their lives every time they left the docks, and illness was often the cause for many deaths on the open seas. Although Ona Staines did not leave personal testimony about the death of her husband, we know he was no longer a part of the Staines family after 1803. The circumstances of Jack Staines's death—Was it protracted illness or sudden? Was it while he was at sea or in his own home?—remains a mystery to this day, but his death notice appeared in the *New-Hampshire Gazette* on May 3, 1803. The specifics are lost, but the endurance of his fugitive wife was not. After only six years of marriage, Ona Staines found herself

alone with young children, with no one but herself to rely upon
financially. Once again, she was reliant upon her network of friends
to find a way to survive.

The Staines family lived close to neighbor John Bartlett, who
offered the young widow a maidservant position. This form of
employment would call for Ona Staines to live with the elderly Ann
and John Bartlett in order to earn wages to support her young family. It is unclear but improbable that Staines was allowed to bring
her children to board with her. In most cases women were forced to
leave their children in the care of family members or friends for long
periods of time. For Staines, this was too much to ask and eventually
she turned to her friends, the Jack family, to save her.

The Jacks (as they were called by their neighbors and friends)
was a free black household that had come to the rescue of the
fugitive on at least one other occasion. In 1799 when Washington's nephew, Bassett, came to Portsmouth looking to reclaim Mrs.
Staines and to take her back to Virginia, the fugitive turned to this
family for help. The Jacks lived outside the city limits of Portsmouth in a small cottage in Greenland, where they harbored Mrs.
Staines and her toddler, Eliza. After Jack Staines died, she found
herself calling upon them again for assistance. But this time it was
at a juncture when the Jack family needed help themselves.

The matriarch of the family, Phillis Jack, had managed to turn
her bondage into opportunity. For unknown reasons, Jack's master,
Deacon James Brackett, decided to let go of his human property
sometime during the 1760s. With no raging abolitionist movement
to propel him, we can only guess his reasons for emancipating a
young slave woman before the Revolution. The only thing more
startling than her freedom was the gift of land that accompanied
it. Brackett gave his former slave a parcel of land and a small home
that was surrounded by swampy wetlands. It wasn't uncommon

for slave owners to move bondwomen, especially those with whom they had an ongoing sexual relationship, out of their homes and into private dwellings. Slave owners built small cottages buried deep in the woods where they could keep their prized possessions out of view from jealous wives, all with the hope of easing marital tensions. Just how Phillis Jack came into her freedom, we don't know, but her status as a free landholding black woman is notable.

Phillis Jack's land lay close to the border between Greenland and Stratham, a location at the center of a property-line battle between the neighboring towns. Existing town records do not cite Phillis Jack as the formal owner of the property, but other accounts and eyewitness reports place the former slave and her family on this parcel of land. Residents of Greenland often referred to the stream that ran through the property as "Phillis's Brook," while less enlightened neighbors simply called it "Nigger's Brook."

The patriarch of the Jack family was enslaved for a much longer stint than was his wife, but he earned his freedom by his service in the Revolutionary War. Like many enslaved people, Jack was called many names, Jack Warner (after his slave owner), John Jack, Black Jack, and Jacks. His daughters would eventually use the surname Jack on formal records and accounts.

When Ona Staines turned to the Jack family again for help, they were themselves in dire straits. Matriarch Phillis Jack died in October of 1804, only a year after the death of Jack Staines, and poverty had already fastened its grip on the family. Although the former slave had found freedom and amassed property, her family had slipped into the ranks of the desperately poor. So impoverished, her family couldn't even pay for an honorable funeral for Phillis Jack. This was the case for many free black families across the Northeast who simply could not afford the cost of a coffin or to hire professional grave diggers. Mutual aid organizations in cities such as Philadelphia and New York provided assistance to black families for this kind of need, however in Greenland, New Hampshire, no such organization existed. Private citizens stepped in to cover the cost of Phillis Jack's funeral and to recognize her passing with the ringing of the town's bell.

Ona Staines and her children eventually moved into the Jack home, fusing two desperate and grieving families into one. Close to thirty years old now, Staines was definitely capable of earning a decent wage, provided she had help raising her own small children. Living at the Jack home was the patriarch and his two daughters, Nancy and Phillis Jr. Like Ona Staines, the women were in their thirties. Similar to other struggling black families, they pooled their meager resources to stay afloat.

But over the next ten years it became nearly impossible for Ona Staines to support her children. In August of 1816, things were so bad for the Staines family that the unthinkable had to be confronted; Ona Staines would place her teenaged daughters into indentured servitude. Her two Northern-born daughters were bound out for a fee. Eliza and Nancy Staines went to work for Nathan Johnson, who lived about a mile away. In return for food and shelter, the sisters worked the fields and served the six members of the Johnson family. Nathan Johnson received thirty-five dollars from the town coffers for agreeing to provide food and shelter to the impoverished teenagers. Johnson was doing the town a favor by taking the teenagers into his home. They would no longer be reliant upon Greenland's charity or considered a financial nuisance. Ona Staines said good-bye to her daughters, now indentured servants, who would serve out an eight-month contract. It was probably at this moment that her son, William, followed in his father's footsteps and left home to look for wages as a sailor. He was only sixteen years old, but life in Greenland had become too difficult, and Ona Staines could do nothing to help. William left Greenland for new East Coast seaports and was never again recorded as a resident in New Hampshire. His mother's depression must have been suffocating.

In April of 1817, the Staines daughters returned home, but Eliza, the eldest, didn't stay long. The Johnsons expected Eliza Staines to serve them for an additional nine months, and this time, she would not have the company of her sister for comfort. As Ona Staines worried about her daughter, still caught in the unpredictable web of servitude, things grew even bleaker. The fall brought the typical cold weather of New England as well as the death of the Jack patriarch. Thirteen years had passed since the death of Phillis Jack, and neighbors came to the family's aid when the family found themselves unable to pay for a funeral. When Eliza Staines returned in January of 1818, she came home to a house full of women trapped in poverty with very little chance of escaping it.

The women in the Jack household did odd jobs, domestic work, and anything that could bring in additional income. Both Nancy and Eliza Staines were known around the town for their artistic abilities, and as they grew into adulthood, they began to sell their sketches to wealthy Portsmouth families. The Jack sisters never married and neither did the Staines girls, leaving the five women to muscle their way through the early years of antebellum America. Little changed in their material lives as their small house began to show signs of aging. The women of the house were simply happy to have a roof over their heads; poverty's roots were deep.

The 1830s tested Ona Staines in ways that were unimaginable. That her Northern-born daughters would die before her was a cruel twist of fate, another unfair and seemingly insurmountable blow.

On February 16, 1832, Eliza Staines died at the age of thirty-four after a "long and distressing illness." She was followed by her sister Nancy on September 11, 1833. Never released from the grasp of poverty, Eliza and Nancy Staines experienced lives that were filled with challenges, concerns about hunger, forced servitude, and the ever-present fear of slave catchers. Ona Staines did the best she could to raise her daughters, and now in her late fifties, she was, once again, alone.

It was her faith in God that carried Ona Staines through the most difficult times in her life. In her later years, Staines reminisced about her sojourn to Christianity and literacy, two silos that she encountered once she fled north. Staines recounted that she "never received the least mental or moral instruction of any kind, while she remained in the Washington family." For many fugitives and former slaves, access to education and the ability to practice religion in their own ways were markers of freedom. By the 1840s, literacy rates among free African Americans were climbing, and Staines linked her newly found literacy to her religious practice, telling another interviewer that the ability to read the Bible and participate in religious events made her "wise unto salvation." She questioned George Washington's religious practice, prompting her interviewer to write, "She never heard Washington pray, and does not believe that he was accustomed to." While there are many accounts of the first president attending church services, Staines questioned his devotion and did not leave Martha Washington out of her commentary. She stated, "Mrs. Washington used to *read* prayers but I do not call that praying." It was Staines's own strong connection to the church that prompted her to question Martha Washington's religious integrity.

Ona Staines probably attended Reverend Samuel Haven's South Church, the place where she married Jack Staines. But she was moved to join the Baptist denomination after hearing the sermons of Elias Smith, an itinerant preacher who traveled around New England during the 1790s, landing permanently in Portsmouth by 1802.

Once she moved in with the Jack family, Staines probably attended the Baptist church in Stratham, only a mile's walk from her home. Decades later, it was this connection that brought Reverend Thomas Archibald to interview the aging fugitive. Archibald published this first interview on May 22, 1845, in the *Granite Freeman*, an abolitionist newspaper. The article appeared on the forty-ninth anniversary of her escape—almost to the day. With her children deceased, the elderly Ona Staines no longer hid from the spotlight. Now in her early seventies, the fear of being returned to the Parke Custis heirs had finally been vanquished. Her *Granite Freeman* interview appeared a week before the paper's announcement of a new publication, a narrative written by a man named Frederick Douglass. It might not have been her intention to be grouped with other famous fugitives such as Frederick Douglass, but she was.

Two years later, on New Year's Day, Ona Staines's story appeared in the leading abolitionist newspaper of the era, the *Liberator*. Her name and life's story were finally known to thousands of readers across the nation, permanently linking her to the crusade for black freedom in the years leading up to the Civil War. Interviewer Benjamin Chase, antislavery convention attendant and ardent abolitionist, was lucky to record his interview with Staines when he did. A little over a year later, in February of 1848, Dr. George Odell paid a call to the Jack household, where Ona Staines and Nancy Jack resided. Nancy's sister, Phillis Jack, had died, so the two elderly women were left alone. Dr. Odell's house call was most likely to treat an ailing Ona Staines, now close to seventy-four years old. But whatever cures or treatment he may have prescribed were unsuccessful. On February 25, 1848, eleven days after the doctor's visit, Ona Maria Staines was carried away, not by slave catchers, but by her God.

Ona's Sister: Philadelphia Costin

Washington, DC, in 1800. Published in 1834.

When Ona Staines was asked to reflect upon her escape, her interviewer put forth a question that could be asked of any successful fugitive who lived a life in the shadows. The interviewer wrote, "When asked if she is not sorry she left Washington, as she has labored so much harder since, than before, her reply is 'No, I am free, and I have, I trust, been made a child of God by the means.'"

Although she never regretted her escape, she could not forget her family members who still lived at Mount Vernon. Leaving them behind was the greatest of sacrifices. The slave woman surely wrestled with her soul, thinking about the consequences of her actions and how they might place her family in harm's way. How could her family ever forgive her for abandoning them? What would become of them? Instead of visualizing their anger and feelings of betrayal, she must have hoped for her family's blessing, imagining them secretly cheering for her as she risked everything to find freedom.

Ona Staines would have no idea that the price of her freedom carried such a steep penalty for her loved ones, most specifically for her younger sister Philadelphia. Staines's escape from a life under the scrutiny of Eliza Custis Law had unintended consequences, and Philadelphia ended up in the very position that Staines had refused to accept. Passed down to the volatile granddaughter of the Washingtons, Philadelphia found herself living the life that was intended for her older sister. The fugitive's younger sister did what most enslaved people were trained to do—she survived the best she could. Philadelphia probably never believed that one day she, too, would be free.

⁕

When the Washingtons returned to Mount Vernon in the early summer of 1796 without Ona Staines, there was no way to prevent the rumors and gossip that spread like contagion through the slave quarters and the Mansion House. Her disappearance served as a reminder to all who labored at Mount Vernon that when given the right opportunity, freedom could be taken. Her departure must have earned her special acknowledgment, perhaps a hero's recognition, among the Washingtons' slaves. But no matter how proud or elated, the slaves at Mount Vernon had to suppress any expression of joy. Driven into the unspoken alcoves of their minds, the fugitive took her place among the fabled stories of other slaves who had risked everything for freedom. The enslaved Harry, Tom, and Will Shag were among the few bondmen at Mount Vernon who had gambled on escape; sometimes they found freedom but most often they met with capture and the auction block. Ona's name was now firmly rooted in the legend of freedom makers.

Not everyone shared the hidden enthusiasm regarding the fugitive's escape. Martha Washington was deeply disturbed by the abandonment of her slave, for not only did her bondwoman break the law by running away, she also destroyed the first lady's plans of assistance for her newly married and now pregnant granddaughter. Martha Washington was forced to make new arrangements regarding Eliza Custis Law, and she turned to a young Philadelphia.

Only sixteen years old, Philadelphia was saddled with the responsibility of serving the new Mrs. Law. Perhaps Philadelphia had proven herself to be trustworthy and reliable and was therefore the natural replacement for her older sister. Or maybe, in a fit of anger, Mrs. Washington purposely selected Philadelphia to serve the new Mrs. Law, a duty that would require her to leave Mount Vernon and head for a new home in the Federal City. If vindictiveness was her motive, Martha Washington was successful. Philadelphia followed in her older sister's footsteps, leaving behind the world she knew at Mount Vernon. Both Ona Staines and Philadelphia traveled through similar rites of passage; torn from their homes, the sisters were sent to live and serve in new cities.

On January 19, 1797, Mrs. Law and her new husband, Thomas, welcomed the arrival of a baby girl, Elizabeth Parke Custis Law. Much like their fast and furious courtship and marriage, the union brought sudden and sweeping change to Mount Vernon. Upon her marriage, Eliza Law received a portion of her inheritance from her late grandfather Daniel Parke Custis, an inheritance that included a significant number of slaves. Eliza's marriage and the birth of a baby expedited Philadelphia's departure from Mount Vernon.

Existing records do not mention her exact date of departure, but according to Washington's records, Philadelphia was still spinning at Mount Vernon as late as April of 1797. Sometime after that, Philadelphia would go to live with the Laws in Georgetown.

When the Congress decided upon the Potomac River location for the nation's new capital, there were two established towns in the area, Alexandria and Georgetown. Located at the southern tip of the District of Columbia, Alexandria was considered to be a handsome Virginia town with attractive homes and a growing population, while Georgetown was separated from the Federal City by Rock Creek and was considered a bit more remote. By 1800, Georgetown counted close to two thousand black residents, the vast majority of whom were enslaved.

Both Philadelphia and Ona Staines witnessed the slow growth of black freedom. For Ona Staines the experience was more dramatic, as slavery was near extinction in her Northern city by the time of her escape. When Philadelphia arrived in Georgetown, she must have taken quick notice of the small but growing number of free black residents. Close to three hundred free blacks lived in Georgetown and more than three hundred and fifty lived in Alexandria. Philadelphia would watch the number of free blacks in the District of Columbia grow steadily, but so too did slavery. Enslavement and liberty wrestled each other in the first two decades of the nineteenth century, with black bondage losing its might by the 1830s.

Just as Ona Staines found marriage and companionship with a husband, so too did Philadelphia. Both women selected free men as spouses, a decision that would help each of them hold on to the elusive grasp of freedom. Although the date is uncertain, Philadelphia eventually married a man named William Costin, who many believe was the son of Ann Dandridge, Martha Washington's legendary interracial half sister. Dandridge was believed, by some, to be the offspring of Martha Washington's father and an enslaved woman. Several oral histories and accounts state that Dandridge eventually gave birth to a son named William whose father was Jacky Custis, the son of Martha Washington. If these accounts and recent genealogy are accurate, William Costin was the nephew and the grandson of the first lady. Whatever Costin's lineage may have been, he was considered a free man, never appearing on the slave inventories at Mount Vernon. Costin eventually moved from Virginia to the new Federal City, harnessing the limited power he possessed as a free black man. Over time, Costin would use his money and his relationships to secure the freedom of his family members and his friends.

As slavery's laws grew more restrictive in Virginia and Maryland, free blacks took flight from these states, bolting for the Capital City. Slave resistance was on the mind of many, as white residents read about bloody slave rebellion in Haiti. Virginians shuddered as they learned of a failed insurrection by an enslaved blacksmith named Gabriel. The bondman from the Prosser estate planned to attack Capitol Square in Richmond, take the governor hostage, and negotiate for black freedom. Liberty became more difficult to secure and harder to maintain in Virginia, a likely reason for William Costin's migration to the Federal City. Or perhaps it was Philadelphia's presence in Georgetown that prompted a young Costin to follow his heart and relocate. The promise of a life in a new city must have been a welcomed option as the home he knew at Mount Vernon came undone.

Martha Washington died on May 22, 1802, and while her family, friends, and the public mourned her death, the dower slaves at Mount Vernon were likely consumed with fear. The day of reckoning had come. Martha Washington's will mandated that all of her slaves were to be divided among her grandchildren, a plan that would break slave families apart.

The Custis grandchildren were all adults at the time of their grandmother's passing, and all except George Washington Parke Custis (Washy) were married. The estate that George and Martha Washington had safeguarded for nearly half a century was to be transferred, and the division of property, including enslaved men and women, would increase the wealth of the Custis grandchildren. Eliza Custis Law was bequeathed forty-three slaves, including Philadelphia, who was assigned a value of eighty pounds. Eliza Law's sisters also inherited a significant number of slaves; Martha Custis Peter received forty-eight enslaved people, and Nelly Custis Lewis was bequeathed thirty-three human souls.

George Washington Parke Custis, the only male grandchild, was allotted thirty-six slaves, one of whom was Elish, Martha Washington's sole slave who was not a part of the Custis estate. A number of slaves who were willed to George Washington Parke Custis came as family units. A slave woman named Caroline and her four daughters, Rachel, Jemima, Leanthe, and Polly, managed to avoid separation and began their new assignment together. Philadelphia's sister-in-law Charlotte, once married to the late Austin, managed to keep her sons, Billy and Tim and her daughters Elvey and Eliza by her side. Betty Davis was also among the fortunate, as she kept her nuclear family together. In 1797 Davis had given birth to a third daughter, named Lucinda, who along with her mother and two sisters, waited for word about their futures. With her sister, Philadelphia, assigned to Eliza Law and another sister (Ona Staines) still on the run, Davis clung desperately to her daughters. Betty Davis, Nancy, Oney, and Lucinda, were all transferred to the estate of George Washington Parke Custis, eventually residing at his home at Arlington. Davis was listed with a value of sixty pounds, Nancy fifty pounds, Oney thirty-five pounds, and Lucinda was worth twenty pounds.

The death of the matriarch ended almost fifty years of tradition at Mount Vernon. Feelings of deep uncertainty touched all who were connected to the estate of the Washingtons; however, for Eliza Law, there were additional matters that troubled her. Aside from losing her grandmother, Mrs. Law observed the deterioration of her marriage, a relationship that had steadily grown more troubled. The whirlwind romance that developed into a marriage had come undone over the course of eight years. Family members and friends commented upon the demise of the Law marriage, suggesting that both parties involved created a host of marital problems. During Martha Washington's last years, the couple stifled their unhappiness in order to spare the family's matriarch from pain or concern. But following Martha Washington's death, Thomas Law traveled to Europe and shortly after his return, the couple made the decision to separate. On August 9, 1804, Thomas and Eliza agreed upon a legal separation, with Thomas Law offering real estate and a $1,500 annuity to his estranged wife. Eliza Law left the District of Columbia for Maryland, where she spent an extended period of time with her aunt and uncle. Rosalie Stier Calvert, Law's aunt, placed the blame of the failed marriage on both Thomas and Eliza, writing, "It is a sad thing to see two people with a child separate without good reason. You know what an odd man [Thomas Law] has always been. She had a disposition completely opposite to his, and she wasn't sensible enough to put up with his peculiarities. The result is that they are both at fault, which is usually the case. . . ."

Just as Eliza and Thomas Law's marriage changed the lives of both Ona Staines and Philadelphia, so too did their eventual divorce. The Laws lived estranged from one another for close to six years, with Law eventually filing a bill of divorce in 1810. Thomas Law was granted custody of their young daughter Eliza, who would eventually attend boarding school in Philadelphia, but what remains unclear was the fate of all the bound laborers who served the Law family. As Eliza Law reclaimed her Custis surname, she began a nomadic life. Custis purchased a small home in Alexandria that she named "Mount Washington" and lived there from 1805 to 1809. At some point during the Law's legal separation, Eliza Custis gave her estranged husband permission to emancipate some of her slaves. On June 13, 1807, Thomas Law gave Philadelphia her freedom, signing her manumission papers in consideration of one dollar.

He may have emancipated her because the maintenance and taxes on slave labor exacerbated his already cash-strapped affairs. And, like Washington, Law had a change of heart about the probity of slavery. Certainly, Law was no strident abolitionist, and while married to Eliza Custis, he lived with and profited from slave labor. But bound labor must not have settled well with Thomas Law, and his belief in gradual emancipation and the eventual relocation of black people emerged after the end of his marriage.

We do know that by the time of her emancipation, Philadelphia was close to twenty-eight years old and was married to William Costin. The couple did not wait for freedom to begin their family, a risky decision given the inheritable slave status that could have locked their children into bound labor. Thomas Law not only emancipated Philadelphia Costin, but he also set free her two children, two-year-old Louisa and four-month-old Ann. That same year, Thomas Law released additional members of the Costin family, most of whom were women and children. Among those emancipated was William Costin's mother, Ann Dandridge, who had married and taken the surname Holmes. The Costins took advantage of their free status and became well-known members of the free black community in

Washington, DC. They expanded their family, purchased property, and assisted men and women who looked desperately for an exit from human bondage.

Although emancipated, Philadelphia Costin understood just how tenuous her free status was. Slavery would live on in the District of Columbia for more than another fifty years, and as long as it existed, Philadelphia Costin could never rest without concern. Kidnappers surveyed the streets of the Federal City, instilling fear and vulnerability into the hearts of men and women who possessed freedom papers—papers that were meaningless to unscrupulous slave catchers. The former slave needed to stay vigilant and not let her family's newly found opportunity take down her guard.

Philadelphia's emancipation was not surprising and was most likely due to the valued relationship between her husband and Martha Washington's grandchildren. William Costin became one of the pillars of early black society in Washington, amassing property and moderate wealth over the course of his lifetime. Landing a job as a porter at the Bank of Washington, a title that he kept for more than twenty-five years, Costin's free status and financial security allowed him to agitate for the rights of free blacks and to help those who were still enslaved. Eliza Custis Law trusted William Costin, calling on his carriage-driving services, and, on occasion, even asking for financial help. Costin obliged whenever he could, which in turn helped to secure his own family's freedom.

Costin must have been a charismatic man, but when natural charm failed him, he could be a force to be reckoned with. When black codes grew tighter in Washington, Costin sued the city. Black codes required that every free black person appear before the mayor with documents signed by three different white citizens, attesting to good character. But white references were not enough for the mayor, so an imposed twenty-dollar peace bond was mandated, requiring free blacks to offer advance payment as a commitment to good behavior. Although the judge believed that Costin should be exempted from the new requirement, the laws remained intact. The personal exemption for Costin was in no way a victory for all free blacks.

When Costin couldn't fight the law and win, he simply used it to his favor. Committed to helping friends and family find their way to freedom, Costin had to play the game; he became a slave owner. Throughout the 1820s, William Costin purchased and emancipated a number of enslaved men and women, many of whom had a direct connection to Mount Vernon. Twenty-eight-year-old Leanthe Brannin, daughter of Caroline, was one of the beneficiaries of Costin's moral compass. She too had been a slave at Mount Vernon, but by 1820, Costin purchased her from George Washington Park Custis and then offered the woman a chance to buy her own freedom for five dollars.

Perhaps Custis's participation in the colonization movement made him more amenable to emancipating Brannin? More likely it was the mutually beneficial relationship between Custis and Costin that allowed for deals to be struck. Costin's work with the Bank of Washington and entrepreneurial spirit placed him in a favorable light with the Custis heirs. On occasion, the grandchildren wrote to Costin, asking him for help with transportation from his hack business. But more important than a carriage ride was Costin's position at the bank, one that allowed for the Washington grandchildren to borrow money when necessary. The agreeable relationship between William Costin (often referred to as Billy) and the Custis heirs placed him in the perfect position to become an agent of change. He leveraged this relationship in order to purchase his family and friends.

As William Costin slowly led his family and friends out of slavery's grasp, Ona Staines remained tucked away in Greenland's seclusion. Perhaps had she known that her younger sister, Philadelphia, lived a good life as a free woman, it would have offered her peace of mind and a temporary salve to the difficult life she lived as a fugitive. If she knew that some of her old friends had managed to make it out of slavery, it might have eased her suffering that came with the loss of a husband and desperate poverty. Certainly, Ona Staines would have rejoiced at the news that her namesake and niece, Oney Fortune, was one of the lucky family members purchased and emancipated by William Costin. Had she known all of this information, it might have erased the only remorse, the only regret she carried with her to the grave. Ona Staines had walked away from her family at Mount Vernon, seizing an opportune moment, and she never looked back. To know that her family would eventually prosper as free people would have confirmed that her choice to escape had been a good one.

Her life had been difficult, but for fifty-two years Ona Staines never lost faith in herself. Every day that the fugitive opened her eyes, she knew one thing to be true: she would "rather suffer death" than return to slavery.

Acknowledgments

ACADEMICS ALMOST ALWAYS THANK THEIR FAMILY OR THEIR "VILLAGE" at the end of their acknowledgments, but I'd like to break from that tradition. It takes a long time for historians to write books, and my family has supported me for many years. I have dedicated this book to two people: my mother, Frances C. Armstrong, and my husband, Jeffrey K. Dunbar. My mother was the first person to read my manuscript, and she did so many times over. She asked good questions and helped me to think about what a more "general" audience expects to read when they pick up a book. Her advice was invaluable. My husband is an incredibly supportive partner. Jeff not only picked up the slack when I was off on research trips or secluded in my office, but he is a closet historian who was just as mesmerized by Ona Judge Staines as I was. His patience and deep pride in my work helped me to make it to the finish line.

My son, Christian A. Dunbar, has grown up with Ona Judge Staines. Thank you for sharing your time with her and for your deepening respect for African American history. My father, Jacob R. Armstrong, my sister, Nicole E. Armstrong, and my niece, Leah G. Armstrong, have supported me in various ways, but remind me of the importance of family. Thank you to my "chosen family"— Raymond, Tracey, Amber, Christian, and Christopher Johnson who loved on me and my family when we needed it the most. I offer special thanks to Tracey, who was always there to help me with my son. You gave me peace of mind, a necessity for all writers.

To my "girls" who continue to entertain and love me—Marjorie DeLaCruz, Lisa Langhart, Rhea Williams, Jessica Davis Ba, Robin Watkins, Dana Baxter, Dawn Baxter Woodhouse, Nichelle Bussey, Christine Bussey Singleton, Dana Thomas Austin, Kysha Harris, Maria Schindler, and Tara Williams—thank you for the energy, the fun, and the memories.

To my "Sistah Scholars" who continue to do "the work"— Gabrielle Foreman, Tiffany Gill, Carole Henderson, Carol Rudisell, Daina Ramey Berry, Jessica Millward, Crystal Feimster, Krystal Appiah, Jessica Johnson, Farah Griffin, Kali Gross, Amrita Chakrabarti Meyers, Barbara Krauthamer, Martha Jones, Thavolia Glymph, Leslie Harris, and Barbara Savage—your work and commitment to the field make academia a better place.

I have benefitted from the careful draft readings, comments, and support from a number of scholars and friends. I offer my deepest appreciation to Evelyn Brooks Higginbotham, Jennifer Morgan, Barbara Savage, Leslie Harris, Mia Bey, Duchess Harris, Krystal Appiah, Annette Gordon Reed, Eric Foner, Susan Strasser, Wunyabari Maloba, Avery Rome, and Jennifer Torpie.

There are many institutions that have offered assistance while I wrote this book. I would like to thank the staff at the Fred W. Smith Library for the Study of George Washington at Mount Vernon. Douglas Bradburn was welcoming and Mary Thompson shared her vast knowledge of all things related to the enslaved at Mount Vernon. Archivist Wendy Kail at Tudor Place sent along helpful information, and the staff at the New Hampshire Historical Society and the Pennsylvania Historical Society were always friendly and helpful. I am fortunate to work with great people at the Library Company of Philadelphia. My "partner in crime," Krystal Appiah, makes directing the Program in African American History an absolute pleasure. I have enjoyed working with scholar Rich Newman, and I offer a special thanks to Nicole Joniec for her help with the images for *Never Caught*. I would be remiss if I did not also thank my graduate student Michael Dickinson for all of his help at very important moments during the production of this book. I can't wait for you to join me on the other side of the profession.

Vicky Avery did what few people do, that is, she accepted a phone call from a stranger and offered her goodwill and assistance. I called upon Vicky a few times during my research trips to New Hampshire, and each time, she was kind enough to point me in the right direction. Most memorable was our trekking through the woods (and poison ivy) to visit what is believed to be Ona Judge's final resting place.

On a cold day in November 2014, I sat shivering on the bleachers at my son's soccer game. I was miserable, but quickly forgot my discontent once I began a delightful conversation with writer Kathy DeMarco Van Cleve. As we suffered through the soccer game together, she asked what I was working on, and I told her about Ona Judge Staines. She immediately said, "you should talk to my agent." It was one of the best pieces of advice I have ever received. Not only did Kathy serve as my compass, but she also read my manuscript and offered a critical eye and thoughtful comments. Thank you for your friendship, encouragement, and for introducing me to Laura Dail.

I tell everyone that I know that "my agent is a beast" . . . but in the best of ways. Laura Dail is quick, bold, extremely savvy, and ethical. She is as much an editor as she is an agent, and I thank her for taking care of me and Ona Judge Staines. She led me to my editor, Dawn Davis, and the Simon & Schuster and Atria team.

I have learned so very much from Dawn, more than I ever

thought possible at this stage in my life. Dawn Davis believed in me and in Ona's story, and her patience and heavy editor's pen helped me to rethink the way that I write and present history. The first time that I sat in her office I knew that she was the one. Smart, fierce, and forthright, Dawn is a force and I thank her for helping me to share Ona Judge Staines with the world. This is a collective win for black women's history.

Notes

Foreword

xv   *nearly six thousand people:* I have drawn from the works of Nash and Soderlund's *Freedom by Degrees* and Nash's *Forging Freedom*, 143. Census records indicate that there were 6,436 black people living in Philadelphia by 1800. That number had more than tripled in just ten years.

xvi   *the capital moved to Philadelphia:* Lawler, "The President's House in Philadelphia: The Rediscovery of a Lost Landmark," 5–95. Also see Nash, *The Forgotten Fifth: African Americans in the Age of Revolution*, 61.

xvi   *the "first lady":* The term "first lady" was not used until the middle of the nineteenth century; however, I use the term throughout the text to refer to Martha Washington.

xvii   *recorded narratives of an eighteenth-century Virginia fugitive:* Scholars have unearthed evidence about the lives of fugitives such as Harry Washington, who escaped slavery through his service to the British during the American Revolution. See Cassandra Pybus's *Epic Journeys of Freedom: Runaway Slaves of the American Revolution and Their Global Quest for Liberty* (New York: Beacon Press, 2006) and Egerton's *Death or Liberty: African Americans and Revolutionary America*.

Chapter One

4   *"It rain'd Hail'd snow'd and was very Cold":* Theodore J. Crackel, *The Papers of George Washington Digital Edition* (University of Virginia Press, Rotunda, 2008) accessed June 7, 2014, http://rotunda.upress.virginia .edu/founders/GEWN-01-03-02-0003-0013-0011. Original source: Diaries (11 March 1748–13 December 1799), vol. 3 (1 January 1771–5 November 1781).

5   *"in better health and spirits":* Crackel, *The Papers of George Washington Digital Edition*, accessed June 9, 2014, http://rotunda.upress .virginia.edu/founders/GEWN-02-09-02-0185. Original source: Colonial Series (7 July 1748–15 June 1775), vol. 9 (8 January 1772–18 March 1774).

5   *only one living child:* For more on the early life of Martha Dandridge Custis, see Joseph E. Fields's *"Worthy Partner": The Papers of Martha Washington* (Westport, CT: Greenwood Press, 1994), xx.

5 *breaking the news of his stepdaughter's death:* Crackel, *The Papers of George Washington Digital Edition,* accessed June 9, 2014, http://rotunda.upress.virginia.edu/founders/GEWN-02-09-02-0185. Original source: Colonial Series (7 July 1748–15 June 1775), vol. 9 (8 January 1772–18 March 1774).

6 *one of the wealthiest widows in the colony of Virginia:* See "Complete Inventory of the Estate of Daniel Parke Custis" and "Account of Land and Acreage" in Fields, *"Worthy Partner,"* 61–76.

7 *Betty was approximately twenty-one years old:* See "List of Artisans and Household Slaves in the Estate c. 1759" in Crackel, *The Papers of George Washington Digital Edition,* accessed April 26, 2014, http://rotunda.upress.virginia.edu/founders/GEWN-02-06-02-0164-0025. Original source: Colonial Series (7 July 1748–15 June 1775), vol. 6 (4 September 1758–26 December 1760). The date of this document is still uncertain; however, Betty is listed as a twenty-one-year-old dower slave and seamstress.

7 *sexual relations with his slaves:* A number of scholars have contributed to the growing literature surrounding rape and sexual power in early America. Sharon Block's *Rape and Sexual Power in Early America,* Jennifer Morgan's *Laboring Women: Reproduction and Gender in New World Slavery* and Clare Lyons's *Sex among the Rabble* are extremely helpful texts.

7 *the poet Frances Ellen Watkins Harper wrote:* See Houston Baker's *Long Black Song: Essays in Black American Literature and Culture* (Charlottesville: University of Virginia Press, 1990), 70. No other children were listed with Betty on the slave inventory lists from the Custis estate. If by 1759 Betty had children other than Austin, they were either deceased or had been sold away.

8 *The highest-valued mother-and-child pair:* Fields, *"Worthy Partner,"* 61.

8 *hired white weaver named Thomas Davis:* I am indebted to the many years of research conducted by research historian Mary Thompson at the Fred W. Smith National Library for the Study of George Washington. Thompson has pored over the records of the estate for decades and was generous with her time and research with me as I completed this book. My analysis regarding the family ties of Ona Judge is in alignment with Thompson's beliefs. I would also like to thank Molly Kerr, Digital Humanities Program manager at the library, for all of her time and thoughtfulness as we went about the difficult work of the genealogy of the enslaved. I believe that Thomas Davis, a white hired weaver who worked at Mount Vernon, fathered at least two of Betty's children. Their textile skills would have placed the slave and servant in direct contact with each other. It is almost impossible to know the exact birth dates of Betty's children. Washington did not keep vital statistics for all of his slaves and therefore did not record their births. There were two extant inventories produced for Washington's slaves: one in 1786 and another in 1799. The 1786 inventory lists the approximate ages of Betty's children as does the inventory from 1799.

8   *knowledge of expert weaving:* See Julie Matthaei's *An Economic History of Women in America,* 43–63. Also see Laurel Thatcher Ulrich's *A Midwife's Tale* and *The Age of Homespun,* 75–174.

9   *a daughter named Ona Maria Judge:* We do not know the exact month in which Ona Judge was born. We know that Judge was born sometime around 1773–1774.

9   *She would be called Oney:* "Oney" was the diminutive of Ona, a nickname that appears in numerous places throughout George Washington's letters, ledgers, and slave inventories. In her interviews that appear in abolitionist newspapers much later in her life, she refers to herself as Ona Maria Judge or Ona Staines. I have chosen to use the name that she called herself and not the diminutive that so often appears in the records and secondary sources.

9   *"Baltimore or any port in America":* George Washington Papers, Library of Congress, 1741–1799, ser. 4. General Correspondence, 1697–1799, Andrew Judge and Alexander Coldclough, 8 July 1772, Printed Indenture.

10   *Andrew Judge entered into service:* See David W. Galenson's "The Rise and Fall of Indentured Servitude in the Americas: An Economic Analysis" in *Journal of Economic History* 44, no. 1 (March 1984): 1–26.

10   *creating the blue uniform worn by Washington:* Lund Washington's Mount Vernon Account Book, 1772–86, f. 32, ViMtvL, http://founders.archives.gov/documents/Washington/02-10-02-0113. According to Lund Washington, in November of 1774 Judge made "1 Suite Regimentals" for George Washington.

11   *the birth of a daughter:* Aside from Andrew Judge, no other person with the same last name lived at Mount Vernon or the surrounding area. Andrew Judge's arrival in 1772 and Ona Judge's birth sometime between 1773 and 1774 make the strongest of cases that the two were related. Descriptions of Ona Judge fashion her as interracial with a light complexion and bushy hair.

11–12   *Andrew Judge lived in his own home:* "Heads of Families, Virginia," *Heads of Families at the First Census of the United States Taken in the Year 1790: Records of the State Enumerations, 1782 to 1785: Virginia* (Washington: BPO, 1908). The home in which Judge lived was either purchased outright or on land that was rented.

12   *Ona and her siblings, including Philadelphia:* Although there are suggestions that Philadelphia was also the daughter of Andrew Judge, I have not been able to track down any slave inventories or records that refer to Philadelphia as "Philadelphia Judge." Philadelphia's manumission papers and obituary do not refer to her as "Judge." While there are existing family letters at the Fred W. Smith National Library for the Study of George Washington from descendants of Philadelphia that name her as "Philadelphia Judge," I have found nothing else that cites her as such. For a complete list of Washington's slave inventories of 1786 and 1799, see "[Diary entry: 18 February 1786]," Founders Online, National Archives (http://founders

.archives.gov/documents/Washington/01-04-02-0003-0002-0018 [last update: 2015-03-20]). Source: Donald Jackson and Dorothy Twohig, eds., *The Diaries of George Washington*, vol. 4, *1784–30 June 1786* (Charlottesville: University Press of Virginia, 1978), 276–83, and "Washington's Slave List, June 1799," Founders Online, National Archives (http://founders.archives.gov/documents /Washington/06-04-02-0405 [last update: 2015-03-20]). Source: W. W. Abbot, ed., *The Papers of George Washington*, Retirement Series, vol. 4, *April–December 1799* (Charlottesville: University Press of Virginia, 1999), 527–42.

12   *The name is both African and Gaelic:* Evelyn Gerson's master's thesis, "A Thirst for Complete Freedom: Why Fugitive Slave Ona Judge Staines Never Returned to Her Master, President George Washington" (Cambridge: Harvard University, 2000), notes that the name "Ona" emerged from three African tribal languages. See Newbell Niles Puckett and Murray Heller's *Black Names in America: Origins and Usage* (Boston: G.K. Hall 1975), 429–30. The text suggests that although the name "Ona" has its roots in African languages, it was used by white women. Nineteenth-century records show that both men and women were named Ona.

12   *House for Families:* The "Quarters [or House] for Families" were eventually torn down in the 1790s. By the early 1790s until George Washington's death, the majority of the slaves at the Mansion House lived in the buildings that flanked the Greenhouse. Some slaves lived in rooms above the kitchen building as well as individual cabins.

13   *Childhood for enslaved girls and boys was fleeting:* For more on childhood and slavery, see Marie Jenkins Schwartz's *Born in Bondage: Growing Up Enslaved in the Antebellum South* (Cambridge: Harvard University Press, 2009). Although this text focuses upon childhood and enslavement in the nineteenth century, it is extremely helpful in lending context to Ona Judge's life in late eighteenth-century Virginia. Chapter three, titled "Young Children in the Quarter," offers a nuanced interpretation of challenges faced by enslaved children.

Chapter Two

18   *unanimously elected to serve as president:* See Gordon Wood's *Revolutionary Characters: What Made the Founders Different* (New York: Penguin, 2006), 46–47.

18   *"President of the United States of America":* Letter from John Langdon to George Washington, 6 April 1789, Manuscript, George Washington Papers, Manuscript Division, Library of Congress [Digital ID# us0071].

18   *"to borrow money upon interest":* Letter to Richard Conway, 4 March 1789, in *The Papers of George Washington*, Presidential Series, vol. 1 (Charlottesville: University Press of Virginia, 1987), 361–62.

19   *Seven slaves would accompany the Washingtons:* As noted before, the absence of a birth record for Ona Judge only allows us to speculate

about her exact age. It is probable that she was either fifteen or sixteen years of age when the Washingtons moved to New York.

19 *things connected to the running of the house:* Gerson, "A Thirst for Complete Freedom," 53.

19 *"I bade adieu to Mount Vernon":* "[Diary entry: 16 April 1789]," Founders Online, National Archives (http://founders.archives.gov/documents /Washington/01-05-02-0005-0001-0001 [last update: 2015-12-30]). Source: Donald Jackson and Dorothy Twohig, eds., *The Diaries of George Washington,* vol. 5, *July 1786–December 1789* (Charlottesville: University Press of Virginia, 1979), 445–47.

19 *"to render service to my country":* Ibid.

20 *Washington's journey north took him through Philadelphia:* Kaminski and McCaughn, *A Great and Good Man,* 104.

20 *"quiet entry devoid of ceremony":* George Washington to George Clinton, 25 March 1789. *The Papers of George Washington Digital Edition.*

20 *"Rooms in a Tavern":* Ibid.

20 *3 Cherry Street:* Chernow, *Washington: A Life,* 564.

20 *a population of about thirty thousand people:* White, *Somewhat More Independent,* 4. The 1790 census reported 31,229 people living in New York City.

20 *The streets of New York:* Ibid. For more on race, slavery, and freedom in New York during the Early National Period, see Leslie Harris's *In the Shadow of Slavery* and Graham Russell Hodges's *Root & Branch.*

21 *Unsettled and displeased:* Martha Washington wrote to a handful of family and friends, describing her unhappiness with the transition to New York and a longing for Mount Vernon. See Martha Washington, "Letter, Martha Washington to Mercy Otis Warren, December 26, 1789," in Martha Washington, Item #25, accessed July 29, 2014, http://www .marthawashington.us/items/show/25 and "Letter, Martha Washington to Fanny Bassett Washington, October 23, 1789," in Martha Washington, Item #13, accessed July 29, 2014, http://marthawashington .us/items/show/13.

21 *"Black Sam as Steward":* Tobias Lear to George Augustine Washington, 3 May 1789, George Washington Manuscript Collection, Book, Manuscript, and Special Collections Library, Duke University.

21 *awaiting the arrival of the first lady:* Ibid.

23 *"Everything appeared to be in confusion":* Robert Lewis, "Journal of a Journey from Fredericksburg, Virginia to New York, May 13–20, 1789," Digital Collections from George Washington's Mount Vernon, http:// cdm16829.contentdm.oclc.org/cdm/compoundobject/collection /p16829coll14/id/45/rec/2.

23 *"these poor wretches seemed greatly* agitated": Ibid.

23 *Austin's wife, Charlotte:* Charlotte was a seamstress at Mount Vernon and married to Austin. Charlotte had at least five children: Billy, Timmy, Elvey, Jenny, and Eliza.

25 *New York enacted a new comprehensive slave law:* See Harris, *In the Shadow of Slavery,* 70–71 and Joanne Pope Melish, *Disowning Slavery,* 64–72.

25   *public sentiment regarding African slavery:* See Harris's *In the Shadow of Slavery,* chapters 3–4.

25   *William Lee was a teenager:* Washington recorded the purchase of a teenage boy named "Mulatto Will" from Mary Lee for the sum of sixty-one pounds.

25   *dressing his master's hair:* See Douglas R. Egerton's *Death or Liberty: African Americans and Revolutionary America*: 4–5.

25   *"fearless horseman":* Ibid., 5.

26   *"calling himself William Lee":* Ibid., 7.

26   *Thomas be allowed to travel to and live with Lee:* Egerton, *Death or Liberty,* 7–8.

27   *"broke the pan of his knee":* Ibid.

28   *Black postilions and footmen:* Edgar J. McManus, *Black Bondage in the North* (Syracuse: Syracuse University Press, 1973), 17.

28   *caps worn by Giles and Paris:* Decatur and Lear, *Private Affairs of George Washington,* 169. This specific request occurred in November of 1790.

30   *with her old friend Mary Morris:* Martha Washington, Martha Washington to Frances B. Washington, 8 June 1789, Gilder Lehrman Institute of American History, http://www.gilderlehrman.org/collections /treasures-from-the-collection/martha-washington-first-lady's-grand children-were-her-top-.

30   *1,800 free blacks:* Nash and Soderlund, *Freedom by Degrees,* 18. The 1790 census, tax assessment list, manumission lists, and Constables' returns counted the total population of Philadelphia (including Southwark and Northern Liberties) as 44,096, of whom 301 were enslaved and 1,849 were free blacks.

30   *The eighteenth-century poster: Description of a Slave Ship* (London), 1789, Rare Books and Special Collections, Princeton University Library, https://blogs.princeton.edu/rarebooks/2008/05/219-years-ago-de scription-of-a/.

31   *Franklin penned several essays:* For more on Benjamin Franklin and his views on slavery, see David Waldstreicher's *Runaway America.*

32   *moon sailed in front of the sun:* Nasa.gov solar eclipse of May 24, 1789. Although myth has it that Banneker predicted an eclipse in April of 1789, NASA reports that the eclipse occurred on May 24, 1798, and was only seen from the region surrounding Papua, New Guinea.

32   *left Philadelphia and headed for New York:* Martha Washington to Frances B. Washington, 8 June 1789.

Chapter Three

34   *Embree would face charges:* See Graham Russel Hodges's *Root & Branch,* 166. Taken from the New York City Manumission Society Reports, 1785–95, *New York Manumission Society Papers,* New York Historical Society, and *People v. Lawrence Embree* (November 5, 1789), New York City Mayor's Court Records, 1789–90, New York Public Library.

34 *African Free Schools for black children:* See Harris's *In the Shadow of Slavery*, 49, and see Christine Pawley's *Reading Places: Literacy, Democracy, and the Public Library in Cold War America* (Amherst: University of Massachusetts Press, 2010), 49. Also see Elizabeth McHenry's *Forgotten Readers*, 31–32.

34 *well-known nineteenth-century black leaders:* "Examination Days: The New York African Free School Collection," New York Historical Society, accessed April 20, 2015, https://www.nyhistory.org/web /africanfreeschool/#.

35 *influential black society:* Alexander, *African or American?*, 9–11.

35 *white students raided black graves:* Ibid., 9.

36 *In Martha's entourage:* Chernow, *Washington: A Life*, 572.

37 *an image for the new American aristocracy:* For more on late eighteenth- and early nineteenth-century women's dress and fashion, see Catherine Kelly's *In the New England Fashion.*

37 *When Mrs. Washington arrived at Cherry Street:* Martha Washington to Frances B. Washington, 8 June 1789.

37 *Rooms were enlarged and remodeled:* Ibid.

38 *third floor and attic:* For more on Washington's living conditions in New York, see Donald Jackson and Dorothy Twohig's *The Diaries of George Washington*, vol. 6, January 1790–December 1799 (Charlottesville: University Press of Virginia, 1979), 26.

38 *Tobias Lear, personal assistant to George Washington:* Chernow, *Washington: A Life*, 583.

39 *Nelly Washington also learned:* Thane, *Mount Vernon Family*, 63; Ribblett, *Nelly Custis*, 17–18.

40 *Martha Washington was homesick:* Lossing, *Martha Washington*, 22.

40 *"I had no leizure to read":* Chernow, *Washington: A Life*, 576. For original source, see "From George Washington to David Stuart, 26 July 1789," Founders Online, National Archives (http://founders.ar chives.gov/?q=george%20washington%20to%20david%20stuart&s =1111311111&sa=&r=190&sr=, ver. 2014-05-09).

41 *Mrs. Washington greeted her guests:* Chernow, *Washington: A Life*, 577–78.

41 *through lower Manhattan:* Brady, *Martha Washington: An American Life*, 172.

42 *Governor George Clinton owned eight slaves:* White, *Somewhat More Independent*, 10.

43 *educate and baptize black New Yorkers:* Harris, *In the Shadow of Slavery*, 48.

43 *Judge was now in the minority:* Although the majority of Mount Vernon's inhabitants were of African descent, Virginia's population was a majority white. In 1790 a little under 300,000 enslaved men and women lived in the state; however, the total population hovered around 747,000.

43 *Ten percent of New York's population:* White, *Somewhat More Independent*, 4.

44 *Stockhouse owned a slave:* Ibid., 6.

44 *the majority of the blacks:* Ibid., 12.

44 *arduous kinds of domestic work:* For additional information about African American women in New York, see Dabel's *A Respectable Woman* and Alexander's *African or American?*.

45 *"Just before them, a Mulatto girl":* Decatur and Lear, *Private Affairs of George Washington*, 135–36.

46 *consumed with fear:* Chernow, *Washington: A Life*, 586.

46 *The surgery was quite serious:* Tobias Lear to Colonel Clement Biddle, 24 June 1789, in William Baker's *Washington After the Revolution 1784–1799* (Philadelphia: J. B. Lippincott Co., 1897).

47 *much larger home on Broadway:* Henry B. Hoffman, "President Washington's Cherry Street Residence," *The New York Historical Society Quarterly Bulletin* 23 (January 1939): 90–103; and Anne H. Wharton, "Washington's New York Residence in 1789," *Lippincott's Monthly Magazine* 43 (1889): 741–45.

47 *"general health seems to be declining":* See Douglas Southall Freeman's *George Washington: A Biography*, vol. 6 (New York: Charles Scribner's Sons, 1948–57), 245.

48 *out of harm's way:* On May 18, 1790, the *New York Journal* reported, "The President of the United States has been exceedingly indisposed for several days past, but we are rejoiced at the authentic information of his being much relieved the last evening." Similar reports appeared in the *Pennsylvania Gazette* on May 19, 1790.

Chapter Four

49 *new site for the nation's capital:* For more on the relocation of the federal capital to Philadelphia, see Gary Nash's *First City: Philadelphia and the Forging of Historical Memory* (Philadelphia: University of Pennsylvania Press, 2011), 123.

49–50 *Judge's sister, Betty Davis:* Nancy's exact birth date is unknown. George Washington's 1799 Slave Inventory lists Nancy as nine years of age, dating her birth year as sometime around 1790.

50 *entrenched system of plantation slavery:* Virginia's 1790 census notes that 12,866 free people of color lived in the state, which at the time included West Virginia. This number would include men and women who were Native American as well as African or African American.

51 *"hurt at the idea of bidding adieu":* The *Federal Gazette*, 1 September 1790.

51 *the site of the nation's capital:* Fergus M. Bordewich, *Washington: How Slaves, Idealists and Scoundrels Created the Nation's Capital* (New York: Amistad Books, 2008), 3–7.

51 *the first Congress:* See Edward M. Riley's "Philadelphia, The Nation's Capital, 1790–1800," *Pennsylvania History* 20, no. 4 (October 1953): 358–359, Pennsylvania State University Press.

53 *"the dirty figures of Mrs. Lewis":* "From George Washington to Tobias Lear, 9 September 1790," Founders Online, National Archives (http://founders.archives.gov/documents/Washington/05-06-02

-0195 [last update: 2015-03-20]). Source: *The Papers of George Washington*, Presidential Series, vol. 6, *1 July 1790–30 November 1790.*

53   *extremely demanding chef:* Gerson, "A Thirst for Complete Freedom," 66.

54   *"the Son of Herculas":* "From George Washington to Tobias Lear, 22 November 1790," Founders Online, National Archives (http://founders .archives.gov/documents/Washington/05-06-02-0331 [last update: 2015-03-20]). Source: *The Papers of George Washington*, Presidential Series, vol. 6, *1 July 1790–30 November 1790*, 682–83.

54   *a ninth slave joining them:* "Postillion Joe" is mentioned by Washington in correspondence dated October 19, 1795. It is believed that he traveled to Philadelphia from Mount Vernon after an eight-day journey. It is uncertain how long Joe remained in Philadelphia, but the 1799 Mount Vernon slave inventory lists him as among the other slaves living at Mount Vernon.

55   *The "President's House" stood at 190 High Street:* Edward Lawler Jr., "The President's House in Philadelphia: The Rediscovery of a Lost Landmark," *The Pennsylvania Magazine of History and Biography* 126, no. 1 (January 2002): 5–95.

55   *the house on High Street:* Ibid., 5.

56   *also known as "Black Sam":* The racial identity of Samuel Fraunces is still unclear, although most scholars believe that he was a man of African descent. Nicknamed "Black Sam," Fraunces was a well-known tavern owner in New York who eventually traveled to Philadelphia to serve as a steward for the Washingtons. Although no documentation of his birth has been uncovered, it is suggested that he came from Barbados or possibly Haiti. In the 1790 census, Fraunces was identified as a free white male who had a history of slave ownership and still clung to one slave in his New York residence. For more on Washington's Steward, see Rice, *A Documentary History of Fraunces Tavern* and Blockson, "Patriot, White House Steward and Restaurateur Par Excellence."

56   *Attached to the kitchen:* Edward Lawler Jr., "The President's House in Philadelphia," 32.

56   *The rear of the property:* There was a bit of controversy about the history of the refitting of the smokehouse. While some at the National Park Service were hesitant to claim that slaves were required to live in the smokehouse, much of the necessary documentation provided by scholar Edward Lawler Jr. allows us to accept that slaves did indeed live in the smokehouse.

56–7   *Friday evening "drawingrooms":* Lawler, "The President's House in Philadelphia," 41.

58   *crude wooden structures:* John Blassingame's groundbreaking work, *The Slave Community*, examines the important role of the slave cabin as a respite from the ever-present watchful eye of the slave master.

58   *slave named Venus:* For centuries, a lingering oral testimony generated by African American descendants who lived at Mount Vernon sug-

gests that a slave named West Ford was Washington's son. According to the oral tradition, Ford's mother, a slave named Venus who was owned by Washington's brother (John Augustine Washington) and lived some ninety-five miles from Mount Vernon, had at least one sexual encounter with Washington that yielded a child. Most historians reject this assertion, as no written evidence exists to prove such a claim. Writer and biographer Henry Wiencek suggests that the possibility of Washington fathering West Ford is strong and points out that Ford was eventually freed by Hannah Bushrod Washington, the president's sister-in-law. Ford was the only slave freed in the will of Hannah Washington, and he was given 160 acres of land adjacent to Mount Vernon—a unique opportunity. For more on this, see Wiencek's *An Imperfect God*, 293–99.

Chapter Five

62 *"take advantage of a law of this State"*: "To George Washington from Tobias Lear, 5 April 1791," Founders Online, National Archives (http://founders .archives.gov/documents/Washington/05-08-02-0050, ver. 2013-08-02). Source: *The Papers of George Washington*, Presidential Series, vol. 8, *22 March 1791–22 September 1791*, 67–68.

63 *"after a residence of six months"*: Ibid.

63 *"the blacks in this family"*: Ibid.

64 *"as a necessity of his employment"*: "From George Washington to Tobias Lear, 12 April 1791," Founders Online, National Archives (http://founders .archives.gov/documents/Washington/05-08-02-0062, ver. 2013-08-02). Source: *The Papers of George Washington*, Presidential Series, vol. 8, *22 March 1791–22 September 1791*, 84–86.

64 *"practice of enticing slaves"*: Ibid.

64 *"too great a temptation"*: Ibid.

65 *strident abolition movement*: New York's first emancipation law was passed in 1799. See Harris, *In the Shadow of Slavery*, 70.

67 *"to deceive" the public if necessary*: "From George Washington to Tobias Lear, 12 April 1791," Founders Online, National Archives (http://founders .archives.gov/documents/Washington/05-08-02-0062, ver. 2013-08-02). Source: *The Papers of George Washington*, Presidential Series, vol. 8, *22 March 1791–22 September 1791*, 84–86.

67 *"none* but yourself & Mrs. Washington"*: Ibid.

67 *they might run off*: Ibid.

68 *allow Austin to reunite with his family*: Martha Washington to Fanny Bassett Washington, 19 April 1791, in Fields, *"Worthy Partner,"* 61.

68 *Austin was given a total of $11.66*: Austin was given $11.66 for the trip to Mount Vernon—passage to Baltimore in the stage cost $4.55, while the leg of the trip from Baltimore to Alexandria required $4.00 for transportation and close to $3.00 for other expenses, such as food and overnight lodging.

69 *"bind them to a master"*: "To George Washington from Tobias Lear, 24 April 1791," Founders Online, National Archives (http://founders .archives.gov/documents/Washington/05-08-02-0099 [last update:

2015-03-20]). Source: *The Papers of George Washington*, Presidential Series, vol. 8, *22 March 1791–22 September 1791*, 129–34. The attorney general's interpretation of the law was incorrect, and in actuality, all members of Congress were protected from the gradual abolition law.

69   *"insolent in the State of Slavery"*: Ibid.

70   *"entice them from their masters"*: Ibid.

70   *"it behooves me to prevent the emancipation"*: Ibid.

71   gold-headed cane and cocked hat: George Washington Parke Custis, *Recollections and Private Memoirs of the Life and Character of Washington* (New York: 1860), 422–24.

72   *"pretty strong proof of his intention"*: "To George Washington from Tobias Lear, 5 June 1791," Founders Online, National Archives (http://founders.archives.gov/documents/Washington/05-08 -02-0172, ver. 2013-08-02). Source: *The Papers of George Washington*, Presidential Series, vol. 8, *22 March 1791–22 September 1791*, 231–35.

73   *"his fidelity or attachment to you"*: Ibid.

73   trip back to Virginia: Decatur and Lear, *Private Affairs of George Washington*, 239.

73   *"his departure for Virginia"*: "To George Washington from Tobias Lear, 5 June 1791," Founders Online, National Archives (http://founders .archives.gov/documents/Washington/05-08-02-0172 [last update: 2015-03-20]). Source: *The Papers of George Washington*, Presidential Series, vol. 8, *22 March 1791–22 September 1791*, 231–235.

73   George Washington's birthday: Hercules successfully ran away from Mount Vernon in early 1797. He escaped after he was demoted from his position as lead chef to a basic manual laborer.

73   *"to prolong the slavery of a human being"*: "To George Washington from Tobias Lear, 24 April 1791," Founders Online, National Archives (http://founders.archives.gov/documents/Washington/05-08 -02-0099 [last update: 2015-12-30]). Source: *The Papers of George Washington*, Presidential Series, vol. 8, *22 March 1791–22 September 1791*, ed. Mark A. Mastromarino (Charlottesville: University Press of Virginia, 1999), 129–34.

74   would eventually release his slaves from bondage: George Washington's views about slavery changed over time. As historian Philip Morgan notes, the first president had no epiphany, but his misgivings about human bondage evolved so that by the end of his life he chose to emancipate his slaves following the death of his wife. See Philip Morgan's "To Get Quit of Negroes," 403–29.

Chapter Six

76   Ona Judge was given permission to attend the same theater: Decatur and Lear, *The Private Affairs of George Washington*, 268.

76   Christopher only received fifty cents: Ibid., 201.

76   disabled William Lee had returned to Mount Vernon: William Lee served the Washingtons while they lived in New York; however, he returned to Mount Vernon in the summer of 1790 before the Washingtons took

up residence in Philadelphia. Lee's disabling knee injuries prevented him from serving the president in a reliable manner.

77   *It was the first black mutual aid society:* William Douglass, *Annals of the First African Church in the United States of America, Now Styled the African Episcopal Church of St Thomas* (Philadelphia: King and Baird, 1862), 12–49.

79   *160 slaves took their chances:* The data concerning runaway slaves comes from Smith and Wojtowicz's *Blacks Who Stole Themselves,* as well as a survey of nineteen other Pennsylvania newspapers by Nash and Soderlund. The number of runaway slaves was probably higher than the 122 counted in the surveys. There are likely to have been omissions due to a lack of reporting by some slave masters.

79   *4,500 blacks living around Mount Vernon:* According to United States census records, there were 12,320 people living in Fairfax County, Virginia, in 1790. See "Heads of Families—Virginia" in *United States Census, 1790.*

79   *5 percent of the city's population:* Billy Smith, *The Lower Sort: Philadelphia's Laboring People 1750–1800* (Ithaca: Cornell University Press, 1994), 193.

81   *remove Giles from service:* Washington explains in a letter to Tobias Lear that Giles would probably "never be able to mount a horse again" following a presumed riding accident. See "From George Washington to Tobias Lear, 19 June 1791," Founders Online, National Archives (http://founders.archives.gov/documents/Washington/05-08 -02-0193, ver. 2014-05-09). Source: *The Papers of George Washington,* Presidential Series, vol. 8, *22 March 1791–22 September 1791,* 275–78.

81   *least desirable for slaves at Mount Vernon:* Giles does not appear on the 1799 Mount Vernon slave inventory; however, a slave named Giles appeared on the 1802 list of slaves who were inherited by Martha Parke Custis Peter, granddaughter to Martha Washington. If this was the same Giles, he was only valued at ten pounds, suggesting that his injuries left him virtually worthless in the eyes of his owners. Or perhaps it was his son, a young child incapable of hard labor.

81   *"Paris has become so lazy":* "From George Washington to Tobias Lear, 19 June 1791," Founders Online, National Archives (http://founders .archives.gov/documents/Washington/05-08-02-0193, ver. 2013-08-02). Source: *The Papers of George Washington,* Presidential Series, vol. 8, *22 March 1791–22 September 1791,* 275–78.

82   *illness claimed his life:* George Washington to William Pearce, 2 November 1794, ser. 4, General Correspondence, George Washington Papers, Library of Congress.

82   *Men and women suffered:* For more on yellow fever throughout American history, see Crosby, *The American Plague.*

82   *Yellow fever sickened and killed many:* Chernow, *Washington: A Life,* 700–702.

83   *Polly Lear died on July 28:* See Decatur and Lear's *The Private Affairs of George Washington,* 181, and Brighton's *The Checkered Career of Tobias Lear,* 115–16.

83 *recruiting black men and women to lend a hand:* Newman, *Freedom's Prophet*, 87–88.

84 *African Americans represented 10 percent of all deaths:* See J. H. Powell's introduction to *Bring Out Your Dead.*

84 *Blacks were accused:* See Newman, *Freedom's Prophet*, 94–95, for more on the most well-known pamphlet printed to defame the character of Philadelphia blacks during the yellow fever epidemic.

84 *Betty Davis had given birth:* Farm reports at Mount Vernon dated January 12, 1793, list Betty Davis as having a baby or being in "childbed." Washington's 1799 Slave Inventory lists Oney as six years old and the daughter of Betty D.

85 *his wife, Charlotte, and their five children:* Charlotte and Austin were close in age, and based upon information contained in the 1786 and 1799 Mount Vernon slave inventories, Charlotte had at least five children: Billy (born c. 1782); Timothy (born in 1785); and three daughters, Elvey, Jenny, and Eliza (no ages were given for the three girls on the 1799 inventory).

85 *He was "likely to Lose his Life":* John H. Barney to Bartholomew Dandridge, 20 December 1794, George Washington Papers, Library of Congress, 1741–1799, ser. 4, General Correspondence, 1697–1799, http://memory.loc.gov/cgi-bin/ampage?collId=mgw4&fileName=gw page106.db&recNum=835.

86 *"her life must have been miserable":* George Washington to William Pearce, 1 February 1795, *The Writings of George Washington*, 34:109.

86 *a new slave by the name of Joe:* Joe Richardson appeared in the 1786 Mount Vernon slave census, suggesting that he was over the age of fourteen. Joe was married to Sall, who was born around 1769, and like Ona Judge's family members, she worked as a seamstress at Mount Vernon. Joe arrived in Philadelphia sometime in 1795 following a journey from Mount Vernon to Philadelphia. See "Letter from George Washington to William Pearce October 19, 1795" in John C. Fitzpatrick's *The Writings of George Washington*, 34:337–38. At the time that Joe came to Philadelphia, he was married to Sall and had three young sons: Henry, 7; Elijah, 3; and Dennis, 1.

Chapter Seven

89 *Thomas Law and Eliza Custis promised themselves:* Henry Wiencek, *An Imperfect God*, 290.

90 *granddaughter's explosive announcement:* John Adams to Abigail Adams, 23 February 1796 [electronic edition]. *Adams Family Papers: An Electronic Archive*, Massachusetts Historical Society. http://www .masshist.org/digitaladams/archive/doc?id=L17960223ja&bc=%2F digitaladams%2Farchive%2Fbrowse%2Fletters_1789_1796.php. For original copy, see John Adams to Abigail Adams, 23 February 1796, p. 1, original manuscript from the Adams Family Papers, Massachusetts Historical Society. Adams writes that he attended an elaborate ball on the twenty-second of February to celebrate the president's birthday. Also see Weld, *Travels through the states.*

90   *George Washington received a letter from Thomas Law:* The letter from
      Thomas Law to George Washington has not been found.

91   *the president sat down to write both his granddaughter and Thomas Law:*
      Crackel, *The Papers of George Washington Digital Edition*, Diaries (11
      March 1748–13 December 1799) "[Diary entry: 10 February 1796]."

91   *"after a careful examination of your heart":* George Washington to
      Eliza Parke Custis, 10 February 1796, *The Papers of George Washing-
      ton*, accessed June 13, 2015, http://gwpapers.virginia.edu/documents
      /george-washington-to-elizabeth-betsey-parke-custis-2/.

91   *the president did nonetheless offer the approval:* George Washington to
      Thomas Law, 10 February 1796, *The Papers of George Washington*,
      accessed June 13, 2015, http://gwpapers.virginia.edu/documents/george
      -washington-to-thomas-law/.

91   *"be fixed in America":* Ibid.

92   *"Betcy Custis is to be married next Month":* John Adams to Abigail
      Adams, 23 February 1796 [electronic edition]. *Adams Family Papers:
      An Electronic Archive*, Massachusetts Historical Society. http://www
      .masshist.org/digitaladams/archive/doc?id=L17960223ja&bc=%2F
      digitaladams%2Farchive%2Fbrowse%2Fletters_1789_1796.php.

93   *a farewell address to the American people:* Ellis, *American Creation*,
      200. Washington thought about retiring after his first term but held
      on until the new nation was relatively stable. James Madison wrote a
      1792 version of a farewell address, but the president turned to Alex-
      ander Hamilton to assist him in the writing of a new farewell address
      that was printed in September of 1796. Also see Chernow's *Washing-
      ton: A Life*, 752–54.

94   *spent their days sewing for the Washingtons:* See overseer John Neale's
      "Weekly Report of Mount Vernon" written to George Washington
      July 30, 1796, in Crackel, *The Papers of George Washington Digital Edi-
      tion*, Retirement Series (4 March 1797–13 December 1799), vol. 1 (4
      March 1797–30 December 1797). Also see Washington's farm reports
      April 23–29, 1797. Betty Davis and Philadelphia (Delphy) both spent
      close to six days making clothing.

94   *"for a more lazy, deceitful & impudent huzzy":* George Washington to
      William Pearce, 8 March 1795, *The Writings of George Washington*,
      34:135.

96   *"she is more man than woman":* See Barratt and Miles, *Gilbert Stuart*
      and Chernow's *Washington: A Life*, 748.

96   *she refused to go to church:* Ibid.

97   *his quick engagement to the president's granddaughter:* Ibid.

98   *"no shadow of law to protect her from insult":* Jacobs, *Incidents in the
      Life*, 34.

Chapter Eight

100   *"fugitive slave problem":* Ibid. During the eighteenth century, slaves
      throughout the Mid-Atlantic and the Upper and Lower South always
      looked north for freedom. It is nearly impossible to chart exactly how
      many men and women were enslaved or fugitives in the Mid-Atlantic,

but 1790 census takers (however flawed their numbers might be) listed a total of 16,422 slaves in Pennsylvania, Delaware, and in southern counties of New Jersey. Although slaves never formed more than 4 to 5 percent of Pennsylvania residents throughout the colonial period, their numbers in the port city of Philadelphia were significant. Black presence reached as high as 28 percent of the population in the early eighteenth century and dipped to about 7 percent by the beginning of the Revolution.

101 *Many lost their lives to hypothermia:* See *Blacks Who Stole Themselves,* 11. Smith and Wojtowicz note that only 11 percent of the 959 runaways advertised in *Pennsylvania Gazette* between 1728 and 1790 attempted to escape in December, January, or February.

101 *drove vegetables and fruits into hibernation:* Ibid.

101 *the forests and wilderness protected:* According to Ira Berlin, between one-half to three-quarters of young enslaved men in the Philadelphia environs fled their masters sometime during the 1780s. The revolutionary era as well as the gradual abolition laws of the North served as ample enticement for slaves to take leave of their masters. See Berlin's *Many Thousands Gone,* 233.

102 *South Carolina and parts of the Upper South:* White, *Ar'n't I A Woman?,* 70. According to White, 77 percent of the runaways advertised in the colonial newspapers of South Carolina were male. Of the 1,500 newspaper advertisements in Williamsburg, Fredericksburg, and Richmond, Virginia, from 1736 to 1801, only 142 were women.

102 *"Abroad marriages":* Camp, *Closer to Freedom,* 25–29. Abroad marriages occurred when enslaved men and women lived on separate farms. According to Camp, it was often the male slave who visited his wife.

103 *twenty-six advertisements appeared in the* Gazette: Smith and Wojtowicz, *Blacks Who Stole Themselves,* 12. Ads ran frequently between 1728 and 1790.

103 *A four-dollar reward: Pennsylvania Gazette,* September 1, 1790, which also appears in *Blacks Who Stole Themselves,* on page 158.

103 *An eight-dollar reward:* Ibid.

104 *"I will ship him off":* George Washington to Anthony Whiting, 3 March 1793, *The Writings of George Washington,* vol. 32, March 10, 1792–June 30, 1793, 366.

104 *In 1791, the enslaved Waggoner Jack was sold:* Thompson, "Control and Resistance."

104 *Charlotte's constant insubordination:* "Anthony Whitting to George Washington, 16 January 1793," Founders Online, National Archives (http://founders.archives.gov/documents/Washington/05-12 -02-0005, ver. 2014–05–09). Charlotte was married to Austin, Ona Judge's brother.

105 *"correction (as the only alternative) must be administered":* "George Washington to Anthony Whitting, 20 January 1793," Founders Online, National Archives (http://founders.archives.gov/documents /Washington/05-12-02-0013 ver. 2014–05–09).

105   *"shall rescue such fugitive"*: Proceedings and Debates of the House of Representatives of the United States at the Second Session of the Second Congress (November 5, 1792 to March 2, 1793).

106   *aid or assistance to a fugitive*: For more on the background of the Fugitive Slave Law of 1793, see Paul Finkelman's *Slavery and the Founders: Race and Liberty in the Age of Jefferson* (Armonk, NY: M. E. Sharpe, 1996), chapter 4.

106   *the Fugitive Slave Law protected their property rights*: See Paul Finkelman's "Chief Justice Hornblower of New Jersey and the Fugitive Slave Law of 1793" in *Slavery and the Law* (New York: Rowman & Littlefield Publishers, 2002), 120–27.

107   *soon climbed up the economic ladder*: Newman, *Freedom's Prophet*, 56–57.

107   *services in March of 1796*: Ibid., 127.

108   *during the spring of 1796*: See "Washington's Household Account Book, 1793–1797," in *Pennsylvania Magazine of History and Biography* 31 (1907), 182. On May 10, 1796, Judge received money from Washington to purchase a new pair of shoes. Not only would the purchase of shoes be a necessity for a fugitive in the making, but it would also have offered Judge the opportunity to visit Richard Allen's home because, in addition to his chimney sweep business, Allen's home also served as a shoe shop.

108   *a shoe shop in his home on Spruce Street*: Newman, *Freedom's Prophet*, 142.

108   *$1.25 to purchase new shoes*: "Washington's Household Account Book, 1793–1797," *Pennsylvania Magazine of History Biography* 31 (1907), 182.

108   *"she should never have a chance to escape"*: Rev. Benjamin Chase, letter to the editor, *Liberator*, January 1, 1847.

108   *she knew that she had to flee*: T. H. Archibald, *Granite Freeman*, May 22, 1845.

108   *"never to be her slave"*: Ibid.

109   *"I never should get my liberty"*: Two published interviews with Ona Judge Staines appeared in abolitionist newspapers during the 1840s, offering her opinion about the events of the eighteenth century. This citation appears in an interview penned by Reverend T. H. Adams entitled "Washington's Runaway Slave," in the *Granite Freeman*, May 22, 1845.

110   *On Saturday, May 21, 1796*: A ten-dollar reward for the capture of Judge was advertised in *Claypoole's American Daily Advertiser*. The ad was published on Monday, May 24, 1796, and stated that Judge escaped on Saturday.

111   *another ad in* Claypoole's American Daily Advertiser: Most of the existing secondary literature about Ona Judge's escape mistakenly cite the *Pennsylvania Gazette* as the publisher of her runaway ad. No such ad exists in Ben Franklin's newspaper; however, ads appear in both *Claypoole's American Daily Advertiser* and the *Philadelphia Gazette*

(also known as the *Federal Gazette*). Kitt's ad appeared in the *Philadelphia Gazette* first, followed by an ad that appeared in *Claypoole's*. The Washingtons stopped their advertising for her return in only a few days, with the last ad appearing in *Claypoole's* on May 27, 1796.

111 *"Absconded from the household of the President"*: Claypoole's American Daily Advertiser, May 24, 1796.

111 *"many changes of very good clothes"*: Ibid.

111 *"she may attempt to escape by water"*: Philadelphia Gazette & Universal Daily Advertiser, May 23, 1796.

112 *"Ten dollars will be paid to any person"*: Claypoole's American Daily Advertiser, May 24, 1796.

113 *notified law-enforcement authorities in New York*: Thomas Lee Jr. to George Washington, 28 June 1796, George Washington Papers, Library of Congress, 1741–1799, ser. 4, General Correspondence, 1697–1799, http://memory.loc.gov/cgi-bin/ampage?collId=mgw4&fileName=gw page109.db&recNum=578.

113 *"I never told his name"*: Granite Freeman, May 22, 1845. Also see *Portsmouth Journal*, July 15, 1837. Bowles died on the evening of Saturday, July 8.

114 *boots, bridles, and saddles*: Bowles and his partner Leigh repeatedly advertised in the *New-Hampshire Gazette*. See June 4, 11, and 25, 1796, for a description of the goods they listed for sale.

114 *his own ship, the* Nancy: Ibid.

114 *Bowles's arrival in the city on May 10*: Philadelphia Gazette & Universal Daily Advertiser, May 10, 1796. Two New York newspapers announce the *Nancy*'s arrival in Philadelphia. See *Argus, or Greenleaf's New Daily Advertiser*, May 12, 1796, and *Minerva*, May 12, 1796.

114 *a sloop that carried molasses, coffee, potatoes*: John Bowles advertised in *Philadelphia Gazette & Universal Daily Advertiser* from May 11 through May 17.

Chapter Nine

120 *black men and women living in New Hampshire*: See Valerie Cunningham's "The First Blacks of Portsmouth." There were 630 free blacks and 158 slaves living in New Hampshire.

121 *along the sea and the rivers*: William D. Pierson, *Black Yankees: The Development of an Afro-American Subculture in Eighteenth-Century New England* (Amherst: University of Massachusetts Press, 1988), 14.

121 *It wouldn't take long*: The number of slaves at Mount Vernon continued to grow. By 1799 there were 318 slaves who lived and labored for the Washingtons.

121 *"lodged at a Free-Negroes"*: Joseph Whipple to George Washington, 22 December 1796, George Washington Papers, Library of Congress, 1741–1799, ser. 4, General Correspondence, 1697–1799. http://memory.loc.gov/cgi-bin/ampage?collId=mgw4&fileName=gw page110.db&recNum=395.

122 *age-old method used in Africa*: Adams and Pleck, *Love of Freedom*, 41.

123   *Judge and other domestics:* Ibid.
123   *dangerous and terribly hot task:* See Tera Hunter's *To 'Joy My Freedom*, 56–65.
124   *did not live beyond the age of forty:* Pleck and Adams, *Love of Freedom*, 42. Also see Susan Klepp's "Seasoning and Society."
124   *Smith sold one human:* Cunningham and Sammons, *Black Portsmouth*, 16–17.
124   *captive who arrived in New England:* Ibid.
125   *The extreme cold:* Piersen, *Black Yankees*, 5.
125   *"slaves cease to be known and held as property":* Cunningham and Sammons, *Black Portsmouth*, 77, and Melish, *Disowning Slavery*, 66.
125   *human bondage disappeared by 1805:* Cunningham and Sammons, *Black Portsmouth*, 77.
126   *It wouldn't be until 1857:* Ibid.

Chapter Ten

130   *senator and a governor of New Hampshire:* For an extensive biography of the New Hampshire senator and governor, see Lawrence Shaw Mayo's *John Langdon of New Hampshire* (Concord, NH: The Rumford Press, 1937).
130   *"contains about 5,000 inhabitants":* *The Diary of George Washington, from the first day of October 1789 to the tenth day of March, 1790.*
132   *before one of the Washingtons' friends:* Caroline Kirkland, *Memoirs of Washington*, 469. Kirkland's biographical account of Washington's life includes a version of the encounter between Eliza Langdon and Judge. Known for her contributions to American literature, Kirkland produced the biography written for juvenile readers with a slant toward young women. Her description of Judge and Langdon's meeting in Portsmouth took dramatic license with the facts and was not in alignment with George Washington's description of the meeting between Langdon and Judge.
133   *the buying and selling of slaves:* Cunningham and Sammons, *Black Portsmouth*, 41.

Chapter Eleven

137   *six letters that would change hands:* There are five letters dated between September 1, 1796, and December 22, 1796, that revolve around the attempted capture of Ona Judge. A sixth letter between Secretary of the Treasury Oliver Wolcott and the customs collector in Portsmouth, Joseph Whipple, is missing.
138   *more like a family member than a slave:* George Washington to Oliver Wolcott, 1 September 1796, Connecticut Historical Society (Box 4, Folder 4).
138   *a freckle-faced ten-year-old:* Ibid.
139   *Someone else must have lured her away:* Washington to Whipple, 28 November 1796. Washington states that a Captain Prescot reported seeing Ona Judge and that she had tried to obtain employment in his

household. According to the president, Ona Judge was homesick and wanted to return to her family and friends.

139 *French boyfriend abandoned Ona Judge:* Ibid.

139–40 *anyone who captured a fugitive:* Proceedings and Debates of the House of Representatives of the United States at the Second Session of the Second Congress (November 5, 1792 to March 2, 1793).

140 *a formal identification of the runaway:* George Washington to Oliver Wolcott, 1 September 1796.

140 *"put her on board a Vessel":* Ibid.

140 *his annoyance with Ona Judge was evident:* Ibid.

140 *"treated more like a child than a Servant":* Ibid.

141 *"with great pleasure execute the Presidents [sic] wishes":* "Joseph Whipple to Oliver Wolcott, Jr., September 10, 1796," in Martha Washington, Item #20, accessed 15 July 2013, http://www.martha washington.us/items/show/20.

141 *he was an entrepreneur:* Joseph Foster's The Soldiers' Memorial. Portsmouth, N.H., 1893–1921: *Storer Post, No. 1, Department of New Hampshire, Grand Army of the Republic, Portsmouth, N.H., with record of presentation of flags and portraits by the post to the city, 1890 and 1891* (Portsmouth, 1921), 20–26.

141 *appointed Whipple as Portsmouth's customs collector:* "John Langdon to George Washington, 17 July 1789," Founders Online, National Archives (http://founders.archives.gov/?q=john%20langdon%20to%20george %20washington%20july%2017%201789&s=1111311111&sa=&r=4&s r=ver.2013-06-26). Whipple had held this position as the new nation was being formed.

142 *his wife, Hannah Billings of Boston:* See Blaine Whipple's *History and Genealogy of "Elder" John Whipple of Ipswich, Massachusetts: his English ancestors and American descendants* (Victoria, BC: Trafford; Portland, OR: Whipple Development Corporation, 2003).

144 *under no circumstances would she return:* "Joseph Whipple to Oliver Wolcott, Jr., 4 October 1796," in Martha Washington, Item #21, http://marthawashington.us/items/show/21 (accessed May 6, 2014).

146 *"the Vessel sailed without her":* Ibid.

146 *"a thirst for compleat freedom":* Ibid.

147 *"her willingness to return & to serve with fidelity":* Ibid.

148 *"in favor of universal freedom":* Ibid.

148 *best for the president to hire a lawyer:* Ibid.

148 *"it is with regret that I give up":* Ibid.

148 *"enter into such a compromise":* George Washington to Joseph Whipple, 28 November 1796, *The Writings of George Washington, 35:296–97.*

149 *"to reward unfaithfulness":* Ibid.

149 *The president's attitudes regarding African slavery:* George Washington to the Marquis de Lafayette, 5 April 1783, *The Writings of George Washington,* 26:300. For more on Washington's evolving sentiments regarding human chattel, see Philip D. Morgan's "To Get Quit of Negroes," 403–29.

149   *"will be forgiven by her Mistress":* Ibid.

150   *"would excite a mob or riot":* Ibid.

151   *"be in a state of pregnancy":* Ibid.

151   *hunting Ona Judge and her unborn child:* Ona Judge never made mention of any pregnancy during the first few months after her escape to Portsmouth, New Hampshire, and there are no existing records to support Washington's claim. Judge did not give birth to a child in 1797. Unless she miscarried the baby, the president's suggestion was simply speculation.

151   *"restore to your Lady her servant":* Joseph Whipple to George Washington, 22 December 1796, George Washington Papers, Library of Congress.

152   *let go of human bondage:* Ibid.

Chapter Twelve

157   *capable of assisting fathers and mothers:* Clark, *The Roots of Rural Capitalism,* 24.

157   *slavery prohibited the legal marriages:* For more on early slave marriages, see chapter 4 of Betty Wood's *Slavery in Colonial America, 1619–1776.*

157   *black jacks suffered racial discrimination:* Bolster, *Black Jacks,* 1–6.

158   *Negro Seamen Act:* See Douglas Egerton's *He Shall Go Out Free.*

158   *imprisoned during their stay:* Edlie L. Wong, *Neither Fugitive nor Free,* 183–84.

159   *application for a marriage certificate:* Joseph Whipple to George Washington, 22 December 1796, Papers of George Washington, Library of Congress.

160   *county clerk Thomas Philbrook:* See Priscilla Hammond's *Vital Records of Greenland, New Hampshire: Compiled from the Town's Original Record Books, earliest and latest dates recorded, 1710–1851* (Salem: Higginson Book Company, 1997). See January 8, 1797. Thomas Philbrook, the clerk of Greenland, New Hampshire, recorded that John Staines and Oney "Gudge" were registered or "published" in the town of Greenland in Rockingham County and that they were married by Samuel Haven. John Staines was also known as Jack Staines.

161   *as the head of household:* See Year: *1800;* Census Place: *Portsmouth, Rockingham, New Hampshire;* Series: *M32;* Roll: *20;* Page: *903;* Image: *513;* Family History Library Film: *218679.* Ona Judge's husband is listed as "Jack Stains."

162   *They would name her Eliza:* We do not have an exact date of birth for Eliza Staines; however, the physician who reported her death in 1832 estimated that Eliza was thirty-four years old, placing her birth sometime around 1798. See "Certificate of Death for Eliza Staines, 16 February 1832," *New Hampshire Vital Statistics,* Concord, NH. Ancestry.com. *New Hampshire, Death and Burial Records Index, 1654–1949* [database online]. Provo, UT: Ancestry.com Operations, Inc., 2011.

163   *John Adams became the second president:* See chapter 8 of David McCullough's *John Adams.*

164   *demand for freedom was denied:* "From George Washington to Burwell
       Bassett, Jr., 11 August 1799," Founders Online, National Archives
       (http://founders.archives.gov/documents/Washington/06-04-02-0197
       [last update: 2015-03-20]). Source: *The Papers of George Washington,*
       Retirement Series, vol. 4, *20 April 1799–13 December 1799.*

164   *"& dangerous precedent":* Ibid.

165   *emancipated and rehired as paid laborers:* Ohline, "Slavery, Economics,
       and Congressional Politics, 1790" in Onuf, *Establishing the New Regime,*
       343. Also see Paul Finkelman's *Slavery and the Founders,* 28–29.

166   *She simply refused:* Benjamin Chase, letter to the editor, *Liberator,* Jan-
       uary 1, 1847.

166   *Bassett sweetened the deal:* Rev. T. H. Adams, *Granite Freeman,* May 22,
       1845.

166   *her final and fierce response:* Ibid.

167   *failed to complete the familial obligation:* In Staines's interviews she
       states that Bassett returned a second time to try to convince her to
       return to Virginia, but that the second time would be via force if
       necessary. Staines does not state how much time passed between the
       two attempted retrievals, and therefore we do not know if Bassett
       made two trips to New Hampshire. In any case, Bassett initiated two
       attempts at recapturing Staines.

Chapter Thirteen

172   *before he retired to bed:* Blanton, "Washington's Medical Knowledge
       and Its Sources." Also see Knox, "The Medical History of George
       Washington, His Physicians, Friends and Advisers."

172   *convulsions and near suffocation:* Chernow, *Washington: A Life,* 806.

173   *"my breath cannot last long":* Dorothy Twohig, *George Washington's
       Diaries: An Abridgement,* 430.

174   *"disagreeable consequences" among slave families:* "George Washington's
       Last Will and Testament, 9 July 1799," Founders Online, National
       Archives (http://founders.archives.gov/documents/Washington/06-04
       -02-0404-0001, ver. 2013-12-27).

175   *"faithful services during the Revolutionary War":* Ibid.

175   *William Lee died in the winter of 1810:* See Mary V. Thompson's "Wil-
       liam Lee & Oney Judge: A Look at George Washington and Slavery"
       in the *Journal of the American Revolution* (June 2014). While there is
       no written source, oral tradition suggests that William Lee was buried
       in the slave burial ground on the estate of Mount Vernon.

175   *"unhappy by the talk in the quarters":* Prussing, *The Estate of George
       Washington, Deceased,* 158.

175   *"[in] their interest to get rid of her":* Fritz Hirschfeld's *George Washington
       and Slavery,* 214. Also see Woody Holton's *Abigail Adams* (New York:
       Simon and Schuster, 2009), 33.

175   *George Washington's slaves were set free:* The transaction regarding the
       emancipation of Washington's slaves is recorded in the abstracts of the
       Fairfax County, Virginia, Court records. Also see John C. Fitzpatrick,
       ed., *The Last Will and Testament of George Washington and Schedule of*

his Property, to which is appended the Last Will and Testament of Martha Washington (Mount Vernon, VA: The Mount Vernon Ladies' Association of the Union, 1939).

177 *Ona Staines and her husband lived with their children:* Many black men and women took in adult boarders to help keep costs to a minimum and to help out free and fugitive blacks in need. While this is a possibility for one of the Staines household members, it is probable that at least two of the occupants of the Staines household were their children.

178 *the family welcomed little Nancy:* Death certificates for Eliza and Nancy Staines place their births around 1798 and 1802. See "Death Certificate of Eliza Staines, 16 February 1832" and "Death Certificate of Nancy Staines, 11 September 1833," Ancestry.com. *New Hampshire, Death and Burial Records Index, 1654–1949* [database online]. Provo, UT: Ancestry.com Operations, Inc., 2011.

178 *a birth date around 1800:* See Gerson's documentation of Seaman's Protection Certificates for Portland, ME, Washington, DC, National Archives in "A Thirst for Complete Freedom." Also see the National Archives and Records Administration; Washington, DC; *Quarterly Abstracts of Seamen's Protection Certificates, New York City, NY 1815–1869*, Ancestry.com. *U.S., Seamen's Protection Certificates, 1792–1869* [database online]. Provo, UT: Ancestry.com Operations, Inc., 2010.

178 *The only Portsmouth family with the surname of Staines:* There is a possibility that William Staines was not the biological son of Ona Staines. If William was the product of an extramarital affair, his absence from census records under the Staines, and later Jack, household is understandable.

179 *following in the shoes of his father:* No other documentation links William Staines to his parents, and census records provide nothing in the way of absolute proof of his familial connection.

179 *the death of her husband:* I cannot find any evidence that offers a cause or exact date of death for Jack Staines. A death announcement appeared on May 3, 1803, in the *New-Hampshire Gazette*. Later, Ona Staines is counted with her two children (daughters) among those living with the Jack family in the 1810 census. They are listed among the six free blacks living in the household, but they are not named.

179 *death notice appeared in the* New-Hampshire Gazette: See *New-Hampshire Gazette*, May 3, 1803. The section of the newspaper noted all of the reported deaths at home and abroad. The death announcement stated, "In this town . . . Mr. Jack Staines, (a man of colour)."

180 *a maidservant position:* The account of Ona Staines living with the Bartlett family comes from Gerson's "A Thirst of Complete Freedom," 113. Gerson's footnotes are a bit murky regarding this employment agreement, making verification quite difficult.

181 *border between Greenland and Stratham:* The town of Greenland claimed the property lived on by the Jacks family, but the final border between the two towns was not established until 1860. See Bouton, *Documents and Records Relating to the Province of New Hampshire*, 12:64, 13:480, 25:552.

181 *the stream that ran through the property:* See Charles Nelson's *History of Stratham*, 200.

181 *The patriarch of the Jack family was enslaved:* Gerson, "A Thirst for Complete Freedom," 114. There were many names used for the Jack family, especially for the patriarch. Daughters Nancy and Phillis Jr. recorded a surname of Jack.

182 *Phillis Jack's funeral:* See *Town Records of Greenland, New Hampshire, 1750–1851* and Hammond's *Vital Records.* Gerson also cites this in "A Thirst for Complete Freedom," 116–18. Gerson states that Jonathan Dockum received $1.90 for digging Phillis Warner's grave and for offering the family three pints of rum. Municipal funds were also used to reimburse Joseph Clark for making a coffin, and Samuel Dearborn was repaid $0.25 for ringing the town bell. My visit to the Greenland Town Vault fifteen years after Gerson's revealed some missing records.

182 *fusing two desperate and grieving families:* The Jack family was indexed anonymously in the 1810 census, counting six free blacks in the household, most likely Jack; his daughters, Nancy and Phillis Jr.; Ona Staines; and her daughters, Eliza and Nancy. Young William was not reported in this census, perhaps because he was under the age of ten, or maybe worse, he had been indentured out. Existing documentation leaves us with little evidence.

182 *Ona Staines said good-bye to her daughters:* This information comes from the *Town Records of Greenland, New Hampshire, 1750–1851* and Hammond's *Vital Records.*

183 *the death of the Jack patriarch:* Jack died on October 19, 1817.

183 *known around the town for their artistic abilities:* See Charles Brewster's "Washington and Slavery: From Mrs. Kirkland's Life of Washington." The addendum appears in the *Portsmouth Journal of Literature and Politics* (7 March 1857).

183 *Little changed in their material lives:* There are two articles that appear in the Greenland section of the *Exeter News-Letter* that give childhood recollections of the property called home by the Jack Staines family. The first article was published on December 18, 1874, by an author who used only the initial "M." The second article was written by Mary Izette Holmes and was published on January 2, 1917. Both of these articles were written many decades after the death of Ona Staines.

184 *Eliza Staines died at the age of thirty-four: New-Hampshire Gazette,* February 28, 1832.

184 *followed by her sister Nancy:* Ancestry.com. *New Hampshire, Death and Burial Records Index, 1654–1949* [database online]. Provo, UT: Ancestry.com Operations, Inc., 2011. Unlike her sister, Eliza, no obituary appeared in the New Hampshire newspapers for Nancy. Original data: "New Hampshire Death Records, 1654–1947." Index. FamilySearch, Salt Lake City, Utah, 2010. New Hampshire Bureau of Vital Records. "Death Records, 1654–1947." Bureau of Vital Records, Concord, NH.

184 *"mental or moral instruction": Liberator,* January 1, 1847.

184 *the ability to read the Bible: Granite Freeman,* May 22, 1845.

184 *"She never heard Washington pray":* Ibid.

184   *"I do not call that praying":* Ibid.
185   *the sermons of Elias Smith:* Reverend Roland D. Sawyer of Kensington, "New Hampshire Pioneers of Religious Liberty," in *Granite Monthly.* Also see *Liberator,* January 1, 1847.
185–6 *Phillis Jack, had died:* For Phillis Jack's obituary, see the *New-Hampshire Gazette,* January 6, 1846. For information about Dr. Odell's visit, see Hammond's *Vital Records* and Gerson's "A Thirst for Complete Freedom." Dr. Odell received $13.16 for his house call.
186   *Ona Maria Staines was carried away:* There were many published death notices for Ona M. Staines, many of which appeared in the spring of 1848. For a few examples, see the *Portsmouth Journal,* April 1, 1848; the *New-Hampshire Gazette,* April 4, 1848; and the *Pennsylvania Freeman* May 11, 1848.

Epilogue

187   *"'No, I am free'":* *Granite Freeman,* May 22, 1845.
190   *Philadelphia was still spinning at Mount Vernon:* Philadelphia is noted among the spinners, sewers, and knitters in the farm reports at Mount Vernon. The last report of "Delphia" spinning was for the week of April 23–29, 1797. Betty Davis (often noted as Betsey Davis) is also listed. Philadelphia spun, while Betty sewed. See "Farm Reports, 23–29 April 1797," Founders Online, National Archives (http://founders.archives.gov/documents/Washington/06-01-02-0047 [last update: 2015-03-20]). Source: *The Papers of George Washington,* Retirement Series, vol. 1, *4 March 1797–30 December 1797.*
190   *Located at the southern tip of the District of Columbia:* Brown, "Residence Patterns of Negroes in the District of Columbia, 1800–1860" in *Records of the Columbia Historical Society* 47:66–79.
190   *three hundred free blacks:* Ibid. According to the United States Census Bureau, there were a total of 3,244 enslaved people living in the District of Columbia with 783 free blacks. More specifically, in Georgetown there were 277 free blacks in 1800, while Alexandria counted 367.
190   *Enslavement and liberty wrestled each other:* The District of Columbia counted an increase in slavery as noted by the 1810 and 1820 census reports. The number of slaves increased from 5,505 in 1810 to 6,277 in 1820. But by 1830, the number of enslaved people began to decrease and for the first time was smaller than the number of free people. In 1830 there were 6,119 enslaved people and 6,152 free blacks. See Letitia Woods Brown's *Free Negroes in the District of Columbia, 1790–1846,* 11.
191   *nephew and the grandson of the first lady:* The story of Martha Washington's interracial sister, Ann Dandridge, and her son, William Costin, is still a debated topic. Henry Wiencek addresses this possible relationship in his text *An Imperfect God,* 283–87. While I find this to be a somewhat plausible account, I have not found existing documents to prove that Dandridge was the half sister of Martha Washington nor that William Costin was the son of Jacky Custis. It is possible that the oral history surrounding this relationship has changed over the years,

leaving historians with little in the way of ironclad proof. This is the case for many interracial children born during the era of slavery in Virginia and throughout the South. Pioneer black historian George Washington Williams, the first to write a comprehensive history of African Americans, hesitated when discussing Costin's paternal lineage. An additional account from the 1860s, penned by the Union spy Elizabeth Van Lew, states that Jacky Custis was William Costin's father. See *Elizabeth Van Lew Album 1845–1897*, in the Manuscripts Collection at the Virginia Historical Society, in Richmond, Virginia.

191   *The bondman from the Prosser estate:* See Doug Egerton's *Gabriel's Rebellion*.

192   *Eliza Custis Law was bequeathed forty-three slaves: The Washington Family Papers* (Container 3, Box 4, Folder 1), Library of Congress. The documents in Box 4 of the *Washington Family Papers* pertain to Martha Washington. Included in the container are copied images from a private collection that was in the possession of Walter G. Peter and offered to the Library of Congress in 1931. Although the slave inventory list is undated, the majority of the files in this folder are dated between 1800 and 1803. The slave inventory was divided into four sections and clearly designates which slaves were sent to the Custis grandchildren. Philadelphia (who was recorded as Delphia) was among forty-three recorded names who were assigned to "Mrs Law."

192   *Nelly Custis Lewis was bequeathed thirty-three:* Ibid.

193   *Lucinda was worth twenty pounds:* Ibid. In this slave inventory, Betty Davis, Nancy, Oney (spelled Anney on this list), and Lucinda were all listed. The value of Davis's younger children, Oney and Lucinda, was significantly lower than that of her daughter Nancy, and this was due to their age. By 1802 Oney was approximately nine years old, and Lucinda was close to six years of age, while Nancy was close to twelve years old. Davis and her children most likely lived at Arlington, an estate that GWP Custis began building in 1802. The other plantations owned by GWP Custis (White House and Romancoc) have existing slave inventories that do not list Betty Davis or her children.

193   *Thomas and Eliza agreed upon a legal separation:* Thomas Law's offer of real estate to Eliza Law was temporary, for in the separation agreement, it stated that upon her death, the property was "to be re-conveyed to Thomas Law and his heirs." See *Adams v. Law* 58 U.S. 417 (1854).

193   *"they are both at fault":* See letter from Rosalie E. Calvert to her father, H. J. Stier, in Calcott, *Mistress of Riversdale*, 97.

194   *Custis purchased a small home:* See Sarah Booth Conroy's "Hoxton House's Secret: The Origins of the Elegant Gray Stucco Mansion Were Obscured Until Researchers Digging Through Old Records Found the Owner: A Granddaughter of Martha Washington." In the *Washington Post*, June 29, 1995.

194   *Thomas Law gave Philadelphia her freedom:* Philadelphia, Louisa, and Ann's manumission agreement was recorded as Liber R No. 17 pg. 409 by the Recorder of Deeds in Washington, DC. Helen

Hoban Rogers compiled thousands of names of enslaved people and slaveholders from deed books and certificates of freedom. Her book *Freedom & Slavery Documents in the District of Columbia* lists the manumissions of most of the Costin family. The original handwritten libers from 1792 through 1869 are located in Record Group 351, Records of the Government of the District of Columbia, Deed book 112 at the National Archives in Washington, DC. Philadelphia, Louisa, and Ann's manumission was signed on June 13 and recorded on June 26, 1807.

194   *his belief in gradual emancipation:* See Thomas Law's correspondence regarding a belief in gradual emancipation and the support of African colonization in an undated letter in the Thomas Law Family Papers, Box 5, Maryland Historical Society.

194   *taken the surname Holmes:* See Deed book 112, Liber R, no. 17, 1807, signed May, 1, 1807, and recorded on May 5, 1807. This manumission released Margaret Costin (age 19) Louisa Costin (age 17) Caroline Costin (age 15), Jemima Costin (age 12), Mary Holmes (age 8), and Eleanor Holmes (age 6). The Costins and the Holmeses were emancipated together by Thomas Law under one agreement for ten cents. Law also emancipated George Costin, the only male relative, in the same year. Oral tradition suggests that Ann Holmes, who was emancipated by Thomas Law shortly after Martha Washington's death, was the mother of William Costin. For her emancipation, see Washington, DC, Deed book, Liber H, no. 8, p. 382, National Archives.

195   *an exit from human bondage:* The Costins had eight biological children (six daughters and two sons). While the Costin daughters Louisa and Ann were born enslaved, I have found records indicating that the Costins welcomed biological daughters Martha, Frances, and Harriet, as well as a son named William G., into the fold, all of whom were born free. According to obituaries for William Costin, there were at least four adopted Costin children. Philadelphia Costin died on December 13, 1831. Her obituary appeared in the *Daily National Intelligencer* (also known as the *National Intelligencer*) on the day of her funeral, December 15, 1831. Costin's death announcement states that she had seven children.

195   *secure his own family's freedom:* See letters from Eliza Parke Custis to John Law, 12 October 1808, and letter from Eleanor Parke Custis Lewis to William Costin, 12 June 1816.

195   *imposed twenty-dollar peace bond:* See *Costin v. Washington* (October 1821), Case No. 3,266, Circuit Court, District of Columbia.

196   *a chance to buy her own freedom:* See Rogers's *Freedom & Slavery Documents in the District of Columbia* 3:114. Originals are recorded as Liber A Z, no. 50, 1820 (23 October 1820) in Record Group 351, Records of the Government of the District of Columbia, Deed book 112 at the National Archives in Washington, DC. Leanthe's surname appears as "Brannin" and not "Branham." It was very common for last names to be misspelled on formal documents.

196 *Washington grandchildren to borrow money:* See letter from Eliza Parke
     Custis to John Law, 12 October 1808, in the Peter Collection, Thomas
     Peter Box: MSSVII Papers of John Law. Also see letter from Eleanor
     Parke Custis Lewis to William Costin, 12 June 1816, Peter Collection,
     Thomas Peter Box: MSSXI. Fred W. Smith National Library for the
     Study of George Washington at Mount Vernon.

197 *her namesake and niece, Oney Fortune:* Rogers, *Freedom & Slavery Docu-
     ments in the District of Columbia* 1:114. The recorded manumission for
     Oney Fortune was signed on October 13, 1827, and recorded on Novem-
     ber 5, 1827. The record notes that William Costin "manumits his slave
     woman named Oney, a bright mulatto who is about thirty-five years old."
     The unusual first name and age matches with a child under the care of
     Betty Davis listed as Oney on George Washington's 1799 slave inventory.
     Oney Fortune was the niece of Ona Judge Staines.

197 *"rather suffer death":* Joseph Whipple to Oliver Wolcott Jr., 4 October
     1796.

Selected Bibliography

Printed and Online Primary Sources

Adams, John. John Adams to Abigail Adams, 23 February 1796 [electronic edition]. In *Adams Family Papers: An Electronic Archive*. Massachusetts Historical Society. http://www.masshist.org/digitaladams/.

Bouton, Nathaniel. *Documents and Records Relating to the Province of New-Hampshire from 1692 to 1722: Being Part II of Papers Relating to That Period; Containing the "Journal of the Council and General Assembly."* Manchester, NH: John B. Clarke, State Printer, 1869.

Brewster, Charles. "Washington and Slavery: From Mrs. Kirkland's Life of Washington." *Portsmouth Journal of Literature and Politics*, 7 March 1857.

Crackel, Theodore, ed. *The Papers of George Washington Digital Edition*. Charlottesville: University of Virginia Press, Rotunda, 2007–.

Description of a Slave Ship. London, 1789. Rare Books and Special Collections, Princeton University Library. https://blogs.princeton.edu/rarebooks/2008/05/219-years-ago-description-of-a/.

Elizabeth Van Lew Album 1845–1897. Manuscripts Collection at the Virginia Historical Society.

"Examination Days: The New York African Free School Collection." New-York Historical Society. https://www.nyhistory.org/web/africanfreeschool/#.

George Washington Papers 1741–1799: Series 4. General Correspondence. 1697–1799. The Library of Congress, Washington, DC.

Lear, Tobias. Tobias Lear to George Augustine Washington, 3 May 1789. George Washington Manuscript Collection. Book, Manuscript, and Special Collections Library, Duke University.

Lewis, Robert. "Journal of a Journey from Fredericksburg, Virginia to New York, May 13–20, 1789." Digital Collections from George Washington's Mount Vernon.

New Hampshire Vital Statistics, Concord, NH. Ancestry.com. *New Hampshire, Death and Burial Records Index, 1654-1949* [database online]. Provo, UT: Ancestry.com Operations, Inc., 2011.

Peter Family Archives, Fred W. Smith National Library for the Study of George Washington at Mount Vernon.

Quarterly Abstracts of Seamen's Protection Certificates, New York City, NY 1815– 1869. National Archives and Records Administration. Washington, DC. Ancestry.com. *U.S., Seamen's Protection Certificates, 1792–1869* [database online]. Provo, UT: Ancestry.com Operations, Inc., 2010.

Records of the Government of the District of Columbia. Record Group 351. National Archives, Washington, DC.

Seaman's Protection Certificates for Portland, ME. National Archives, Washington, DC.

Thomas Law Family Papers. Collections of the Maryland Historical Society.

Town Records of Greenland, New Hampshire, 1750–1851. Greenland Town Vault, Town Hall, Greenland, New Hampshire.

The Washington Family Papers. Collections at the Library of Congress.

Washington, George. George Washington to Oliver Wolcott, 1 September 1796. Collections of the Connecticut Historical Society.

———. *The Diary of George Washington, from the first day of October 1789 to the tenth day of March, 1790.* New York: New York Public Library. https://archive.org/details/diarywashington00lossgoog.

———. *The Papers of George Washington.* Vol. 2, *April–June 1789.* Edited by W. W. Abbott. Charlottesville: University of Virginia Press, 1987.

Washington, Martha. Martha Washington to Frances B. Washington, 8 June 1789. Gilder Lehrman Institute of American History. http://www.gilderlehrman.org/collections/treasures-from-the-collection/martha-washington-first-lady's-grandchildren-were-her-top-.

———. Martha Washington to Fanny Bassett Washington, 23 October 1789, in Martha Washington. http://www.marthawashington.us/items/show/25.

Weld, Isaac Jr. *Travels through the states of North America and the provinces of Upper and Lower Canada during the years 1795, 1796, and 1797.* London, 1799.

Newspapers

Argus, or Greenleaf's New Daily Advertiser (New York, NY)

Claypoole's American Daily Advertiser (Philadelphia, PA)

Daily National Intelligencer (Washington, DC)

Exeter News-Letter (Portsmouth, NH)

Finlay's American Naval and Commercial Register (Philadelphia)

Granite Freeman (Concord, NH)

Liberator (Boston, MA)

Minerva (New York, NY)

New-Hampshire Gazette (Portsmouth, NH)

New York Journal (New York, NY)

Oracle of the Day (Portsmouth, NH)

Pennsylvania Freeman (Philadelphia)

Pennsylvania Gazette (Philadelphia)

Philadelphia (PA) Gazette (Federal Gazette)

Portsmouth (NH) Journal

Published Secondary Sources

Adams, Catherine, and Elizabeth H. Pleck. *Love of Freedom: Black Women in Colonial and Revolutionary New England*. Oxford: Oxford University Press, 2010.

Alexander, Leslie M. *African or American?: Black Identity and Political Activism in New York City, 1784–1861*. Urbana: University of Illinois Press, 2008.

Baker, William Spohn. *Washington after the Revolution; 1784–1799*. Philadelphia: n.p., 1897.

Barratt, Carrie Rebora, Gilbert Stuart, and Ellen Gross Miles. *Gilbert Stuart*. New York: Metropolitan Museum of Art, 2004.

Berlin, Ira. *Many Thousands Gone: The First Two Centuries of Slavery in North America*. Cambridge: Harvard University Press, 2000.

Berry, Daina Ramey. *"Swing the Sickle for the Harvest Is Ripe": Gender and Slavery in Antebellum Georgia*. Urbana: University of Illinois Press, 2007.

Blanton, Wyndham. "Washington's Medical Knowledge and Its Sources." *Annals of Medical History* 4.932 (1932): 52–61. Web.

Blassingame, John W. *The Slave Community: Plantation Life in the Antebellum South*. New York: Oxford University Press, 1972.

Block, Sharon. *Rape and Sexual Power in Early America*. Chapel Hill: The University of North Carolina Press, 2006.

Blockson, Charles L. "Patriot, White House Steward and Restaurateur Par Excellence." 20 November 2014. http://library.temple.edu/collections /blockson/fraunces. Web.

Bolster, W. Jeffrey. *Black Jacks: African American Seamen in the Age of Sail*. Cambridge, MA: Harvard University Press, 1997.

Brady, Patricia. *Martha Washington: An American Life*. New York: Viking, 2005.

Brighton, Ray. *The Checkered Career of Tobias Lear*. Portsmouth, NH: Portsmouth Marine Society, 1985.

Brookhiser, Richard. *James Madison*. New York: Basic, 2011.

Brown, Letitia Woods. *Free Negroes in the District of Columbia, 1790–1846*. New York: Oxford University Press, 1972.

Brown, Letitia Woods. "Residence Patterns of Negroes in the District of Columbia, 1800–1860." In *Records of the Columbia Historical Society*. Vol. 47. Washington, DC: Columbia Historical Society, 1971.

Brown, Warren. *History of the Town of Hampton Falls, New Hampshire: From the Time of the First Settlement Within Its Borders, 1640 until 1900*. Manchester, NH: John B. Clarke, 1900.

Bryan, Helen. *Martha Washington: First Lady of Liberty*. New Jersey: Wiley, 2002.

Callcott, Margaret Law. *Mistress of Riversdale: The Plantation Letters of Rosalie Stier Calvert*. Baltimore: Johns Hopkins, 1992.

Camp, Stephanie M. H. *Closer to Freedom: Enslaved Women and Everyday Resistance in the Plantation South*. Chapel Hill: The University of North Carolina Press, 2004.

Carretta, Vincent. *Phillis Wheatley: Biography of a Genius in Bondage*. Athens, GA: University of Georgia Press, 2011.

Chernow, Ron. *Washington: A Life*. New York: Penguin, 2010.

Clark, Christopher. *The Roots of Rural Capitalism: Western Massachusetts, 1780–1860*. Ithaca: Cornell University Press, 1990.

Craft, William, and Ellen Craft. *Running a Thousand Miles for Freedom*. New York: Arno, 1969.

Crosby, Molly Caldwell. *The American Plague: The Untold Story of Yellow Fever, the Epidemic That Shaped Our History*. New York: Berkley, 2006.

Cunningham, Valerie. "The First Blacks of Portsmouth." *Historical New Hampshire* 41, no. 4 (Winter 1989). Web.

Dabel, Jane E. *A Respectable Woman: The Public Roles of African American Women in 19th-Century New York*. New York: New York University Press, 2008.

Decatur, Stephen, and Tobias Lear. *Private Affairs of George Washington, from the Records and Accounts of Tobias Lear, Esquire, His Secretary*. Boston: Houghton Mifflin, 1933.

Douglass, William. *Annals of the First African Church, in the United States of America Now Styled the African Episcopal Church of St. Thomas, Philadelphia, in Its Connection with the Early Struggles of the Colored People to Improve Their Condition, with the Co-operation of the Friends, and Other Philanthropists; Partly Derived from the Minutes of a Beneficial Society,*

Established by Absalom Jones, Richard Allen and Others, in 1787, and Partly from the Minutes of the Aforesaid Church. Philadelphia: King & Baird, Printers, 1862.

Dunbar, Erica Armstrong. *A Fragile Freedom: African American Women and Emancipation in the Antebellum City.* New Haven: Yale University Press, 2008.

Egerton, Douglas R. *Death or Liberty: African Americans and Revolutionary America.* Oxford: Oxford University Press, 2009.

———. *Gabriel's Rebellion: The Virginia Slave Conspiracies of 1800 and 1802.* Chapel Hill: The University of North Carolina Press, 1993.

———. *He Shall Go Out Free: The Lives of Denmark Vesey.* Lanham, MD: Rowman & Littlefield, 2004.

Ellis, Joseph J. *American Creation: Triumphs and Tragedies at the Founding of the Republic.* New York: Alfred A. Knopf, 2007.

Fields, Joseph E. *Worthy Partner: The Papers of Martha Washington.* Westport, CT: Greenwood, 1994.

Finkelman, Paul. *Slavery and the Founders: Race and Liberty in the Age of Jefferson.* Armonk, NY: M. E. Sharpe, 1996.

First Census of the United States, 1790: Records of the State Enumerations, 1782 to 1785: Virginia. Spartanburg, SC: Reprint, 1974.

Fitzpatrick, John C. *The Writings of George Washington: From the Original Manuscript Sources 1745–1799.* Washington, DC: United States Government Printing Office, 1931.

Flexner, James Thomas. *George Washington.* Boston: Little, Brown, 1972.

"Founders Online: Washington's Slave List, June 1799." *Washington's Slave List, June 1799.* 15 June 2015. http://founders.archives.gov/documents /Washington/06-04-02-0405.

Freeman, Douglas Southall. *George Washington: A Biography.* 7 vols. New York: Charles Scribner's Sons, 1948–57. Volume 7 completed by John A. Caroll and Mary Wells Ashworth.

Furstenburg, Francois. *In the Name of the Father: Washington's Legacy, Slavery, and the Making of a Nation.* New York: Penguin Books, 2006.

Galenson, David W. "The Rise and Fall of Indentured Servitude in the Americas: An Economic Analysis." *The Journal of Economic History* 44.01 (1984): 1. Web.

Gerson, Evelyn B. "A Thirst for Complete Freedom: Why Fugitive Slave Ona Judge Staines Never Returned to Her Master, President George Washington." Thesis. Harvard University.

Girard, Philippe R. *The Slaves Who Defeated Napoleon: Toussaint Louverture and the Haitian War of Independence, 1801–1804.* Tuscaloosa: The University of Alabama Press, 2011.

Gordon-Reed, Annette. *The Hemingses of Monticello: An American Family.* New York: W. W. Norton, 2009.

Grizzard, Frank E. *George Washington: A Biographical Companion.* Santa Barbara, CA: ABC-CLIO, 2002.

Harris, Leslie M. *In the Shadow of Slavery: African Americans in New York City, 1626–1863.* Chicago: University of Chicago Press, 2003.

Harvey, Tamara, and Greg O'Brien, eds. *George Washington's South.* Gainesville: University Press of Florida, 2004.

Heads of Families at the First Census of the United States, Taken in the Year 1790: New Hampshire. Spartanburg, SC: Reprint, 1964.

Heads of Families at the First Census of the United States Taken in the Year 1790; Records of the State Enumerations: 1782–1785, Virginia. Baltimore: Genealogical Pub., 1970.

Herbert, Catherine A. "The French Element in Pennsylvania in the 1790s: The Francophone Immigrants' Impact." *Pennsylvania Magazine of History and Biography* 108 (1984): 451–70. Web.

Hirschfeld, Fritz. *George Washington and Slavery: A Documentary Portrayal.* Columbia: University of Missouri, 1997.

Hodges, Graham Russell. *Root & Branch: African Americans in New York and East Jersey, 1613–1863.* Chapel Hill: The University of North Carolina Press, 1999.

Hoffman, Henry B. "President Washington's Cherry Street Residence." *The New York Historical Society Quarterly Bulletin* 23 (1939): 90–103.

Hunter, Tera W. *To 'Joy My Freedom: Southern Black Women's Lives and Labors after the Civil War.* Cambridge, MA: Harvard University Press, 1997.

Jacobs, Harriet A., John S. Jacobs, and Jean Fagan Yellin. *Incidents in the Life of a Slave Girl: Written by Herself, Now with "A True Tale of Slavery" by John S. Jacobs.* Cambridge, MA: Belknap, 2009.

Jones, Jacqueline. *Labor of Love, Labor of Sorrow: Black Women, Work, and the Family from Slavery to the Present.* New York: Basic, 1985.

Kaminski, John P., and Jill Adair McCaughan. *A Great and Good Man: George Washington in the Eyes of His Contemporaries.* Madison, WI: Madison House, 1989.

Kelly, Catherine E. *In the New England Fashion: Reshaping Women's Lives in the Nineteenth Century.* Ithaca, NY: Cornell University Press, 1999.

Kirkland, Caroline M. *Memoirs of Washington.* New York: D. Appleton, 1857.

Klepp, Susan. "Seasoning and Society: Racial Differences in Mortality in Eighteenth-Century Philadelphia." *William and Mary Quarterly* 51 (1994): 473–506. Web.

Knox, J. H. Mason, Jr. "The Medical History of George Washington, His Physicians, Friends, and Advisers." *Bulletin of the Institute of the History of Medicine* 1 (1933): 174–91. Web.

Lawler, Edward, Jr. "The President's House in Philadelphia: The Rediscovery of a Lost Landmark." *Pennsylvania Magazine of History and Biography* 126, no.1 (2002): 5–95. Web.

Lossing, Benson John. *Martha Washington*. New York: J. C. Buttre, 1865.

Lyons, Clare A. *Sex among the Rabble: An Intimate History of Gender & Power in the Age of Revolution, Philadelphia, 1730–1830*. Chapel Hill: Published for the Omohundro Institute of Early American History and Culture, Williamsburg, Virginia, by the University of North Carolina Press, 2006.

Married Women and the Law. Coverture in England and the Common Law World. Montreal: McGill-Queen's University Press, 2013.

Matthaei, Julie A. *An Economic History of Women in America: Women's Work, the Sexual Division of Labor, and the Development of Capitalism*. New York: Schocken, 1982.

McCullough, David G. *John Adams*. New York: Simon & Schuster, 2001.

McHenry, Elizabeth. *Forgotten Readers: Recovering the Lost History of African American Literary Societies*. Durham: Duke University Press, 2002.

McManus, Edgar J. *Black Bondage in the North*. Syracuse, NY: Syracuse University Press, 1973.

Melish, Joanne Pope. *Disowning Slavery: Gradual Emancipation and "Race" in New England, 1780–1860*. Ithaca: Cornell University Press, 1998.

Moore, Lindsay. "Women and Property Litigation in Seventeenth-Century England and North America." In *Married Women and the Law: Coverture in England and the Common Law World*, edited by Tim Stretton and K. J. Kesselring. Canada: McGill-Queen's University Press, 2013.

Morgan, Jennifer L. *Laboring Women: Reproduction and Gender in New World Slavery*. Philadelphia: University of Pennsylvania Press, 2004.

Morgan, Philip D., and Michael L. Nicholls. "Slave Flight: Mount Vernon, Virginia, and the Wider Atlantic World." In *George Washington's South*, edited by Tamara Harvey and Greg O'Brien, 199–222. Gainesville: University Press of Florida, 2004.

Morgan, Philip. "'To Get Quit of Negroes': George Washington and Slavery." *Journal of American Studies* 39.3 (2005): 403–29. Web.

Nash, Gary B., and Jean R. Soderlund. *Freedom by Degrees: Emancipation in Pennsylvania and Its Aftermath*. New York: Oxford University Press, 1991.

———. *First City: Philadelphia and the Forging of Historical Memory*. Philadelphia: University of Pennsylvania Press, 2002.

———. *Forging Freedom: The Formation of Philadelphia's Black Community, 1720–1840*. Cambridge, MA: Harvard University Press, 1988.

———. *The Forgotten Fifth: African Americans in the Age of Revolution*. Cambridge, MA: Harvard University Press, 2006.

Nelson, Charles B. *History of Stratham, New Hampshire, 1631–1900*. Somersworth, NH: New Hampshire Publishing Company, 1965.

Newman, Richard S. *Freedom's Prophet: Bishop Richard Allen, the AME Church, and the Black Founding Fathers*. New York: New York University Press, 2008.

Ohline, Howard A. "Slavery, Economics, and Congressional Politics." In *Establishing the New Regime: The Washington Administration*, edited by Peter Onuf. New York: Routledge, 1991. 335–60.

"Our House? The President's House at Independence National Historical Park." *The Pennsylvania Magazine of History and Biography* 135.2 (2011): 191–97.

Pawley, Christine. *Reading Places: Literacy, Democracy, and the Public Library in Cold War America*. Amherst: University of Massachusetts Press, 2010.

"Philadelphia Household Account Book, 1793–1797." *Pennsylvania Magazine of History and Biography* 30.3 (1906): 47–48. Web.

Piersen, William Dillon. *Black Yankees: The Development of an Afro-American Subculture in Eighteenth-Century New England*. Amherst: University of Massachusetts Press, 1988.

Powell, J. H. *Bring Out Your Dead; the Great Plague of Yellow Fever in Philadelphia in 1793*. Edited by J. Kenneth Foster, Mary F. Jenkins, and Anna Coxe Toogood. Philadelphia: University of Pennsylvania Press, 1949.

Prussing, Eugene Ernst. *The Estate of George Washington, Deceased*. Boston: Little, Brown, 1927.

Puckett, Newbell Niles, and Murray Heller. *Black Names in America: Origins and Usage*. Boston: G. K. Hall, 1975.

Quarles, Benjamin. *The Negro in the Making of America*. New York: Collier, 1969.

Ribblett, David L. *Nelly Custis: Child of Mount Vernon*. Mount Vernon, VA: Mount Vernon Ladies' Association, 1993.

Rice, Kym. *A Documentary History of Fraunces Tavern: The 18th Century*. New York: Fraunces Tavern Museum, 1985.

Riley, Edward M. "Philadelphia, The Nation's Capital, 1790–1800." *Pennsylvania History* 20.4 (1953): 357–79. Web.

Rogers, Helen Hoban. *Freedom & Slavery Documents in the District of Columbia*. Baltimore: Published for the Author by Gateway, 2007.

Rothman, Adam. *Slave Country: American Expansion and the Origins of the Deep South*. Cambridge, MA: Harvard University Press, 2005.

Sammons, Mark J., and Valerie Cunningham. *Black Portsmouth: Three Centuries of African-American Heritage*. Durham: University of New Hampshire Press, 2004.

Sawyer, Roland D. "New Hampshire Pioneers of Religious Liberty: Rev. Elias

Smith of Portsmouth, New Hampshire's Theodore Parker." In *The Granite Monthly: A New Hampshire Magazine Devoted to History, Biography, and State Progress*. Concord, NH, 1918.

Schwartz, Marie Jenkins. *Born in Bondage: Growing up Enslaved in the Antebellum South*. Cambridge, MA: Harvard University Press, 2000.

Schwartz, Philip J., ed. *Slavery at the Home of George Washington*. Mount Vernon, VA: The Mount Vernon Ladies' Association, 2001.

Smith, Billy, and Richard Wojtowicz. *Blacks Who Stole Themselves: Advertisements for Runaways in the Pennsylvania Gazette, 1728–1790*. Philadelphia: University of Pennsylvania Press, 1989.

Smith, Billy G. *The "Lower Sort": Philadelphia's Laboring People, 1750–1800*. Ithaca, NY: Cornell University Press, 1990.

Thane, Elswyth. *Mount Vernon Family*. New York: Crowell-Collier, 1968.

Thompson, Mary V. "Control and Resistance: A Study of George Washington and Slavery." The Historical Society of Western Pennsylvania. Oct. 2000. Lecture.

Ulrich, Laurel Thatcher. *The Age of Homespun: Objects and Stories in the Creation of an American Myth*. New York: Knopf, 2001.

———. *A Midwife's Tale: The Life of Martha Ballard, Based on Her Diary, 1785–1812*. New York: Knopf, 1990.

United States. *Proceedings and Debates of the House of Representatives of the United States at the Second Session of the Second Congress, Begun at the City of Philadelphia, November 5, 1792. "Annals of Congress, 2nd Congress, 2nd Session (November 5, 1792 to March 2, 1793),"* 2nd Cong., 2nd sess. Cong. Rept., 1414–15. Web. Mar. 2014. http://memory.loc.gov/cgi-bin/ampage?collId=llac&fileName=003/llac003.db&recNum=702.

Waldstreicher, David. *Runaway America: Benjamin Franklin, Slavery, and the American Revolution*. New York: Hill and Wang, 2004.

———. "The Wheatleyan Moment." *Early American Studies: An Interdisciplinary Journal* 9.3 (2011): 522–51. Web.

Washington, George. *The Diaries of George Washington*. Edited by Donald Jackson and Dorothy Twohig. Vol. 6. Charlottesville: University of Virginia Press, 1976.

———. *George Washington's Diaries: An Abridgement*. Edited by Dorothy Twohig. Charlottesville: University of Virginia Press, 1999.

"Washington's Household Account Book 1793–1797." *Pennsylvania Magazine of History and Biography* 31 (1907): 142. Web.

Weld, Isaac. *Travels through the States of North America and the Provinces of Upper and Lower Canada during the Years 1795, 1796, and 1797*. London: Printed for John Stockdale, 1799.

Wharton, Anne H. "Washington's New York Residence in 1789." *Lippincott's Monthly Magazine* 43 (1889): 741–45. Web.

Whipple, Blaine. *History and Genealogy of "Elder" John Whipple of Ipswich, Massachusetts: His English Ancestors and American Descendants.* Victoria, BC: Trafford, 2003.

White, Ashli. *Encountering Revolution: Haiti and the Making of the Early Republic.* Baltimore: Johns Hopkins University Press, 2010.

White, Deborah G. *Ar'n't I a Woman?: Female Slaves in the Plantation South.* New York: W. W. Norton, 1985.

White, Shane. *Somewhat More Independent: The End of Slavery in New York City, 1770–1810.* Athens: University of Georgia Press, 1991.

Whitman, T. Stephen. *The Price of Freedom: Slavery and Manumission in Baltimore and Early National Maryland.* Lexington, KY: University Press of Kentucky, 1997.

Wiencek, Henry. *An Imperfect God: George Washington, His Slaves, and the Creation of America.* New York: Farrar, Straus and Giroux, 2003.

Williams, Heather Andrea. *Self-Taught: African American Education in Slavery and Freedom.* Chapel Hill: The University of North Carolina Press, 2005.

Wong, Edlie L. *Neither Fugitive nor Free: Atlantic Slavery, Freedom Suits, and the Legal Culture of Travel.* New York: New York University Press, 2009.

Wood, Betty. *Slavery in Colonial America, 1619–1776.* Lanham, MD: Rowman & Littlefield, 2005.

Wood, Gordon S. *Revolutionary Characters: What Made the Founders Different.* New York: Penguin Books, 2007.

Illustration Credits

Chapter One Courtesy of Mount Vernon Ladies' Association.

Chapter Two Guiseppe Guidicini, *President Washington Taking the Oath, 1789*; 1812–1868; 1839, Oil on fine linen, 52½ x 72 in., New-York Historical Society. Courtesy of the Collection of the New-York Historical Society.

Chapter Three Schomburg Center for Research in Black Culture, Photographs and Prints Division, the New York Public Library (1789-03-30).

Chapter Four Lithograph by William L. Breton. From John Fanning Watson's *Annals of Philadelphia* (1830). Courtesy of the Historical Society of Pennsylvania.

Chapter Five Courtesy of the Historical Society of Pennsylvania.

Chapter Six Schomburg Center for Research in Black Culture, Manuscripts, Archives and Rare Books Division, New York Public Library. 1910.

Chapter Seven Courtesy of the Miriam and Ira D. Wallach Division of Art, Prints and Photographs: Print Collection, New York Public Library.

Chapter Eight Courtesy of the Historical Society of Pennsylvania.

Chapter Nine Courtesy of the Library Company of Philadelphia.

Chapter Ten Courtesy of the New York Public Library Digital Collections.

Chapter Eleven Courtesy of the Library Company of Philadelphia.

Chapter Twelve Courtesy of the New Hampshire Historical Society.

Chapter Thirteen Courtesy of the New Hampshire Historical Society.

Epilogue Courtesy of the Library of Congress.

Index

Page numbers of illustrations appear in *italics*.

About the Author

Erica Armstrong Dunbar is the Blue and Gold Distinguished Professor of Black Studies and History at the University of Delaware. She received her BA from the University of Pennsylvania and her PhD in American history from Columbia University. In 2008 she published *A Fragile Freedom: African American Women and Emancipation in the Antebellum City* with Yale University Press. In 2011, she was appointed the first director of the Program in African American History at the Library Company of Philadelphia. She has been the recipient of Ford, Mellon, and Social Science Research Council fellowships and is an Organization of American Historians Distinguished Lecturer. She lives just outside of Philadelphia with her husband and son.